CONQUERING CORPORATE CODEPENDENCE

LIFESKILLS FOR MAKING IT WITHIN OR WITHOUT THE CORPORATION

CAROLYN CORBIN
WITH GENE BUSNAR

PRENTICE HALL
Englewood Cliffs, New Jersey 07632

Prentice-Hall International (UK) Limited, *London*
Prentice-Hall of Australia Pty. Limited, *Sydney*
Prentice-Hall Canada, Inc., *Toronto*
Prentice-Hall Hispanoamericana, S.A., *Mexico*
Prentice-Hall of India Private Limited, *New Delhi*
Prentice-Hall of Japan, Inc., *Tokyo*
Simon & Schuster Asia Pte. Ltd., *Singapore*
Editora Prentice-Hall do Brasil, Ltda., *Rio de Janeiro*

©1993 *by*
CAROLYN CORBIN

10 9 8 7 6 5 4 3 2 1

Library of Congress Cataloging-in-Publication Data

Corbin, Carolyn.
  Conquering corporate codependence /
Carolyn Corbin, Gene Busnar.
      p. cm.
  Includes bibliographical references and index.
  ISBN 0-13-145848-5
  1. Job security. 2. Work—Psychological aspects.
3. Psychology, Industrial. 4. Corporate culture.
5. Autonomy (Psychology) 6. Employees—Life skills
guides. 7. Unemployed—Life skills guides.
I. Busnar, Gene. II. Title.
HD5708.4.C67 1993   93-5905
650.1—dc20   CIP

ISBN 0-13-145848-5

PRENTICE HALL
Career & Personal Development
Englewood Cliffs, NJ 07632

Simon & Schuster, A Paramount Communications Company

Printed in the United States of America

Dedicated to

Ray Corbin

my husband, love, teacher
and friend

Dedicated to

Nadine Belinda Busnar

whose joy and youthful spirit
keep us on track as we strive
to optimize the future

Acknowledgments

No book is ever written without the help of many people who offer professional expertise, friendship, and support. There are many individuals who give us ideas and become our teachers without ever directly knowing the impact they have on our lives.

Heartfelt thanks go to the following people for their tremendous influence on this project:

Orene Pitts and the late Ben Pitts, my parents, for modeling the indipreneurial lifeskills to me;

Ray, Sr., Coretta, and Linda Corbin, my in-laws, for their constant encouragement;

Rosemary Beckelman, my cousin and friend, whose excellence in parenting, teaching, and leadership skills

viii ✦ *Acknowledgements*

helped me to formulate many theories which are tested and applied in this work;

Juanell Teague, Dallas speaking business consultant, for caring enough about this project to introduce me to the network that made mere ideas become a book;

Kelly Robinson and Shannon Edwards, my colleagues and special friends who constantly help me formulate ideas and concepts while efficiently executing all the marketing and administrative work at Carolyn Corbin, Inc.;

Dr. Jim George, Vice President, Professional Development Institute for the University of North Texas, an excellent educator and wordsmith, who stimulated my thinking, edited this work, and helped me organize the Center for the 21st Century;

Tom Keel, my mentor and friend, who spent untold hours editing this material and meticulously reviewing my thoughts to strengthen the cohesiveness of this book;

Joe Shaw, Dallas graphics specialist, for his excellent graphics in this text. His precision, pleasant personality, and willingness to work long hours helped us make our deadline.

Dr. Paden Neeley, President of the Professional Development Institute for the University of North Texas, for his contagious vision, energy, and enthusiasm in establishing our joint venture, the Center for the 21st Century;

Sara Recer, owner of Recer Management Company in Hollywood and associate with Carol Burnett's Kalola Productions, who not only spent numerous hours in telephone interviews but also graciously offered ideas and suggestions for endorsements;

Reba Anderson, Director of Pharmacy, RHD Memorial Medical Center, my friend since childhood, for her support, manuscript reading, suggestions for self-assessment instruments, interview time, and organizational insight;

All those not previously mentioned whom we interviewed to solidify our perspective: Harry Gossett, Vice President of Corporate Services, Whirlpool Financial Corporation; Linnet F. Deily, CEO, First Interstate Bank of Texas N.A.; Ellen Matsumoto, Public Information Officer, Clovis Unified School District, California; Randy Robason, Tax Partner, Arthur Andersen & Co.; Richard C. Bartlett, Vice Chairman, Mary Kay Corporation; Dick Rivera, President, TGI Friday's, Inc.; Eileen Beasley, Director, Human Resources, RHD Memorial Medical Center, Dallas; Bill Miller, Vice President, In-flight Services, Southwest Airlines; Nick Galanos, Executive Vice President, TGI Friday's, Inc.;

Euna Brady, Carolyn Corbin Inc.'s Director of Marketing at the beginning of this project, for enthusiastic insight and coordination of much of the initial material;

Arnett Peel, President of Mother Dubbers, Inc., and all the staff for rapid turnaround time in the production of audio tape duplications containing the many hours of transcription. Their enthusiasm for the project was a source of constant encouragement.

Jeff Herman, New York literary agent, whose dedication, sincerity, persistence and honesty are unsurpassed. He continually spurred my optimism until my dream became a reality.

Tom Power, Senior Editor at Prentice-Hall, for his positive approach, patience, and constructive suggestions;

Jamie Forbes for many hours of input editing, very professional guidance, and suggestions for content and structure;

Gene Busnar, this book's collaborator, whose enduring patience and writing expertise were invaluable.

INTRODUCTION

Americans are more determined than ever to take responsibility for their own destinies. In a recent survey of corporate employees conducted by Yankelovich Partners, 70 percent of the respondents agreed with the statement, "I'm the one in charge of my own life." At the same time, a mere 12 percent of those surveyed said that they trust public statements made by corporations.[1]

In the wake of the massive layoffs and downsizings of recent years, such skepticism is hardly surprising. Once upon a time, corporations were comfortable places where people who did competent work and fit into the culture felt secure and cared for. Those days are gone—probably forever. Millions of men and women on all levels of the corporate ladder have been let go, and not necessarily because their work was below par.

Today, entitlements are a thing of the past. To make it in this brave, new downsized world, mere competence is no longer enough. You'd better be able to render superior performance—or you're history. This is, of course, a hard pill for people of all ages to swallow. Still, the group most profoundly affected are the so-called baby boomers who are reaching middle age while the world in which they grew up is struggling through its own version of a midlife crisis.

The onset of middle age tends to be accompanied by a good deal of turbulence, which can cause us to question our most basic values. It seems to me that people often go through a kind of second adolescence during this period of their lives. From an emotional standpoint, this is an especially tough time to have to worry about losing your job and trying to start over.

The sad fact is that many people have never been taught how to cope without the protective umbrella they thought corporations and other institutions would provide. In clinging to the mistaken belief that they were entitled to regular raises, good working conditions, and a comprehensive benefits package, these individuals have become overly dependent on the corporations for which they work. Now, for better or worse, that seductive, entitlement-based world is collapsing—and this is generating a tremendous amount of pain.

In Chapter One, I explore the issue of corporate codependence. I'm well aware that the term *codependence* has become an overused buzzword. Nevertheless, it provides an apt description of a destructive and widespread phenomenon. To instill loyalty, too many companies have fostered a false sense of security among employees. By doing so, these companies and their leaders have become accomplices in perpetuating dependence. And, like parties to any codependent situation, organizations that encourage unrealistic expectations are bound to suffer profound consequences.

Not surprisingly, some corporate leaders try to duck responsibility and place the onus on the shattered people who have been let go. "We never promised them a rose garden," said one defensive CEO whose company had recently cut almost a fifth of its work force. "It's not our problem if these people feel like rejected children or jilted lovers."

It didn't take long for this CEO to find out that the pain in his corporation went well beyond the men and women who had been fired. Before long, a tremendous amount of stress and depression began to surface among the people who were still on the payroll. Absenteeism and sick leave had never been higher. Several of the best middle managers defected to competing firms. A number of others quit to start their own businesses. Profits started to shrink. It had, indeed, become "*our* problem."

When I decided to name this book *Conquering Corporate Codependence,* my husband wondered if senior managers and other corporate leaders might take offense. I think not. As I note in Chapter 2: "If you want to create conditions that will motivate the best people to stay, you have to help them develop the skills and allow them the freedoms that will enable them to leave."

A few years ago, this may have been a radical notion. But, as we come face to face with the realities of a new century, the need for what I call *indipreneurship* is gaining widespread acceptance among both individuals and organizations. This combination of independence and entrepreneurship is what it's going to take to make it in the twenty-first century—both within and without the corporation.

Today, we hear a great deal of talk about empowerment. Unfortunately, much of it is just that—talk! Even corporate leaders who sincerely want to empower their employees soon discover that this cannot be accomplished without making profound systemic changes. Before you can empower people, you must show them how to access specific lifeskills and spread them into every pore of the organization.

Part II of this book focuses on what I originally conceived to be *preempowerment* skills. I have since come to recognize that *tracking, resourcing, futuring, optimizing,* and *balancing* are the essential lifeskills all individuals and organizations need to become truly indipreneurial. Men and women who develop these lifeskills will have the flexibility and strength to realize their goals in the face of change and uncertainty. Organizations that invest in fostering indipreneurial lifeskills will be protecting their future in an ever-more-competitive and turbulent business environment.

In Part III of the book, we explore a systemic approach to change that stresses the interdependence between all participating entities. This gets right to the heart of why corporations need to be concerned that their people have high self-esteem and lead balanced lives.

Not so many years ago, corporations felt that they did not have to take an interest in what happened to their people outside the workplace. As long as an employee came to work on time and was reasonably productive, there was no need to be concerned about what went on elsewhere.

Today, we are helping forward-looking business leaders recognize that each individual comprises an interactive system that cannot be divided up into separate and discrete compartments. Clearly, if a person has profound emotional or family problems, his or her work is bound to suffer. At the same time, workaholics who neglect other key aspects of their lives often experience stress, burnout, and medical problems that wind up costing their companies time and money.

As Randy D. Robason, tax partner at Arthur Andersen & Co., noted in a recent interview: "In the past, we looked primarily at technical and work-related skills. It has become clear, however, that we're hiring a whole person—not just someone who does a specific job. We now understand that helping people improve their lifeskills and become more fulfilled benefits the organization as well as the individual."

In my view, the importance of fostering indipreneurial lifeskills goes well beyond the needs of corporations. I have made it my mission to share these principles and techniques with people of all ages and organizations of every size and description. I have joined forces with the University of North Texas in creating *The Center for the 21st Century* to spread this critical message worldwide.

It is important to keep in mind that even the largest organizations are made up of people. Therefore, as more women and men continue to master the lifeskills and become indipreneurial, the stronger all the systems of which they are a part will be. I truly believe that reading this book and following its principles will make you a stronger and happier person. This, in turn, will have a positive impact on your systemic environment, which will pervade every aspect of your life.

As you read the pages that follow, you and I will develop a personal and direct connection that I hope will continue into the future. I'm excited about working with you and look forward to embarking on our journey together.

Carolyn Corbin
Dallas, Texas

Endnote

1. The Yankelovich findings are cited in Stratford Sherman, "A Brave New Darwinian Workplace," *Fortune,* January 22, 1993.

CONTENTS

PART II
DEVELOPING INDIPRENEURIAL
LIFESKILLS 67

PART I

THE CORPORATION AND YOU

CHAPTER 1

DECLARE
YOUR
INDEPENDENCE!

Do you feel more insecure and uncertain about your future than at any other time in your life?

Are you experiencing undue stress and burnout on your present job?

Are you depressed as a result of having been laid off or fired from your job?

Are you currently employed, but living in fear that you may soon be axed?

Would you like to change careers or start your own business, but fear that you don't have what it takes?

If your answer to one or more of these questions is yes, you may be impaired by a set of unhealthy attitudes and behaviors that center on your relationship with the company you work for—or from which you were fired.

In the wake of the massive layoffs of recent years, job-related stress and depression have become so widespread that a growing number of companies are offering free therapeutic counseling to employees who feel they have no control over their future. And what of those who are no longer working? As you might imagine, the extent of their suffering is far worse.

A source at one major airline reports over 100 cases of attempted suicide among workers who'd been laid off by that company within an 18-month period. The source noted that, in most of those cases, the driving force behind the despair was emotional, not financial.

WHAT IS CORPORATE CODEPENDENCE?

You've probably heard the term codependence used in discussions of alcohol and drug abuse. What you might not know is that reliance on substances is not a necessary precondition for codependence to exist. Consider the following generally accepted definitions of codependence and descriptions of codependent persons.

✦ Codependence is an emotional state perpetuated by fear and low self-worth that results in neglect of personal needs and goals.

✦ Codependence is a condition caused by a family or other system

> that controls behavior with inflexible rules and unexpressed emotions.
>
> ✦ A codependent person comes from a dysfunctional family or other system, and generally finds his or her identity primarily through relationships within that system.
>
> ✦ Codependents tend to be loyal to a fault, remaining in the dependent relationship no matter what.

I believe that corporate codependence is the term that best describes many of the problems affecting people and businesses today. I imagine that some of you will respond skeptically when I say that this affliction now poses a threat to the survival of millions of people—as well as the companies for which they work. Maybe you're asking yourself if corporate codependence is just another one of those snappy slogans without much substance to back it up.

Can it really be that millions of otherwise stable men and women are walking around with some terrible condition that is potentially as life threatening as alcoholism or drug abuse, and that you may be among those suffering from this disorder? Ask yourself if you know anyone who displays one or more of the eight behaviors or attitudes described here.

Eight Ways to Recognize Corporate Codependence

> 1. A person who, after being fired or laid off, is paralyzed by a sense that his irrevocable right to job security has been violated.
>
> 2. An employed person who becomes depressed or obsessed by the

thought that he can be fired at any time.

3. A person who will sacrifice the best interests of her department or company to look good to her superiors.

4. A person who withdraws from interactions with coworkers.

5. A person who is a workaholic or otherwise ready to do anything to please others at the expense of her own self-interest.

6. A person who unrealistically thinks that he or she can solve the problems of others—that is, play the hero.

7. A person who is often out sick or who frequently complains about physical symptoms while on the job.

8. A person who is obviously suffering from excessive related stress, but refuses to discuss or acknowledge her problem.

IDENTIFYING HEALTHY AND UNHEALTHY FAMILY SYSTEMS

When the term "codependence" comes up, it is most often linked to the issue of dysfunctional families. Perhaps you think it's a stretch to view corporations in that light.

You may never have thought about it in this way, but every company is a distinct family unit—as is each department within an organization. A close look at the dynamics in most of these units or groups of people reveals a structure of power and authority that closely resembles that which exists among parents and children.

"Entering into a corporate family for the first time is a lot like being born," say Drs. Ona Robinson and Edward Stephens, two New York–based psychotherapists who are partners in the consulting firm, On Step. "As you grow up, you learn about the way your family works. To survive, you adapt your attitudes and behaviors in ways that enable you to get along in that particular family."[1]

Just as children in codependent biological families often take on the destructive response patterns of an abusive or addicted parent, people who work in dysfunctional corporations can take on the negative behaviors that characterize leaders of those institutions. Here's the bottom line: An unhealthy family will produce unhealthy family members— whether that family is biological or corporate.

There are, of course, some important distinctions between corporate and other forms of codependence. For one thing, the corporate variety is not directly related to abuse or other traumatic events that may have taken place in early childhood. Most people suffering from the symptoms of corporate codependence don't require psychotherapy or a 12-step program to reverse the condition. What they do need is a better understanding of their circumstances, as well as the lifeskills that will enable them to prosper in this performance-based environment.

Later in this chapter, I'm going to ask you to complete a questionnaire that will help you evaluate the extent and nature of your particular corporate codependent tendencies. Please don't feel bad if you find that you exhibit some of the thoughts and attitudes that characterize this condition. Let me assure you that they can be reversed in a relatively short time. Besides, you've got plenty of company.

Just as certain economically disadvantaged persons have grown dependent on welfare and other government programs, many middle-class individuals have become overly reliant on the protection furnished by corporations.

Men and women who've never been taught to be independent can become emotionally and financially addicted to their good salaries, well-appointed offices, and corporate-benefits programs. When people are fired or laid off in an era of extensive and irreversible corporate cutbacks, they come to realize that they may never be able to replace the salaries and perks to which they have grown accustomed. This realization can pose a severe threat to their identity as well as their economic survival.

If you look at the changes corporate America has experienced in recent years, it's not hard to understand why so much corporate codependence is surfacing at this time. Not long ago, people entered the corporate world believing that companies would furnish not only jobs—but also protection from the "what-ifs" of life. They provided vacations, health benefits and retirement plans—even friends and a social life. Now that entitlement-based world is collapsing, and many of us are finding it difficult to cut the cord.

As more and more corporations pare down to stay competitive, millions of loyal and competent people are being unceremoniously fired. No industry or category of employees is safe. Downsizing is a phenomenon that has hit automobile manufacturing as well as banking, managers with six-figure salaries as well as support staff and assembly-line workers.

There are, of course, many who will continue to remain on the corporate payroll. But those men and women have now been forced to evaluate their prospects in a far more skeptical light. "How do I know I won't be next to get the ax?" people often ask these days. The answer, of course, is that they don't know—and this uncertainty is the trigger for a good deal of anxiety.

Until recently, there was an unwritten contract between corporations and their employees that went something like this: "You give us good and faithful service, and we'll give you job security and all the benefits that go with it."

In the new corporate America, the implicit agreement between company and employee has been revised. What we're now looking at is a short-term contract—one that can be severed by either side on short notice.

Unfortunately, many people have a hard time coming to terms with that reality, even after they've been fired. To the extent that they cannot let go of their unrealistic expectations, these men and women are suffering from corporate codependence. At the same time, companies that intentionally or inadvertently encourage such false hopes on the part of their employees had best recognize that they are equal partners in perpetuating this unhealthy condition, and at risk of suffering its consequences.

If we, as individuals, are going to survive and thrive, we must develop skills that enable us to be both independent and entrepreneurial. I call people who combine these two traits *indipreneurs*. It is my feeling that, in the coming years, we are going to need to be *indipreneurial*—not just with respect to our careers, but in everything we do.

At the same time, corporations that want to ensure growth and profitability must recognize the importance of nurturing indipreneurial qualities in their employees. Otherwise, they will continue to wonder why their most talented people are defecting to the competition—and why those that remain are lacking in motivation.

*I*NDIPRENEURIAL LIFESKILLS

1. Tracking

2. Resourcing

3. Futuring

4. Balancing

5. Optimizing

DEVELOPING THE FIVE
INDIPRENEURIAL LIFESKILLS

When men and women talk about feeling burned out and rudderless in their lives, they generally focus on symptoms such as losing their jobs, career dissatisfaction or anxiety about finances. But the real issues cut much deeper.

The sad fact is that many people have never been taught how to cope without the protective umbrella they thought corporations and other institutions would provide. In clinging to the mistaken belief that they were entitled to regular raises, good working conditions and a comprehensive benefits package, these individuals have never learned to rely on themselves. Now that this seductive, entitlement-based world is changing into one in which nothing is guaranteed, millions of people are being left out in the cold—financially and emotionally.

Just as we can no longer count on the companies for which we work to meet our financial or career needs, we also can't count on our government to look after us in our old age or to subsidize our children's college education. Suddenly, we are being told: "Sorry, pal. We're clean out of money. You're just going to have to learn to fend for yourself."

To maintain financial viability and ensure a good quality of life in the coming years, we must develop skills that address the new performance-based environment. We need to be able to critically evaluate situations, to maximize our resources, to envision the future, to be responsible for our own physical and psychic wellness—and to show our children how to do the same.

Unfortunately, most of us have been educated only to master academic subjects or trained to perform specific job tasks. If you're like many people born after World War II, it's a good bet that you've never been taught at least some of the essential skills needed to overcome adversity in your career as well as in your personal life. These success skills are what we teach at The PDI/CCI Center for the 21st Century,[2] and the results have been dramatic.

We've helped men and women in crisis turn their lives around. We've shown salespeople and job seekers how to remain optimistic in the face of rejection and tough economic times. We've put faltering companies back on the road to profitability. We've even helped school systems use lifeskills techniques to improve the motivation and performance of their students. Now I'm pleased to have this opportunity to show you how to achieve these same positive changes—and to help you reverse the conditions that may have made you overly dependent on corporations and other institutions.

Mastering the five indipreneurial lifeskills will enable you to:

- ✦ Develop greater self-reliance.
- ✦ Function as an indipreneur—both inside and outside the corporation.
- ✦ Prepare for predictable uncertainty.
- ✦ Learn to manage change effectively.
- ✦ Take control of events that appear to be uncontrollable.

APPRECIATING THE BENEFITS OF THE HARD ROAD

After living so long with the tenuous assumption that others are going to take care of us, a tremendous amount of pain is generated when we suddenly realize that the responsibility for our well-being falls squarely on our own shoulders. But, in the end, that is the bottom line. I guess I should consider myself lucky. My family owned a small farm, and I was introduced to the hard road early on. Life on our little farm was a constant struggle. To survive, we had to learn to live with uncertainty and to plan ahead. Circumstances demanded that we manage on a limited budget, value family relationships, and have faith in the future. I believe that many of the lifeskills we learned on the farm are the same ones people need today. If we're going to move ahead, we must be able to think creatively, work independently as well as in teams, plan for adversity, and assume responsibility for our actions. On the farm, it was essential that everyone be a productive contributor. Productivity was directly related to results: there was simply no place for deadwood, nor was there any way to cover up mistakes. When I was 6, it was my job to feed the orphaned lambs who had been rejected by their mothers. One day, I ran off to play with my friends and neglected my responsibilities. When I came home for dinner that night, my parents glumly informed me that one of the lambs had died. They didn't yell, nor did they administer any punishment. Although I was very young, I could clearly see the direct consequences of my actions—and so could everyone else.

Today, we are faced with similar circumstances. People who don't pull their load are going to have a tough time. Beyond that, job security in virtually every industry has become as unpredictable as next season's crop yield was on our farm. That's why it's so important to develop the skills that help you become an *indipreneur*. But before you can do that, you have to let go of the unrealistic expectations that have been holding you back.

How to Use Pain as an Agent for Positive Change

One of the first things that motivates us to implement positive change in our business and personal lives is the recognition of pain—be it economic, emotional, spiritual, or physical.

Most of the men and women who attend our seminars are in pain. Some have lost their jobs or are experiencing various forms of career-related anxiety. Others are divorced, alienated from their children, trying to cope with aging parents, or experiencing some sort of emotional crisis. Many talk about feeling drained, disappointed with life, and pessimistic about the future.

The corporations that retain our services are also experiencing various forms of pain:

✧ Many companies call us in because they are experiencing chaos caused by rapid growth. I've worked with a number of profitable corporations that expanded their businesses without hiring additional personnel. Everyone from top management on down is made to understand that they are expected to do more with less. In many cases, these added responsibilities are heaped on without the requisite resources and freedoms needed to carry them out.

✧ Companies that mistakenly thought they were sailing along in calm and stable waters suddenly find themselves beset by all sorts of turbulence. The quality of their products and services has been slipping over a period of time, often in almost imperceptible increments. Their profits are shrinking. Their best people are defecting to competing firms, and many of the ones who remain are depressed and burned out. Consequently, people feel over burdened and stressed out. Those that don't quit become less productive on their jobs.

✧ Even those companies that are willing to hire additional personnel in times of growth may face unanticipated problems. Adding people is one thing. Training them to be productive team players is quite another. In the face of tough economic times, people may be thrilled just to have a job when so many others are out of work. But, when people are unable to contribute, even a regular paycheck is not enough to prevent this initial excitement from turning into depression and frustration.

Each of these circumstances creates its own kind of pain—on both a corporate and personal level. We are called in to evaluate and reverse these conditions. One of the first things we do is help clients understand that pain in and of itself is no guarantee that positive change will occur.

Many organizations and individuals feel pain, yet they continue to ignore it. Eventually, this kind of dysfunctional behavior causes the pain to become more intense. In some cases, the increase in discomfort is enough to force some kind of change. Unfortunately, there are those individuals and companies who continue the same dysfunctional behaviors until they suffer economic or personal bankruptcy.

The fact that you're reading these words demonstrates a willingness to expose yourself to new and more productive problem-solving methods. If you succeed in mastering the skills in this book, you may one day reach a point where you feel comfortable with the way things are going. But this is only the beginning.

If anything is certain in life—and in business—it is that nothing remains the same for very long. That's why it's important to recognize that no matter how well your particular actions and strategies are working at a given time, chances are they will not continue to work down the road.

In the short term, the lifeskills you learn in these chapters will help you deal effectively with the particular adversities you're currently facing. However, the long-range purpose of developing these skills is to anticipate and effectively manage change. That's why I'm going to show you how to master a change management process that will enable you to employ the lifeskills *before* you are faced with a crisis.

*S*ELF-EVALUATION EXERCISE:
HOW MUCH DO YOU RELY ON YOUR JOB?

✦ ✦ ✦

I'd like you to complete a short exercise designed to help you to begin evaluating the extent to which you may be corporate codependent.

Instructions I've listed 20 questions that I want you to answer either yes or no. If you are presently unemployed, answer as you would have on your last job.

1. Do you become overly upset when your boss or job supervisor criticizes your work?

2. If a coworker was given a promotion that you felt you deserved, would you keep your feelings hidden from your boss or supervisor?

3. If you were fired from your job after ten years of loyal service, would you consider that a violation of an unwritten agreement with your employer?

4. Do you find yourself obsessing over job-related matters on weekends and vacations?

5. Do you accept virtually any decision your organization makes without question?

6. Do you depend solely on your company to train you and upgrade your skills?

7. Do you feel it's not your responsibility to independently evaluate your company's economic stability?

8. Are you unaware of the details of your employee benefits plans?

9. Are the pension and health, disability and life insurance plans provided by your employer the only policies that you carry?

10. Do you feel it's your employer's responsibility to make certain that you are employed at your highest skill-level?

11. Do you become so preoccupied with problems at work that you can't enjoy time with family and friends?

12. Have you neglected to make contingency plans for when you are no longer on the corporate payroll?

13. Have you determined that your skills and temperament are best suited for being in business for yourself, but feel afraid and ill equipped to strike out on your own?

14. Are most of your close friends from the workplace?

15. Do your accomplishments at work give you a sense of power and self-esteem that you can't find elsewhere?

16. Do you have few hobbies or interests that are not work-related?

17. Will you do virtually anything to please your bosses to get ahead on your job?

18. Are you more concerned with being adept at corporate politics than with superior job performance?

19. Do your feelings of self-worth hinge on success in the workplace?

20. If you could somehow continue to receive your current salary and benefits, would you still feel devastated if you lost your job?

Scoring For each yes answer, give yourself 5 points. The higher your score, the higher the degree of corporate codependence. Each of the issues raised in this questionnaire will be discussed more fully in subsequent chapters. For now, you can use the following guidelines to determine the extent to which you rely on the company for which you work.[3]

Total: ____

0–25 = Relatively few codependent tendencies; high sense of freedom and independence

30–65 = Moderately codependent; able to think and act independently in certain situations

70–100 = High degree of corporate codependence

If your test results indicate that you have relatively few corporate codependent qualities, you will still find the subsequent chapters useful for honing your lifeskills and helping you strengthen your independence. Should your answers indicate that you have more corporate codependent symptoms than you had anticipated, don't despair. Everything you will need to reverse the condition can be found right here in this book, including:

✦ Exercises and questionnaires to help you understand the particular circumstances and response mechanisms that caused the condition to develop.

✦ Training in the basic lifeskills you will need to become an indipreneur and reach your potential.

✦ Innovative techniques to help you manage change and build self-esteem.

Before I show you how to strengthen the lifeskills that will enable you to make it—within or without the corporation—I'd like to share with you two particularly instructive cases of people with relatively severe codependency symptoms who successfully used the lifeskills you will learn in this book to turn things around.

CASE STUDY 1:
FORCED TO BECOME
AN INDIPRENEUR

When Fred was laid off from his job as a systems analyst, he felt devastated. At his first indipreneuring seminar, he talked about the unfairness of his being fired.

"There were people who had less seniority than I did," he complained bitterly. "And I'm not being immodest when I say that I was better at my job than most of them."

At age 47, Fred had never known what it was like to get along outside the corporate womb. Upon graduating from college, he entered that world with a specific set of job skills that had served him well—or so he thought—until the day he got fired. By the time Fred attended the seminar, he had been without work for eight months, with no prospects in sight. The strain had started to take its toll.

Fred and his wife, a high school teacher, had one 14-year-old daughter. Because the couple had always been relatively frugal with money, Fred's unemployment did not pose an immediate financial threat. Nevertheless, Fred was going through a full-blown crisis.

For the first time in his life, Fred started to drink heavily. When his wife suggested that he might have a problem, a bitter fight ensued. Fred's daughter picked up on the growing dissension between her parents, and it was starting to affect her schoolwork.

To his credit, Fred was able to stop drinking on his own. Shortly thereafter, he took the positive step of attending the indipreneuring seminar. This proved to be the impetus he needed to get back on track. Fred was encouraged to participate in a *motivational resourcing group*[4] and a *thinktank*. These groups helped Fred sharpen his *tracking* and *futuring* skills.

Rather than seek another corporate position, Fred decided that he would attempt to set up his own small business. By using the tracking methods we will explore in Chapter Three, Fred was able to pinpoint an area of expertise that suited his unique talents.

One of the things Fred enjoyed doing in his spare time was putting together computer hardware systems. He often went to computer shows and flea markets and bought parts from which he constructed integrated units. After researching and analyzing the market, Fred started to believe that this talent was something he might be able to turn into a viable business.

The members of Fred's thinktank agreed that this was a potentially lucrative area for him to pursue. At the same time, they helped to pinpoint the skill areas that Fred needed to strengthen.

During Fred's years in the corporate world, he had been well paid for performing specific tasks. Although he had what is generally considered a highly skilled job, those skills had proven to be insufficient for him to remain employed.

To make a living running his own business, Fred needed to develop new skills in areas like negotiation and sales. Beyond that, he had to be willing to do whatever it took to keep his new enterprise afloat—regardless of whether that meant answering phones, sweeping floors, or working on weekends. Furthermore, there would be no benefits programs beyond those Fred could provide for himself.

Like all people who launch new business ventures, Fred had no way of knowing whether his would succeed. In any case, he had come to the realization that the same skills that would help him create a viable business would also make him more employable should he ever have to look for another job.

Like so many people coping with corporate codependence, Fred had always concentrated on learning the skills that would allow him to work for someone else. He never valued, nor was he taught to master, the skills that are needed to be an indipreneur.

Fred came to understand that the same indipreneurial skills are essential—whether you decide to work for yourself, if you want to get ahead in the corporate world, or even if you simply want to remain employable so that you don't suddenly find yourself without a job.

Today, Fred is the owner of a successful small business that assembles computers and sells them exclusively through mail order. "It wasn't an easy road," he says in retrospect. "But it's great to be making a living at what I used to do for free in my garage.

"I can't believe I'm saying this, but being forced to become an *indipreneur* was the best thing that could have happened. I thought I could get by relying on others to be responsible for my welfare, but losing my job made me painfully aware of the dark side of that equation.

"I can honestly say that I feel better about myself than I have in years. I work harder than I ever did as an employee, but there's nothing like the feeling of being in control of your own destiny."

Case Study 2:
HOW TO PLEASE OTHERS
BY ADDRESSING YOUR
NEEDS FIRST

Jan was an administrative assistant who was constantly trying to please her boss by overworking. She always arrived at the office early and was the last one to punch out. If the boss asked her to take work home on evenings and weekends, she felt unable to say no.

As Jan was to discover, her automatic response style was that of a *rescuer*. Rescuers have relatively low self-esteem coupled with a low degree of entitlement. They tend to be reactors who feel controlled by circumstances. Rescuers are subject to health problems—particularly those related to stress. This type of person often works tirelessly, hoping to gain acceptance, attention, and affection from others. Unfortunately, these efforts almost always prove insufficient.

Like many rescuers, Jan was a workaholic—someone who is driven by fear rather than by the desire to achieve. What are people like Jan so terrified of? Perhaps they're afraid of being laid off, or of not having money—or simply of being rejected.

Whatever it is they fear, workaholics like Jan exert themselves for negative reasons. Jan had been doing this kind of thing since graduating from high school. Because her stress level had been so high for so long, Jan had been in a state of perpetual crisis for years. Now, at age 39, she was experiencing severe stomach problems and migraine headaches. Far too often, her lunch consisted of two buffered aspirin and an antacid.

At her last checkup, Jan's physician warned her that, unless she slowed down, she might soon develop colitis, a serious stress-related disease. Jan needed to recognize that her behavior was also potentially damaging to her boss, who would lose her services if she became too sick to work, not to speak of her company, which would have to foot the medical bills. But the first thing Jan had to do was come to terms with the negative impact her codependent fears and behaviors were having on her.

After Jan discussed her problems during one of my corporate seminars, she and three other participants were encouraged to set up a *self-esteem resourcing group*. By engaging in dialogues—both with herself and the group—Jan learned how to adopt a more productive approach to resolving her difficulties.

Jan was able to acknowledge that, in playing the role of rescuer, she felt compelled to sacrifice her own needs for the sake of her boss. The key shift in her thinking came when Jan recognized that, by setting realistic limits on the number of hours she would work, she would also be doing what was best for her boss and her company.

Before she could move out of her destructive patterns, Jan had to ask herself the following questions:

✧ Why am I driving myself so hard?

✧ What fears do I have?

✧ Why do I expect so much of myself?

✧ Why can't I tell my boss no?

✧ What is the solution that best serves my interests—as well as the interests of all parties?

Jan credits her self-esteem resourcing group with helping her maintain a sense of balance during this difficult period. Just as important, she was able to help other members of the group work out some of their problems. By participating with others in a creative resourcing process, Jan was able to exercise some of her own inner strengths. For Jan, *optimizing* this situation meant coming to grips with her needs and boundaries and conveying them to her boss. Ultimately, the question we all must answer before we can overcome our fears is: "Can I take what I perceive to be the worst possible consequences?" If you can accept this scenario, you will be home free. With the help of her group, Jan created scenarios based on her worst fears. Part of the dialogue went something like this: "What would happen if I did lose my job? Or if my boss became angry? Would the consequences really be any worse than what I'm experiencing now?" Once she felt more secure about her competence on the job and recognized the critical changes that needed to be made, Jan went to her boss and took a stand: "I would like to continue working with you," she told him, "but you must recognize that I have certain limits. You can count on my best efforts during business hours, but I will no longer be able to take work home on evenings and weekends. I have some ideas about streamlining procedures and increasing our productivity during normal working hours. Perhaps we can work together on implementing them." Jan's boss wasn't thrilled with this change, but he really had no choice but to accept these new terms: Jan was an especially efficient administrative assistant, and he didn't want to lose her.

Jan reports that, despite her working far fewer hours, her evaluations are as good as ever. Even more important, she feels less stressed out and far more energetic both in and out of the workplace.

CONCLUSION: THE FUTURE IS IN YOUR HANDS

I'm not about to tell you that it will be easy to overcome fears and reverse behavior patterns that have developed over a period of years. Still, at The Center for the 21st Century, we see it happen every day—and I have confidence that yours will be yet another of our success stories.

As you've seen in the cases of Jan and Fred, this is a process that takes work. To reverse counterproductive patterns, you may first need to engage in self-talk or join a resourcing group to help you muster up the courage to address the situation. You may need to create a scenario addressing your particular fears. To role-play the interactions and potential consequences—both with yourself and others.

These chapters are designed to teach you these and many other skills. I'm here to help you develop those tools, and to provide encouragement and inspiration along the way. But ultimately, it's up to you to turn the knowledge on these pages into positive action.

The future is in your hands. Let me show you how to make the most of it!

ENDNOTES

1. The Stephens–Robinson quote regarding the corporation as a family is cited in Edward Stephens and Ona Robinson, *Compelled to Compete*, Corporate Training Workbook (New York: On Step, 1991).

2. The PDI/CCI Center for the 21st Century is a joint venture between the Professional Development Institute for the University of North Texas and Carolyn Corbin, Inc. It shall be referred to, hereafter, as The Center for the 21st Century.

3. All instruments in this book are designed for the sole purpose of improving self-awareness. These instruments are not scientific—nor are they meant to be used in lieu of psychotherapy or professional counseling.

4. *Highlighted* terms indicate that the topic will be fully explored in a subsequent chapter.

CHAPTER 2

CREATING A HEALTHY CORPORATE CLIMATE

Helping human beings fulfill their potential is of course a moral responsibility, but it's also good business. . . . Learning, striving people are happy people and good workers. They have initiative and imagination, and the companies they work for are rarely caught napping.

Ralph Stayer,
CEO of Johnsonville Sausage[1]

A middle manager at a large communications company recently told me a joke that had been going around his department:

Two men are sentenced to death—one is an executive in a large Japanese corporation, the other holds a comparable position in an American firm. Both men are granted one wish before they are to be executed. The Japanese man asks that he be permitted to recite a four-hour presentation on the advantages of the Japanese way of doing business. His request is granted.

When the American is asked to state his wish, he gets down on his knees and beseeches his executioners to end his life immediately so that he can be spared from listening to yet another speech on the virtues of Japanese corporations.

This little allegory sums up how tired many of us have grown of hearing about how wonderful the Japanese are at running their corporations. As I speak to people in both large and small companies, they tell me that "they've had it up to here" with such rhetoric about empowerment, cooperation, flattening the pyramid, flipping the pyramid, and on and on.

Some of these folks have been to seminar after seminar to learn these supposedly cutting-edge management styles. While nobody questions the theoretical merit of these techniques, there is a prevailing skepticism among the people in many companies about the sincerity on the part of those entrenched corporate leaders who are suddenly trying to pass themselves off as harbingers of change.

"We are being preached all this garbage about teamwork and trust," managers and front-line employees confide. "But nothing has really changed—except the rhetoric. As far as I can tell, it's pretty much business as usual."

When a company's leaders espouse one set of values while acting in a totally contradictory way, there's bound to be a credibility problem that will at some point translate into poor corporate health.

We've worked with any number of corporations whose leaders spoke as if they recognized the need to empower people on every rung of the ladder. Some had spent tens of thousands of dollars on seminars designed to apprise middle management and front-line employees of new, more democratic ways of doing things. More often than not, however, such measures are met with a great deal of skepticism—and rightfully so!

When the people who hold power in an organization start talking about sharing it with those who for years have been following orders, there is bound to be a credibility gap. When we ask employees to interpret their company's sudden interest in empowerment, we typically receive the following responses:

"A ploy by management to gain more control."

"A superficial public relations effort that nobody believes."

"Empty promises designed to placate a dissatisfied and unproductive work force."

If management says one thing and then does another, employee mistrust will be the order of the day. We've been working with one company that was experiencing a trust gap that pervaded the entire organization. For the sake of this discussion, let's call it the Acme Data Organization (ADO).

Several years back, ADO decided to streamline its operation. In a letter to employees announcing the company's new belt-tightening policy, the CEO asked that everyone pull together and sacrifice for the greater good. It was also decided that, for the next two years, raises would not exceed 5 percent for middle managers and front-line employees.

Nobody in the company was particularly thrilled about these limitations on salary increases. Nevertheless, there was a general acceptance of the new policy. But then, six months later, top-echelon management rewarded itself for two profitable quarters with what was perceived to be a gigantic bonus.

Around that time, ADO's leaders began to invest heavily in seminars on empowerment. This was met with an anger that soon began to impact the bottom line. Some of the company's most productive people took early retirement. Others started seeking opportunities elsewhere. Absenteeism and lateness increased dramatically. By the time we were called in, ADO was in a state of severe corporate pain.

For a company's leaders to ask people to tighten their belts and then give themselves substantial bonuses is bad enough. To then exacerbate the situation by asking those same people to believe they are being empowered is, to say the least, the act of leaders who don't have a clue about motivating human beings to do their best work.

It is one thing for the leaders of a company to talk about trust and quite another for them to create the conditions that make it a reality. Just as some governments call themselves democracies but stifle free enterprise, some corporations speak the language of trust but refuse to abandon their need to exert total control.

History has shown that, to endure, nations and companies must encourage people to take responsibility for their behavior and common initiative. Those countries and businesses that fail to marshal these forces will not be able to compete on a global level. There's a saying: "If you're going to talk the talk, you've got to walk the walk." As Peter Block observes in *The Empowered Manager*, "If you fundamentally believe that leadership, direction and control are best exercised at the top of our institutions and our society, then just . . . be the best parent you can be. Don't create expectations of partnership that ultimately you will not fulfill."[2]

Part of what we try to impart to our corporate clients is the importance of raising the self-esteem of each employee, whatever his or her position in the organization. The best gift you can give someone is a feeling of self-worth and pride in what they do. This also turns out to be a highly cost-effective business strategy that pays handsome dividends to those organizations with the courage and foresight to invest in it.

Nine Ways to Increase Corporate Trust

The creation of trust is an ongoing reciprocal process that cannot be established overnight. When there is a widespread perception of deceit and hypocrisy on the part of senior management, reparative measures must be instituted and the process takes longer. But, whatever has transpired in the past, there are certain precepts of corporate trust that can be initiated at any point. For the most part, these require little or no monetary expenditure—just a shift in attitude and perception.

1. *Consider employees an asset rather than an expense to the organization.* Companies that value each person's contribution and convey that message to them are making a wise investment in the future.

2. *Treat people as you would like to be treated.* Let the people who work for and with you know that you are interested in their needs and are open to hearing their complaints. Never create expectations that you're not willing to apply to yourself. If you expect people to be honest and abide by the golden rule, you must be prepared to do likewise.

3. *Create an atmosphere that is supportive, not threatening.* Accept responsibility and blame when it is yours to accept. Treat your mistakes and those of others as opportunities for growth and learning.

4. *Encourage team spirit among people at every level.* A team does not exist outside its leadership. Every team member—from the front-line worker to the CEO—should be seen as cogs of the same greater wheel. Create job titles that reflect the team ethic.

5. *Practice what you preach.* Language and rhetoric are not going to get the job done unless they are backed up by

meaningful action. To have a team spirit, each member must feel that he or she has an investment in the team's success. Therefore, everyone must be allowed to share in the good times as well as the bad.

If an organization is going to ask people to forgo raises when business is off, it should also have some sort of profit-sharing program that kicks in when things are good. Such a program must include everybody—not just the people on top.

6. Convey as much permanency as possible without making false promises or raising unrealistic hopes. People are apt to operate better when they feel the leader is with the organization for the long haul. A sense of long-term commitment inspires security and hope for the future.

7. As much as possible, close the distance between the way team members are compensated. In a team-oriented company where everyone is contributing, there is no justification for the 85:1 ratio in salaries between upper management and lower-level employees one finds in many large corporations.

Peter Drucker is one of many management experts who feel that American businesses are out of balance in this respect—and that this is eroding their competitive edge. The ratio in most European and Japanese corporations is about 10:1. Drucker believes that a healthy ratio should be no more than 20:1. Surveys indicate that employees believe that their shares and those of stockholders are about where they should be. In their estimation, it is only top management that they feel are being grossly overpaid.[3]

Narrowing the salary gap may cause some upper-level people to leave. In many corporate cultures, the amount of money one earns has a social and emotional value that goes beyond economic considerations. Some people may not be ready to give that up. The question that must then be asked is: How committed are those individuals to their people and to the company's long-term welfare?

8. Eliminate perks that exacerbate differences between team members and serve no practical purpose. Even if upper management is reluctant to give up a piece of their hefty paychecks, there are a number of less painful sacrifices that can be made to create a team atmosphere.

The more managerial distance can be decreased in an organization, the more trust there will be. Start by eliminating such unnecessary perks as separate parking places, separate dining rooms, and separate social events. We have found, for example, that in companies where leaders regularly visit with team members on all levels and discuss matters of mutual concern, valuable information is exchanged. At the same time, an immeasurable amount of trust is generated.

9. Encourage contact and communication between team members on every level. Keep the lines of communication open. Don't allow organizational hierarchies to become barriers that prevent people from talking to one another. Encourage a free exchange of ideas and information. Leaders need to set the tone by being receptive to suggestions from all quarters, and to reward positive input accordingly.

Use instruments like the ones provided in this chapter to survey individual and collective attitudes. The information gleaned from such surveys can identify problems before they become crises. When using such instruments on a departmental or companywide basis, share findings with all team members and apprise them of all subsequent decisions.

Make everyone aware of both the good and bad news in a timely fashion. Whatever the message, deliver it in person. Leaders who are visible and forthcoming with other team members generate loyalty and high levels of motivation throughout the organization.

IDENTIFYING THE SIX PSYCHIC REWARDS PEOPLE WANT MOST

When a company's leaders take the nine steps just cited, they create a climate in which people are more likely to put forth their best. While the creation of basic trust is essential to any company's well-being, ongoing maintenance requires paying careful attention to team members' changing needs.

When we start working with a company, we often ask its leaders what they perceive as being most important to their employees. In general, the answers are bigger raises and bonuses, more extensive medical coverage, and better pension programs.

These issues are, indeed, matters of concern to most people. Nevertheless, there is mounting evidence that employee dissatisfaction and lack of motivation are linked more to nonmonetary issues. Consider the following:

An *Industry Week* survey found that there is widespread dissatisfaction in the workplace on all levels. Work is no fun anymore, and the problem is not money. The survey, which targeted mostly middle managers and first-line supervisors, found the level of dissatisfaction to be pretty much the same in virtually all industries.

When asked what was eroding their enjoyment of work, almost half of the survey respondents blamed the absence of teamwork and existence of a dog-eat-dog climate in their organizations. Thirty percent complained that their efforts were not being acknowledged. Only 10 percent blamed insufficient pay.

Nearly 60 percent of the people surveyed said working was once fun at their companies, though not in recent years. When asked what might improve the situation, the suggestions most often proposed were creating a team atmosphere, abolishing titles, providing more individual nonmonetary recognition for employees' efforts, and having a boss who cares.[4]

A Louis Harris poll found a growing "perception gap" between what employees really want and what top management *thinks* they want. For example, managers assume that pay and job security are of paramount importance to employees. In fact, these meat-and-potatoes issues rank lower than such psychic factors as:

1. Respect

2. Increased opportunities and recognition for making meaningful contributions

3. A higher standard of management ethics in deeds—not just words

4. Closer and more honest communications with senior management

5. More reliable information on where the company is heading

6. A better understanding of how their jobs fit into the total scheme[5]

Our own corporate training work confirms the *Industry Week* and Harris findings that the things employees value most can't be measured in dollars. One would think that this would be welcome news to upper management. Imagine the joy of learning that you can satisfy people's wants and needs without spending a lot of money. The problem is, most business leaders never even bother to ask their people what's important to them.

A. Foster Higgins and Co., an employee-benefits consulting firm, finds that only 45 percent of large employers make regular use of worker opinion surveys.[6] It's a good bet that the other 55 percent of these organizations audit their financial resources on a regular basis—yet they neglect im-

plementing simple and inexpensive steps to gauge the feelings of employees.

The most glaring lesson that has emerged from our own
work with corporations is the mutuality of interests between
a company and the people who work there. If people are
unhappy and feel undervalued, this will ultimately impact
negatively on a business's bottom line. By the same token, a
happy and highly motivated work force is almost always a
sign of good corporate health and productivity.

I recall walking into my bank several years ago and
noticing a big difference in the general attitude of employees.
Everyone was smiling and going out of their way to be
cordial. In the past, employees always seemed subdued and
preoccupied. When I asked my favorite teller what happened
to cause the change, here's what she said:

"A number of years ago, First Interstate Bancorp based
in California bought us. The transition around here really
began at that time. But the major influence is the CEO, Linnet
F. Deily, who has become a great role model for all of us. It
makes all the difference to have someone in charge who
really cares and shows it.

"The great thing is, she takes an interest in our personal
lives as well as our performance and comments about the
bank. My husband recently had surgery. When Ms. Deily
visited the branch, she remembered to ask about him. She
doesn't have a big intimidating ego like some CEOs. Instead,
she is quietly confident—and that makes us all feel more secure.

"Ms. Deily's intelligence has taken the bank to new
heights in profitability. Beyond that, people see her as a good
friend who listens and makes you feel important. I realize
that this may sound too good to be true, but her interest in
our feelings and what we have to say makes everyone want
to pull together for the success of First Interstate."

Just as senior management needs to know how employees feel about their company, it is important that each woman

and man makes her or his own assessment of the corporate environment. For only after companies and the people who work there acknowledge problems and identify their source can positive steps be taken. Once the leaders of a company determine that people are unhappy and why, they can begin assessing and implementing various options for change. By the same token, there is often a great deal those of us who work for corporations can do to improve the conditions under which we work, once we recognize the prevailing problems.

There is no question that making such workplace assessments can be a chancy proposition for both individuals and companies. Nevertheless, we believe such risks, once acknowledged, are well worth taking.

As individuals, we may conclude that our current work situation is beyond repair. If so, we may have to consider plying our skills elsewhere. This is a frightening prospect to some people, who would rather remain in an unhealthy situation and delude themselves that all is well—or at least tolerable.

At the same time, it takes courage for companies to invite employees to take a clear-eyed look at how they feel about their jobs, knowing that the ensuing assessment may cause some good people to leave. In the final analysis, a company's leaders need to ask themselves the following question: *Do we want people to work here out of choice or out of fear?*

Show me a company with a highly motivated work force, and I'll show you a flexible situation where people feel free to choose. As I often find myself telling CEOs and other top-management people:

"If you want to create conditions that will motivate the best people to stay, you have to help them develop the skills and allow them the freedoms that will enable them to leave.'

In Chapter One, we discussed the importance of fam: systems. It was noted that the negative attitudes and be:

iors exhibited by corporate leaders can impact employees in much the same way that a dysfunctional parent can cause codependence on the part of other family members. Companies that try to exert too tight a grip on their employees are very much like parents who are afraid to let go of their children. In the end, the only way to feel comfortable staying somewhere is the knowledge that you are free to go. Here's the bottom line:

✦ Healthy families foster choice and independence.

✦ Unhealthy families promote fear and codependence.

ASSESSING YOUR COMPANY'S WELLNESS QUOTIENT

We have noted that the first step in creating a healthy corporate environment is to assess current conditions. When I ask corporate leaders if they believe their people are happy, they will generally answer in the affirmative. More often than not, though, this assessment turns out to be inaccurate. If you want to find out how people feel, you need to ask them. Then you must give them an opportunity to respond candidly and without fear.

The two evaluation tools in this chapter are adapted from ones we use in our corporate and organizational work. They are designed to serve a twofold purpose.

1. From the perspective of the individual, these tools are helpful for evaluating objective conditions and subjective feelings about current or former working environments.

2. These instruments provide valuable feedback to businesses that administer them on a departmental or companywide basis. To ensure that employees are candid in assessing their work environment and the effect this

might be having on productivity, we suggest that respondents not be required to identify themselves.

Collectively, the scores on these two instruments can be used to assess an organization's health—or wellness quotient. We also suggest that senior management take this test from the point of view of a hypothetically typical worker. The distance between the way a company's leaders think people will respond and the actual cumulative response patterns of that company's employees provides a good gauge of how much work needs to be done to close the gap.

Exercise:
HOW FLEXIBLE IS MY COMPANY?

✦ ✦ ✦

Instructions   Please respond to each of the following statements by filling in the blanks with a "0" if the statement never applies to you, a "1" if it sometimes applies to you, and a "2" if it always applies to you.

1. I am unhappy with my job.
2. I feel that I am restricted to my assigned tasks.
3. I fear the consequences of making independent decisions.
4. My job bogs me down in paperwork and other meaningless tasks.
5. I feel disconnected and isolated from my organization.
6. I feel that I don't really count here.
7. I don't trust upper management.
8. People in my organization expend a lot of energy competing for turf.
9. I do not feel psychologically rewarded by my organization.
10. I do not respect upper management.
11. As time goes on, management is requiring more of me while providing fewer resources with which to work.

12. I do just enough work to get by.

13. I'm working mostly for money, time off, and the benefits package.

14. The main thing that keeps me working here is fear of the unknown.

15. I feel that, no matter how well I perform, I'm unlikely to receive a raise or promotion.

16. My manager gives me some power and then takes it back when he doesn't approve of my decisions.

17. The atmosphere in my organization stifles creativity.

Scoring   Add up your score and write down the total in the space provided.

Total:___

   0–10 = Great flexibility

   11–19 = Good flexibility

   20–26 = Very little flexibility

   27–34 = Paralyzed, rigid

The score on this exercise reveals the extent to which the corporate climate fosters flexibility or rigidity among its members. Individual respondents can use this instrument to evaluate their own situations. Managers who wish to evaluate the overall climate in their organizations should compute the average scores of respondents who complete the exercise.

The foregoing questions raise myriad concerns for both individuals and companies. When we speak of flexibility, we are addressing the organizational quality that frees people to be creative and express their ideas.

Not so long ago, flexibility wasn't thought to be a particularly critical factor in an organization's success. But today, we are living in a new economy with new rules and standards. Some of the underlying reasons why flexibility has become more of a factor as we edge closer to the twenty-first century include:

✧ Technological innovations

✧ The globalization of economic activity

✧ An ever-more-diverse work force

✧ An increasing emphasis on the value of time

When workers and managers feel hemmed in by rigid, authoritarian rules, there will be widespread dissatisfaction that ultimately impacts the bottom line. Businesses that succeed in the new economy will be those that can get the most out of their people—and this hinges on maximizing the skills and creativity of each team member.

"The game of economic competition has new rules, requiring great speed and flexibility on the part of business organizations," observes Anthony Carnevale, chief economist at the American Society for Training and Development. Once productivity was the key to success, notes Carnevale. "Today the new competitive standards include quality, variety, customization, convenience, and timeliness.

"Meeting the new standards requires that companies organize work and the way they use their human resources. New-economy organizations operate as flexible networks of information rather than rigid pyramids of power. Authority in these organizations tends to move where knowledge moves—across traditional boundaries and out to where people work face to face with customers, suppliers and even competitors."[7]

We've worked with a number of corporations whose lack of flexibility was not yet affecting the bottom line. Fortunately, the leaders of these companies understood the importance of taking an interest in what their people had to say before they were faced with an imminent crisis. We helped them recognize that flexibility in an organization is not only a key to worker satisfaction. Ultimately, it is a determining factor in corporate survival.

CREATING A FLEXIBLE CORPORATE ENVIRONMENT

To foster the kind of flexible corporate environment where people feel free to be creative contributors, senior management must evaluate their particular leadership style. In our corporate work, we find that these styles fall into three basic categories:

1. Command and control
2. Contracted trust
3. Indipreneurial

Most often, a company's organizational style can be gleaned from the way employees respond to the questionnaire on pages 37–38. The correlation generally looks something like this:

LEADERSHIP STYLE EMPLOYEES' FLEXIBILITY ASSESSMENT

Command and control	Rigid, highly inflexible
Contracted trust	Moderately inflexible
Indipreneurial	Highly flexible

Command-and-Control Companies

Command-and-control companies operate in what we call survival mode. On the top, you have a handful of upper-management types—predominantly white males—who are losing touch with the rest of an increasingly diverse work force. Directives are handed down from above with the expectation that they will be fulfilled—or else!

I would estimate that, prior to the 1990s, 75 to 80 percent of large corporations operated in this mode. However, the realities of the new economy are forcing companies to change their ways—or their leadership. The leaders of command-and-control companies resemble political dictators in the way they govern. They don't trust their people and, therefore, don't engender trust from them.

When I describe command-and-control organizations in my speeches, employees and middle managers often confide that this is indeed the mode their companies are in. Not surprisingly, top-level management at these companies rarely share in that assessment.

What we have here is another example of the perception gap between leadership and everyone else. Then again, why should those who rule wonder about what their underlings think? The answer is simply that the command-and-control strategy no longer works.

In both nations and businesses, leadership sets the stage for how everyone else acts. In far too many cases, the leaders of command-and-control companies suffer from what a *Business Week* cover story called CEO disease.[8] The symptoms of this malady include:

✦ An inability or unwillingness to admit mistakes

✦ A propensity for rewarding "yes people" rather than those who make meaningful contributions

✦ A need to make every decision without necessarily bothering to gather all relevant facts

As a result of these nonproductive attitudes and actions among command-and-control leaders, their companies have become dysfunctional. The problem goes beyond the relations between people within an organization. Too many top managers have effectively walled themselves off from vital information about markets, competitors, opportunities, and employee productivity—and this has created all sorts of problems.

Typically, the leaders of command-and-control companies pride themselves on being competitive. Ironically, the tone their behavior sets for everyone else winds up undermining a business's competitive edge. The *Business Week* article on CEO disease warns what can happen to a company afflicted by this form of leadership:

> Much of the damage . . . is insidious, striking at the heart of a corporation's ability to compete. . . . As the rank and file lose faith in top leadership, morale often collapses. Employees fail to generate the new ideas that are the lifeblood of any renewing enterprise. A we vs. them attitude prevails. Sometimes it can be a contributing factor in bringing a company down.[9]

Just as many political dictatorships are falling by the wayside, I believe that corporate cultures based on telling people what to do—and supposedly taking care of them—are on the way out. Tomorrow's successful companies will be those that encourage their people to think in terms of alternatives and options. This belief is based not on idealism, but on hard-edge social and economic realities.

In my travels, I find that the corporations that are hurting most are those inflexibly bound up in a command-and-control mode. There are, of course, some paternalistic companies that are still in the black. It's worth noting, however, that the leadership in a growing number of these organizations are in the process of changing over to more forward-looking management styles. As one such CEO recently confided:

"We're holding our own at the moment, but I'd be a fool not to recognize the writing on the wall. Economic realities are changing—as are the needs of our people. If we fail to respond to those changes, we're doomed to failure. At some point, we may be merged, bought out or taken over. I can't say exactly what might happen, but I do know that we have to change as conditions warrant or we will not continue to be viable."

Contracted-Trust Companies

Corporate leaders who want their people to be motivated in a reasonably positive way have come to recognize that they must move into an organizational mode that entails a sharing of power. Companies that take some initial steps in that direction are often operating in what I call a contracted-trust basis.

People who work at contracted-trust companies have a spirit of cooperation and negotiation that surpasses anything you'll find in command-and-control organizations. But, from my perspective, contracted-trust organizations are not innovative because the trust they engender isn't genuine. To the extent that shared power exists, it requires constant surveillance.

W. C. Fields aptly described the corporate culture of the contracted-trust organization when he said, "Trust everybody but cut the cards." Eventually, the energy spent on policing activity—that is, constantly cutting the cards—results in an organizational bog that erodes a company's ability to maximize flexibility.

Organizations based on contracted trust are often beset by all sorts of manipulative politics. People feel that if they don't watch their backs they will either be stepped over or undermined. This self-protective attitude can pervade every level of a company and eventually erode the bottom line. Ask yourself if the actions and attitudes in the following list characterize the people in your organization:

FIVE NONPRODUCTIVE BEHAVIORS FOUND
AT CONTRACTED-TRUST COMPANIES

1. Constant attempts at manipulating people and situations
2. Managing information and plans with an eye toward personal gain rather than the benefit of the group
3. Making personnel decisions based on favoritism rather than merit
4. Concentrating on pleasing superiors rather than doing excellent work
5. Lying or distorting the truth to get ahead

When I think about companies based on contracted trust, I am reminded of the economic agreements the United States has with Japan, or the arms agreements it had with the Commonwealth of Independent States (formerly the USSR). Nations can agree to share the power on a worldwide basis, but all treaties must be constantly policed to assure compliance. In addition, specific consequences must be spelled out should one of the parties violate the terms of the agreement. This is not the kind of heartfelt trust that twenty-first-century organizations need to foster among their people.

Indipreneurial Companies

In my opinion, the only organizations that are likely to sustain in the new economy are those whose employees work there out of choice rather than need. As Figure 2.1 indicates, this kind of organization is circular in nature.

FIGURE 2.1
✧
The Indipreneurial Organization

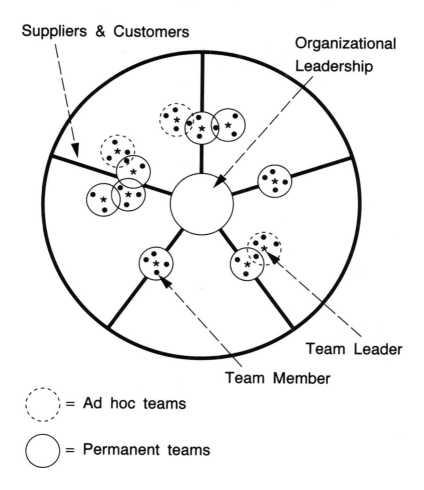

The hub at the middle represents the leadership. The authority within the organization is divided up into many other smaller circles that have permanent and ad hoc team leaders and members involved. Radiating out from that are suppliers and customers that form the spokes of the wheel. There has been much discussion of the benefits and virtues of the circular organization. With respect to our present discussion, I would like to consider this type of organizational structure in terms of earned trust and indipreneurship.

Unlike contracted trust, earned trust is based on the *words and actions* of a people-centered leadership. In this kind of organization, senior management does not feel entitled to loyalty. Instead, they recognize that true loyalty and trust must be nurtured. Trust exists only to the extent that it can be demonstrated by a company's leadership. In such organizations, people follow the lead and are likewise worthy of trust.

For a company to become truly indipreneurial, its people must be able to function as both independent thinkers and team players. This is one of the primary goals we try to help organizations realize. Before we can do that, we often have to dispel a good deal of skepticism. Why should a company's leaders and employees believe that the concept of the indipreneurial organization is nothing more than another piece of mushy rhetoric that can never be made to work?

I see no contradiction between being a hard-nosed business person and having lofty visions. I believe it was George Bernard Shaw who coined a phrase that the late Robert Kennedy made famous:

> Some (people) see things as they are and say why. But I dream things that never were and say—why not?[10]

Until recently, few business leaders could conceive of anything more than a streamlined hierarchical structure. But, today, more and more decision makers are starting to understand the necessity of changing the way things get done in their organizations. The demands of the new economy have propelled some visionary leaders to move their companies into an organizational mode that comes close to the indipreneurial standard.

Once a leader recognizes that the aggregate performance of its people is the key to an organization's success, he or she must assume the responsibility of creating conditions under which superb performance serves both the company's and the individual's best interests.

An indipreneurial organization does not overly concern itself with status. Its leaders recognize that line workers are every bit as important as managers. One step is doing away with traditional hierarchical terminology. At many indipreneurial organizations, for example, employees are called associates or members, while managers are called coaches or facilitators.

Here again, it's essential that changes in terminology be supported by substantive steps. In many contracted-trust organizations, for example, the largest salaries are doled out to managers. Consequently, the most talented people at some companies are often promoted to administrative positions where they in effect become paper shufflers whose creative skills are not being utilized.

Many managers have confided that they felt compelled to accept their current positions because of better remuneration. At the same time, they missed being involved in hands-on functions and felt stifled. To prevent this, the 3M company has created a two-path system that allows the creative staff to make as much as or even more money than their supervisors.[11]

Indipreneurial companies recognize that people who feel happy tend to be more productive. Part of that state of being comes from feeling that one has control over one's destiny. One study conducted at the Westinghouse Electric

Company found a strong link between job conditions and mental health. The study debunks the myth that stress is worse at higher levels of management. In fact, the more control a person has at his or her job, the less the level of stress.[12]

SEVEN WAYS TO TURN A JOB INTO A CAREER

What do you want to be when you grow up? This is a question most of us pondered when we were young. What we were thinking about were careers rather than jobs—pursuits that brought us psychic income as well as money. In corporate America today, what we too often find are people working at jobs simply to earn a paycheck.

Ideally, if people could do what they liked, they would work even if there were no remuneration. Of course, the realities of day-to-day living often make that impractical if not impossible. Still, the more psychic rewards and self-esteem we can bundle into a job, the more productive a person will be.

To a great extent, it's not so much what a person does, but the conditions under which he or she must function. I very much enjoy working with people and companies in helping them reach their potential. But, if I had to do that work in a claustrophobic environment where I was harassed by a supervisor and pressed for time, I might not like it so much.

Employers may not always be able to provide everything a worker needs to consider her job a career. Still, it's in an organization's best interests to provide everything possible to make people feel that they are exchanging their skills for something more than money.

It has been my experience that rigid organizations tend to attract and keep fearful people—men and women who will remain in negative circumstances mostly because they are afraid to risk leaving. Only flexible organizations can provide the kinds of psychic rewards creative people want and need. People who remain on jobs without receiving psychic rewards will eventually experience burnout. Consequently, they will be functioning as automatons incapable of making productive contributions.

Corporate cultures that do not build in psychic rewards often experience a large turnover in good times, when more appealing jobs are easier to come by. During tough economic times, turnover may still be high if people feel burned out and used up. I meet a growing number of dissatisfied men and women who are quitting their jobs and simplifying their life-styles. These folks are opting to sell their homes and cars to get out of financial debt and pursue more rewarding career options.

People who do not receive all the psychic rewards they require from their jobs can sometimes make up the deficit through hobbies and volunteerism. However, these supplementary activities are effective only for those whose jobs supply at least a modicum of psychic nourishment.

To maximize psychic rewards within an organization and move toward the indipreneurial model, there are seven key requirements:

1. Trust must be earned by management, not demanded of the people.

2. The organization must be centered on the needs of people, not just the pursuit of profit.

3. The organization must foster a sense of community between all team members. In a society where family and religious values are not what they once were, people have a tremendous need to belong to something greater than themselves.

4. Power, responsibility, and decision making must be distributed equitably throughout the organization.

5. Environmental dynamism must pervade the organization. Senior management must foster a sense that the team as a whole represents something greater than the sum of its parts. By definition, an indipreneurial organization negotiates its competitive marketplace as a team, not as an extension of a few powerful leaders.

6. Coming to work must be perceived as a positive experience. This feeling is reinforced by many things—including a pleasant physical environment, rules and dress codes that reflect the spirit of the team, and a sense of humor and fun. The people who build their careers at indipreneurial companies are excited about what they and their teams are doing. They actually look forward to coming to work.

7. Indipreneurial companies must be good training grounds that provide a variety of opportunities for team members to grow and advance. The idea of investing heavily in training as a way of providing psychic rewards to employees is one that the leaders of some organizations find problematic. Why, they ask, should they teach their employees skills that don't directly relate to their tasks?

For one thing, talented and highly motivated people want to work in a place where they can advance themselves—if not in their present company, then elsewhere. They will not accept outmoded equipment, dead-end jobs, or a bleak atmosphere. Only people who work out of fear will accept such conditions for long.

There is a good deal of data suggesting that employees tend to stay with companies that provide training. Here again, we see an example of the reciprocal needs of organizations and their members.

In theory, the purpose of training is to make people more valuable to the company. But, at the same time, a company that provides training and educational opportunities is making itself more valuable to its people. A closer examination reveals that the reciprocal relationship between companies and their employees cuts even more deeply.

If we as individuals can no longer count on security by virtue of being employed, we must make sure that we possess the job and lifeskills that make us employable. This is equally important—whether you wish to remain with your present organization, move to another company, or launch your own business venture.

At the same time, organizations that offer their members the opportunity to be more creative and indipreneurial will have a competitive edge in recruiting and retaining the best people. Let me now share with you the seven-point program we use to help organizations in this area.

SEVEN WAYS TO PROMOTE AN ATMOSPHERE THAT NURTURES CREATIVITY

1. As in all matters, an organization's leaders must set the stage for creativity. By definition, it is impossible for rigid leadership to foster creativity. The leaders of indipreneurial organizations make it known that they are open to new ideas from all team members. These leaders are spontaneous in their dealings and encourage spontaneity from others. They create a relaxed atmosphere throughout the organization by demonstrating that they themselves are relaxed.

2. Set up a work environment that fosters relaxation and resourcefulness. Most indipreneurial companies are attractive and relaxed places in which to work. The buildings convey a feeling of freedom in their design and architecture. The work spaces are physically comfortable and well lit. One is often struck by the abundance of bright sunlight, green plants, and fresh air as one walks around.

Several years ago, I took time to set my office at home up as a kind of creativity center, and it has enhanced my work immeasurably. Aside from implementing all the aspects just discussed, I have made my environment noise and interruption free. Whenever necessary, I defer phone calls until I am through creating. I have a small refrigerator filled with healthful and energizing snacks. The room looks out on a garden full of trees, flowers, and singing birds. It is truly a great place to create. I find pleasure in helping others customize similar creativity centers to meet their particular needs.

There are all sorts of things that can be done to develop the kind of relaxed work environment that fosters creativity. I encourage my corporate clients to allow people to wear comfortable clothing. Bill Miller, vice president of in-flight services for the highly profitable Southwest Airlines, says that all employees are encouraged to dress casually during the summer months.

"At times, we even allow our flight attendants to wear tennis shoes," Bill told me. "These folks have to walk and stand for so many hours on end, it makes sense to let them loosen up a bit."

There may, of course, be occasions when more formal attire is called for. But forcing people to wear suits and ties always can cause the work environment to become stiff and stifled.

Companies with rigid dress codes also tend to have cubicles and offices that look exactly the same as one another. As with dress, I believe that letting people decorate their own offices is another simple way companies can encourage creativity.

3. *View mistakes and problems as opportunities for growth.* Creativity cannot flourish in an organization that punishes

mistakes and fails to recognize that without problems there would be no way to break new ground.

Conventional wisdom equates ducking problems with the avoidance of pain, but the two are not equal. While it's true that confronting a problem often involves the acknowledgment of pain, this recognition is the first step to coming up with creative solutions that engender growth. All of us have varying degrees of fear about uncovering problems. Organizations and people who welcome problems as opportunities are exhibiting courage and faith in the future. Here are some of the things the indipreneurial organizations we work with do to reduce such fears:

✧ One communications company gives out a weekly award for the worst error, on the theory that this creates the most fortuitous chance to unearth new discoveries.

✧ One national restaurant chain assigns people to search out problems in various phases of the operation. Once problems are identified, teams are given the responsibility to come up with creative solutions.

✧ A well-known electronics manufacturer rewards team members for trying to fix a problem—as well as for finding the fix to the problem. The leaders of this organization have concluded that generating multiple solutions to problems is an exciting process that fosters a creative mind-set throughout the organization.

4. Celebrate diversity and differences. In setting up teams, it is essential to emphasize diversity in such areas as age, gender, and cultural background. This approach fosters creativity because it brings to the table a variety of styles, backgrounds, viewpoints, and problem-solving menus.

While there may be a tendency on the part of some people to want to be grouped with others like themselves, most women and men learn to appreciate the importance diversity plays in coming up with creative solutions.

In dealing with diverse teams, it is important to welcome conflict and to manage it effectively. Differences between the individual styles of team members are bound to surface. We work with organizations in fostering an atmosphere where conflicts are centered on issues—not personalities.

5. *Take specific steps to nurture increased creativity—and make these programs accessible throughout the organization.* Set up idea days or weeks—even creativity sabbaticals—so that people have time to be thoughtful and creative.

Not all creative pursuits can be accomplished in the confines of the normal work setting. Some companies have discovered the value of providing time in retreat environments for team members.

We have been conducting an increasing amount of our creativity programs in various retreat and off-site situations. A change of scenery can be a good way to relax, rekindle the creative juices, and renew the way we view the world, the competition, and ourselves.

Time away from the workplace gives us a chance to indulge in a process I call "creative daydreaming." Having a sense that there are absolutely no boundaries to what one can think or feel is essential when trying to come up with new ideas.

In addition to time spent alone, people attempting to be creative need opportunities for brainstorming with others. Whatever the environment, there must be a balance of time spent alone and time spent collaborating with others. The exact mix depends on the nature of the specific project and the people who are involved.

6. *Build as much humor as possible in to every pore of the work environment.* Humor, fun, laughter, play: these notions

sound like the antithesis of what work is supposed to be. But, in fact, humor is a feeling that pervades just about everything else. If you are smiling and laughing on a regular basis, it's a good bet that you're going to have a more positive feeling about where you are and what you're doing.

It's possible to have fun in any kind of work setting—even hospitals. "Everything is so serious in a hospital," says Eileen Beasley, human resources director for RHD Memorial Medical Center in Dallas, Texas. "We have to remember that we are human and need to laugh once in a while—even if it's at ourselves."

Reba Anderson, director of pharmacy for RHD Memorial, smiles when she talks about the fun she and her coworkers have. "The pharmacy is an exacting place," says Reba. "Because accuracy is of utmost importance, the stress factor is high.

"One of the many things we do is prepare a five-minute Halloween performance that we put on for each department. The fun we have putting our performance together really helps us stay loose. I'm convinced this and similar activities have resulted in far less human error."

No matter what the context, there is evidence that laughter reduces stress, improves the immune system, and increases the level of endorphins in our bodies. Humor can make a person more creative and even increase learning capacity. When you have fun, you can eventually reach a state of flow called *in fun*. This euphoric state stimulates additional chemical changes that produce even higher levels of creativity.

7. *The organization must take responsibility for establishing specific rules or guidelines for creativity so that people can understand how to become more creative.* Here are ten guidelines we use with our clients:

Ten Steps to Creative Problem Solving

1. Define the problem as a problem. Look at the parameters of the problem and understand that a problem is always the seed that propels the creative process into motion. Problems lead to ideas. Ideas generate innovations and/or solutions.

2. Establish a deadline for coming up with a solution. The mind tends to work toward closure. If there is a deadline, it is more likely that the problem will be addressed and resolved in a timely fashion.

3. Relax and don't panic if solutions aren't immediately forthcoming. Creative ideas and solutions will come in their own time. Sometimes, it helps to bombard yourself with information. At other times, it's helpful to take time to relax and clear your mind before returning to the matter at hand.

4. Work in a pleasant place, free of distractions and interruptions.

5. Read, interview, investigate, and bombard your mind without sorting, parameterizing, or closing yourself off from new ideas.

6. In the course of creating, be sure to think, daydream, make connections, and have fun. When you feel overwhelmed or at an impasse, do something to break out of your mold. Rest, take a walk, work on another project, take a short nap—then try again.

7. Listen to your body. Never deprive yourself of the nourishment, exercise, or sleep you need to be at your best. Learn the best times for you to do different kinds of tasks—and use that awareness to your advantage.

8. Don't get overwhelmed. Work on solving one small part of the problem at a time, while keeping the big picture in sight. There is a stacking effect that occurs when one part of the problem is solved successfully. This tends to enhance the development of creative solutions to subsequent parts of the problem.

9. When you feel ready, communicate your ideas to others and encourage their response. This can result in a positive creative chain that engenders faster and more productive solutions.

10. Develop positive and negative scenarios concerning how things might be as a result of specific solutions. Test these scenarios on others to determine their plausibility. Ask for alternative scenarios. Then test these in the same way.

Before an organization's leaders can establish a flexible environment where meaningful creativity can flourish, they must first establish a long-range focus that lends meaningful structure to day-to-day activities. This focus must then be communicated to everyone in the organization; if not, true teamwork will be impossible.

One reason so many corporations are in pain is the feeling among employees that top management has no overriding plan or vision for the future. Such feelings, however well founded, cause an erosion in confidence with respect to everything leadership says and does.

The following instrument measures the extent to which an organization knows where it is heading. As with the preceding exercise, "How Flexible Is My Company?" we suggest that organizations using this exercise on a departmental or companywide basis do not ask respondents to identify themselves. This anonymity encourages straightforward responses on the part of those assessing their work environment. Such meaningful feedback can, in turn, serve as a springboard for meaningful change.

*E*XERCISE:
HOW WELL FOCUSED IS MY COMPANY?

✦ ✦ ✦

Instructions Please respond to the following statements by filling in the blank at the end of each statement with a "0" if the statement never applies to you, a "1" if it sometimes applies to you, and a "2" if it always applies to you.

1. I don't have time to do all that is expected of me. ____

2. I have to jump from one task to another before I have a chance to complete what I'm working on. ____

3. I often feel stressed and burned out. ____

4. I don't know what management expects of me. ____

5. I often feel that I'm going to fail at my assigned tasks. ____

6. I feel confused most of the time. ____

7. I need more training to do my job well. ____

8. Management doesn't seem interested in what I'm doing. ____

9. Management talks about empowering employees, but, in reality, all that means is that someone on a higher rung has shoved something off on me that he'd rather not deal with. ____

10. Management does not give me the tools and support I need to do my job well. ____

11. I'm working without any clearly defined goals. ____

12. I'm often asked to sacrifice tangible incentives for vague and unnamed future rewards. ____

13. There seems to be more concern with punishing mistakes than with rewarding achievement. ____

14. My manager is almost always too busy to pay attention to me. ____

15. There is great deal of talk about trust, yet much important information concerning goals, budgets, progress and problems is withheld from the vast majority of employees. ____

Scoring Add up your score and put the total in the space provided.

Total___

>0–8 = A very well-focused company whose employees feel empowered and in touch with corporate and departmental goals
>
>9–15 = A moderately well-focused company
>
>16–22 = A poorly focused company whose employees feel out of touch with corporate and departmental goals
>
>23–28 = A very troubled company

The score on this exercise indicates the extent to which the corporate climate fosters meaningful structure or chaos among its members. Readers can use this instrument to evaluate their own situations. Managers who wish to evaluate the overall climate in their organizations should compute the average scores of respondents who complete the exercise.

A THREE-STEP PROGRAM FOR CREATING MEANINGFUL CORPORATE VISION

To establish and maintain a clearly defined vision, an organization must have its people understand the three different areas designated as follows:

1. The mission
2. The message
3. The method

The *mission* must represent something far more than a high-minded statement on the wall. In a well-focused organization, the mission encompasses the ideas that are to be embraced by everybody involved with the organization. The best mission statements are short and to the point, as is the case of the one that follows from Litton Industries:

> [Litton Industries is] a technology-based company applying advanced electronics products and services to business opportunities in defense, industrial automation, and geophysical markets.[13]

Before a mission can be accomplished, people must be adequately trained and motivated. As was noted in the previous section, these hinge on the flexibility and creativity engendered by indipreneurial organizations. One good model for understanding the relationship between a mission and an organization's ability to carry it out is a successful athletic team.

There are 12 players on a professional basketball team—5 who start each game. Of the remaining 7 players, between 3 and 5 usually enter the game for significant periods of time. Assuming that there are no injuries, the remaining team members may see little or no game action—although they may be instrumental in practice sessions.

On a winning team, each player understands and accepts his role relative to the team's mission. Any player who makes it to the professional level was probably the star of his high school and college teams. As a pro, he may be expected to assume a more supportive or subordinate role for the sake of the team. The best basketball teams don't necessarily possess the 12 most talented individual players. What they do possess is the best *blend* of talent.

Each player understands his role on the team. Each trains and practices continuously to maximize his contribution to the team effort. It is hoped that the combination of individuals collaborating in the service of their mission amount to something more than a combination of parts— that is, a team.

Whether in sports or in business, I view a team as the energetic and enthusiastic movement of two or more cooperating individuals toward a common mission. Keep in mind that there is a difference between a mission and a goal. A mission is complex, repeatable, improvable, and emotionally involving. It is created within the organizational culture and pursued through the attainment of long-range goals that are broken down into smaller achievable units.

In Chapter Three, we will further explore the setting and achievement of goals. With respect to our present discussion, however, the key difference to grasp between a mission and a goal is that a goal is short term and obtained only once, whereas a mission is a set of behaviors that are continually repeated throughout the life of the organization and can be achieved over and over again.

The *message* is the next logical step in creating meaningful corporate vision. The message is, in effect, the culture of an organization as expressed in the values it deems to be important. The message of an organization must speak of the real values that are consistent with the culture, or there is bound to be a trust gap.

One of my corporate clients is T.G.I. Friday's, Inc., the international restaurant chain. Friday's prides itself on having a corporate culture that cares about its people. As you will see shortly, this company isn't just spouting a bunch of rhetoric. It goes all out to demonstrate to its employees how much it cares for them.

Frankly, I've always been skeptical when corporations make a big issue about how much they care for their employees. When I was younger, I worked for a company that spent thousands of dollars on printed materials about how much they valued their employees. After a few weeks of working there, I was disappointed to learn that management really looked upon employees as numbers.

In a sense, this kind of situation harks back to our earlier discussion of dysfunctional or unhealthy family systems. In such families, it is not uncommon for parents to tell children that they love them while demonstrating indifferent or even abusive behavior. As with the kind of situation I faced at my former company, it doesn't take people long to recognize the difference between what a parent or business leader says versus what he or she does.

The *method* is the way an organization's message is actually delivered. I mentioned that T.G.I. Friday's has a corporate culture that sends out a message of concern about its people. Let me give you a poignant example of how this concern is expressed:

Recently, T.G.I. Friday's home office scheduled an all-day management development meeting. When it was learned that an ailing manager who was facing imminent surgery felt disappointed that he wouldn't be able to attend, the company's leaders decided to go all out to make this team member's presence at the event a reality.

A special recliner was purchased for the meeting so that the gentleman would be able to attend without disturbing his delicate medical condition. I consider this an extraordinary step for an organization to take in methodizing its message, and I applaud T.G.I. Friday's for it.

Aside from being ready to stand fully behind its message, an organization's success in achieving appropriate and effective methods is closely linked with *tracking*—the lifeskill we will explore in Chapter Three.

In much the same way that an individual must find a unique track for achieving her potential, an organization needs to find a way of developing and pursuing a vision that maximizes the potential of the team.

Rᴇᴀʟɪᴢɪɴɢ ᴛʜᴇ Vɪsɪᴏɴ

In establishing a suitable method, an organization paints a clear picture of a vision that is, in turn, communicated to all team members. The leadership in coordination with the people must understand and buy into that vision.

Richard C. Bartlett, vice chairman of Mary Kay Corporation, is a leader who has demonstrated a commitment to communicating the organization's vision to his team. The company's phenomenal worldwide growth and high-quality product line reflect Mr. Bartlett's success at motivating every member of the corporate staff and sales force to participate in the pursuit of the Mary Kay vision, which reads as follows:

✧ *To be preeminent in the manufacturing, distribution, and marketing of personal care products through our independent sales force.*

✧ *To provide our sales force an unparalleled opportunity for financial independence, career achievement, and personal fulfillment.*

✧ *To achieve total customer satisfaction worldwide by focusing on quality, value, convenience, innovation, and personal service.*

You will note that this vision statement contains a clearly defined three-part mission:

1. *to be preeminent in the manufacturing, distribution, and marketing of personal care products;*
2. *to provide our sales force an unparalleled opportunity for financial independence, career achievement, and personal fulfillment;*
3. *to achieve total customer satisfaction worldwide.*

It has a well-defined message, which is expressed in the words—*by focusing on quality, value, convenience, innovation, and personal service.*

Finally, the method for achieving the Mary Kay vision is revealed in the words—*through our independent sales force.*

Like all teams, a successful corporation must not reflect anything less than the sum of its parts. Ideally, it can evolve into an amalgam of positive attributes that add up to something greater than its components. Today, the leaders of many organizations have come to recognize that their human resources are being squandered or underutilized—and that this is impacting the bottom line.

When an organization's leaders start to understand the pragmatic value of receiving positive contributions from all quarters, they often begin talking about change. As we have seen, however, talking is just the first step in attempting to become a truly indipreneurial organization.

In the late 1980s, companies began calling us in to help make their people more productive contributors. The usual request was that we train people in what everyone then referred to as empowerment skills. What we quickly learned was that many organizations had people who were not ready to be empowered. They simply did not possess the requisite lifeskills.

Empowerment is considered an overused term in some quarters. To my mind, it never did adequately pinpoint the most pressing needs of organizations or individuals. We began using the term *indipreneurial* to describe the independence and entrepreneurial spirit people and companies require to meet today's challenges—and those that await us in the future.

Part II of this book teaches the indipreneurial lifeskills we will all need to survive and thrive in the twenty-first century. These step-by-step techniques have been used to advantage by CEOs of large corporations, middle managers, and front-line employees. They are equally relevant to a self-employed person, to a civil service employee or someone who has spent his or her entire career working for the same company.

As we close in on the twenty-first century, it is clear that indipreneurial lifeskills are needed by people of all ages. Nobody is too old or too young to benefit from them: the student who wants to learn how to learn, the college graduate who is starting out on a career path, the middle manager with 20 years of experience who has recently been laid off, the employee who feels stifled by her job, the retiree who seeks to redirect his life.

Whatever your age or situation, we at The Center for the 21st Century have helped people in similar circumstances. As you will learn, the lifeskills can be applied in virtually any workplace or personal situation. I sincerely hope you will make the most of these principles and techniques.

ENDNOTES

1. Ralph Stayer, "How I Learned to Let My Workers Lead," *Harvard Business Review,* November 1990.

2. Peter Block, *The Empowered Manager* (San Francisco: Jossey Bass, 1991).

3. Peter Drucker is cited by Alan Farnham in "The Trust Gap," *Fortune,* December 4, 1989.

4. The *Industry Week* magazine survey is cited in *The Dallas Times Herald,* March 2, 1991.

5. The Louis Harris poll is cited by Alan Farnham in "The Trust Gap," *Fortune,* December 4, 1989.

6. The Foster Higgins survey is cited in ibid.

7. Anthony Carnevale, *America and the New Economy* (Alexandria, VA: American Society for Training and Development and the U.S. Department of Labor, 1990).

8. John A. Byrne and William C. Symonds, "CEO Disease," *Business Week,* April 1, 1991.

9. Ibid.

10. George Bernard Shaw/Robert Kennedy quote was attributed to Senator Robert F. Kennedy of New York by his brother, Senator Edward M. Kennedy of Massachusetts, at memorial service in New York following the assassination of Robert, June 9, 1968.

11. Judy Waldrop, "Meet the New Boss," *American Demographics,* June 1991.

12. Ibid.

13. Litton Industries' mission statement is cited by Burt Nanus in *Visionary Leadership* (San Francisco: Jossey Bass, 1992).

PART II

DEVELOPING INDIPRENEURIAL LIFESKILLS

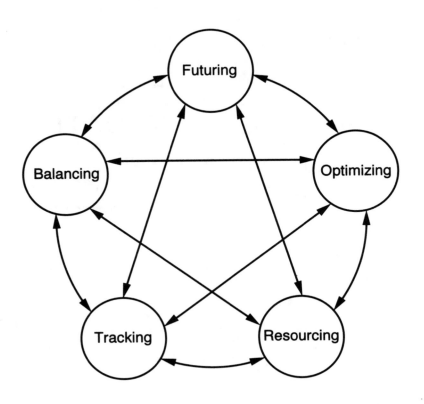

CHAPTER 3

TRACKING: DISCOVERING YOUR UNIQUE PATH

MAXIMIZING YOURSELF AS A RESOURCE

As we've seen, many people who work in the corporate world have never learned to take charge of the psychic rewards that come from exchanging their skills for income. Consequently, they've become overly dependent on their companies for financial security as well as ego strength. Let's face it: when everything in your life—from your friends to the payment of your doctor bills—is provided by the work-place, the very thought of losing this stabilizing force can pose a severe threat to your identity and self-esteem.

If you are going to achieve your full potential—be it in a corporate setting or your own business venture—it is essential to move out of this paralyzing mind-set. The first step in this process is to understand that no person or organization can provide the psychic nourishment necessary for sustenance and growth. This is something each of us must do for ourselves.

Accepting the responsibility for controlling as many occurrences as possible is the first giant step you must take if you are going to anticipate and effectively manage the following kinds of probable life events:

*P*REDICTABLE UNCERTAINTIES

- ✦ Career interruption
- ✦ Illness or disability
- ✦ Property loss
- ✦ Raising and educating children
- ✦ Coping with aging parents
- ✦ Divorce
- ✦ Death of a spouse or significant other
- ✦ Retirement

I'm sure this isn't the first time you've been reminded about the importance of taking responsibility. Unfortunately, such solid but well-meaning advice often goes in one ear and out the other. Here's why.

I've stated my belief in the virtues of embracing the hard road. This requires, among other things, that a person focus on long-term growth rather than short-term gratification. Think about it: if I'm not in touch with the qualities and attributes that make me unique, why should I assume the responsibility for doing all the work it takes to realize my potential?

In our competitive society, we hear a great deal of talk about being a winner—but what does that really mean? In my view, winners are people who have taken the time to find their special place and are running on that singular track that is right for them. I call this lifeskill *tracking*.

Beyond mastering the specific skills cluster we cover in this chapter, tracking entails two underlying beliefs:

1. Each of us is a truly unique being.
2. That uniqueness is worth pursuing.

Although I have not yet had the opportunity to meet many of you, there is no question in my mind that you have a special place in the world, and that you are here to make a difference. But, to achieve that potential, you must develop the skills that will enable you to discover your unique track.

When I speak of tracking as a lifeskill, I'm not just referring to succeeding in your career or in business. Discovering your unique path will have a positive impact on every area of your life. It will raise your self-esteem, improve your personal and business relationships, and place you in sync with the rhythms of the universe.

MASTERING THE THREE-PHASE TRACKING SKILLS CLUSTER

The three phases that concern us in this discussion are:

Phase 1: Master planning

Phase 2: Measuring

Phase 3: Feedback analysis

In recent years, people have expressed strong concern about improving their tracking skills with respect to their careers. This turns out to be as good a place as any to dig in.

Men and women who learn how to get their careers on track are usually able to extend this lifeskill into the personal realm, which, in turn, serves to make them even more productive in their work-related endeavors.

On-track men and women who are passionate about their careers tend to be highly successful. At the same time, the true measure of their success does not hinge on material possessions or other external criteria. Beautiful houses and luxurious automobiles are nice, but they tend to assume a secondary role for people who are in touch with their gifts and driven by their passions.

As you think about your career, ask yourself the following questions:

✧ Do you have a realistic assessment of your abilities and talents?

✧ Are you aware of those strengths that make you stand out?

✧ Are you pursuing a direction that provides you with opportunities to maximize those strengths?

These are just some of the issues that must be addressed before you can find the track on which you are uniquely suited to run. While some of you will probably have to do a good deal of work in this area, there's no need to be overwhelmed. Together, we are going to go through this process step by manageable step. Once you begin to discover the track that's right for you, the positive energy created will keep propelling you forward.

THE FIVE P'S OF MASTER PLANNING

1. Purpose
2. Perspective
3. Plans
4. Priorities
5. Pieces

PHASE 1:
MASTER PLANNING

Planning Your Undertaking

STEP 1: STATE YOUR PURPOSE A statement of purpose is nothing more than the verbal reflection of a dream. In this phase of master planning, you are not yet concerned with implementation. The object here is simply to define the principles on which your plans and goals will hinge. Individuals need a defined purpose for the same reasons that organizations need missions. In fact, the two terms can be used interchangeably in this context. A purpose or mission statement provides focus for its creator, as well as a tool for communicating with others.

As we noted in Chapter Two, a mission is more general and complex than a goal. Just as an organization's mission enables it to set parameters for the team, an individual's statement of purpose provides the conceptual basis for action. An individual mission statement should be no more than about 50 key words—as is the case with my own professional mission statement, which I have hanging on the wall of my office:

> To help people identify and develop the indipreneurial lifeskills necessary to achieve personal and professional fulfillment in the 21st century.

As we've seen, a mission is realized through the pursuit and attainment of long-range goals that are broken down into smaller achievable units. One of the long-range goals I set with respect to my particular mission was to write this book. Some of the specific steps entailed in that process are discussed in this chapter.

STEP 2: ENGINEER YOUR PERSPECTIVE Before you embark on any project, it is important to formulate a vision—that is, a mental picture of its outcome. Since the idea of a mission is to give you a basis for action, you need a blueprint that allows you to visualize the end result. It is instructive to compare the kind of perspective you need for effective tracking to the advanced design engineers must consider when constructing a master-planned community.

Before construction begins, there is a detailed blueprint or layout of the entire community. This gives people both inside and outside the project a complete picture of, among other things, where houses and businesses will be located, where trees, hedges, and plants can be positioned, and where parking and recreational facilities will be placed.

Perspective is no less important in the development of smaller projects. Consequently, building a house requires the same kind of process as creating an entire community. Before a builder starts work, he will visualize and illustrate every detail in advance. This gives the builder—as well as potential buyers—an opportunity to glimpse the end product before construction ever begins.

Formulating a perspective lets you make conceptual changes before actually getting down to the nuts and bolts. It also helps reduce the number of surprises you are likely to encounter along the way, while giving you an opportunity to clarify your preferences and values.

Now that you've seen why perspective is an essential part of tracking, it is important to understand the relationship between the two ingredients necessary for its development: *knowledge* and *vision*.

There would be no way to construct a blueprint for a house unless you first knew something about its structural and aesthetic requirements. At the same time, you need some kind of vision to conceive of the kind of house you want.

In a sense, knowledge and vision complement each other. Your vision is, to a great extent, restricted by your knowledge. At the same time, it is often one's vision that motivates a person to seek knowledge in a particular area.

Think of it like this: What you know—your knowledge—determines what you see; what you see—your vision—determines the road you take in life and how far you will go. A lack of vision will make it impossible for you to maximize the knowledge at your disposal. At the same time, limited knowledge can cause a narrowing of vision.

I recall a time when I was flying from Chicago's O'Hare airport to the Dallas-Ft. Worth airport. We boarded the plane and waited on the runway for two and a half hours. At the end of that time, the pilot informed us that we were returning to the gate. After checking all the instruments, it was found that the right wing compass was out of order.

The pilot explained that without a compass, we would have no direction-finding instrument. As far as he was concerned, that constituted a no-go situation. I submit that without using vision and knowledge to lend perspective to your dream, you too will be facing a no-go situation.

STEP 3: CREATE YOUR PLANS Planning is the road map for realizing your purpose. Once you know what your focus is and have a perspective on what you would like the end result to be, you are in a position to start planning. To plan effectively, you need to gather a good deal of pertinent information—especially if you are pursuing unfamiliar goals.

For example, when I decided to write a book, I started gathering the information I would need to create an effective plan. This included:

✧ Information about the book publishing business.

✧ Information about the potential market for the kind of book I wanted to write.

✧ Information of what specific tasks would be required to complete the book.

✧ Information about obstacles I might encounter along the way.

✧ Information that would enable me to make a realistic projection of the time frames needed to complete various phases of the process.

✧ Information about the people and services I would require.

✧ Resources that could help me find information I was lacking in any of the preceding areas.

In Chapter Four, we will discuss the best ways to unearth and maximize both informational and human resources. For now, I want you to recognize the value of effective planning—a process that one time-efficiency expert Robert Moskowitz describes as "the mechanism that lets you get out of the crush and constant flow of events."[1]

I've seen too many talented men and women jump into projects without first creating a road map. People who do this are sometimes characterized as running around like chickens without heads. They can articulate their purpose, and they seem to have loads of energy and desire. But without viable plans, they tend to waste time, soon get frustrated, and wind up quitting in discouragement.

STEP 4: SET YOUR PRIORITIES "I'm going to get around to it as soon as I have a chance." Whenever somebody says these words, they are revealing that *it* is not a priority for them. Once you set your plans and have an idea of the nuts and bolts that are involved, you have to start ranking things in order of importance. Failing to do so can make it next to impossible to get anything done.

As you consider your plans, you will find that some require immediate action, while others can be dealt with at a later date. Time limitations are key in setting priorities—and not only yours.

Consider what might happen if you needed a specific person's counsel and he was only going to be available for the next two days. In creating your plan, you didn't anticipate the need to contact that individual for another three months. In fact, you had scheduled in some intensive work that would make you unavailable for the entire week. Now someone else's priorities are making it necessary for you to reorder yours.

This busy and important person has offered to have lunch with you tomorrow to discuss your needs. Your plans are important too. Still, this unexpected change is a priority that you should try to address if at all possible. Think of it this way:

> If you were embarking on a trip, you would have to be prepared to alter your road map if conditions so warranted no matter how much effort you spent organizing it. The same principle applies to any sort of planning. You have to be flexible enough to make appropriate adjustments—that is, alter your priorities—in response to prevailing conditions.

There is another way that priorities interface with the use of time, and that has to do with the issue of delegation. In any sort of master plan, there will be many things that need to get done. Fortunately, not all of them require your personal attention.

As I write this, for example, there is a pile of important papers that need to be photocopied and mailed in the next few hours. This work is going to get done on time—but that's not to say I'm going to attend to it personally.

In a little while, someone who helps me with such matters is going to take care of my impending clerical tasks.

Because time is such a precious commodity, tracking necessitates doing only those things that others can't accomplish for you.

As you will discover in Chapter Six, which deals with response styles, some people have difficulty trusting others to take care of the most minute details. People who exhibit this kind of behavior have a *controlling* response style.

Others who have trouble delegating are pennywise and pound foolish about paying people to do things for them. I submit that such individuals are undermining their chances for success. I found out a long time ago that it's wasteful to spend two hundred dollars trying to solve a five-dollar problem. That's why I advise you to do the following:

✧ Place a dollar value on your time.

✧ Estimate the dollar value of the task that needs to get done.

✧ Delegate to others all tasks that do not compensate you in accordance with your worth.

STEP 5: DIVIDE YOUR PRIORITIZED PLANS INTO ACTIONABLE PIECES
What is usually referred to as goals or objectives are, in effect, the tangible things that must get done if you are to achieve your master plan. Thinking of goals as pieces of a puzzle may be a less intimidating way of visualizing the actions that must be pursued in an attempt to realize your mission. But, since the word *goal* has a nicer ring to it than *piece*, we'll continue to use that term.

Before I show you how to integrate your goals into a master plan that will enable you to get and stay on track, let's briefly review some basic dimensions in establishing and achieving goals:

1. A goal must be tangible. As noted earlier, goals are on the opposite end of the master planning spectrum from missions. While a mission or purpose can be long term and even somewhat abstract, a goal is firmly grounded in day-to-day reality. Therefore, each goal must be measurable by specific criteria and have a specific target date for its completion.

If, for example, my goal is to increase my income, I have to state that in specific terms. Am I setting out to double my income or to increase it by 10 percent? Without a specific criterion, I will have no tangible measurement of success.

2. A goal must be attainable. One of the things that removes goals from the realm of the abstract is making them reachable by self-defined measures that can be attained within a given time frame. Dealing in achievable steps helps us get and stay motivated because we are able to see the light at the end of the tunnel. Setting a specific time for achievement also gives us a way to measure our progress.

In the preceding example that referred to a goal of earning more money, an appropriate statement that includes dimensions 1 and 2 would be: "My goal is to double my current income within one year."

3. A goal must be divisible. As I mentioned earlier, writing this book was a long-term goal that grew out of my professional mission. In thinking about the relationship between long- and short-term goals, it is useful to visualize a series of steps leading to a plateau.

Each short-term goal is a step you must climb before you can reach the plateau that signifies the realization of your long-term goal. Depending on the scope of that long-term goal, it may be helpful to develop more modest plateaus that identify major steps on the road to completion. Think of a series of well-defined plateaus—each of which is reached by climbing a series of successive steps. I'll use my writing of this book as a case in point.

I've described the way I proceeded in the planning stage to gather the information I needed to pursue my long-term goal of writing a book. Based on that information, I broke this complex pursuit down in the following way:

> *Long-Term Goal.* To write and publish a book that helps people identify and develop the indipreneurial lifeskills necessary to achieve personal and professional fulfillment in the twenty-first century.

> *Criteria.* To have the book released and distributed by a major publisher so that it can get into the hands of individuals and organizations who need the information.

> *Deadline: Fall 1993*

Confronting Plateaus

In the course of this process, I encountered the following plateaus:

1. Write a book proposal.
2. Find a literary agent.
3. Negotiate an appropriate book publishing contract.
4. Gather the necessary research and interview materials.
5. Write a first draft.
6. Make any revisions that are deemed necessary.
7. Set up public appearances to promote the book.

Let's look at how the first of these plateaus was broken down into steps upon which I was able to act. Please note that each plateau has its own criterion and completion date.

The specific criteria involved in writing a book proposal are (1) complete a sales proposal, (2) develop a table of contents, and (3) write a chapter outline and sample chapter that are ready to be submitted to prospective literary agents and book publishers. My deadline for this was nine weeks.

To accomplish these tasks within the time frame assigned, I undertook to complete the following steps:

1. Input all relevant written information into computer. Deadline: one week.
2. Write first draft of outline and table of contents. Deadline: two weeks.
3. Write first draft of sales proposal and sample chapter. Deadline: three weeks.
4. Get relevant feedback, make appropriate revisions. Deadline: three weeks.

Depending on your particular comfort level and time management needs, steps such as these can be broken down into even smaller substeps. The idea is to keep things at a level that minimizes frustration while maximizing the motivation necessary to keep you on track.

Keep in mind that *a goal must be* ***worthwhile***. This is an issue that has been neglected in much of the literature and thinking regarding goals. In a sense, it preempts the first three dimensions we discussed. Obviously, if you don't believe a goal is worthwhile from the start, there would be no reason to pursue it. Nevertheless, I see individuals and organizations spending their time on endeavors that detract from their purpose.

We live in a world of limited resources. Even the wealthiest organizations and individuals don't possess unlimited amounts of money, and time is a finite commodity for us all—irrespective of finances.

Individuals and organizations that are on track are always cognizant that when they set about achieving one goal, they are declining the opportunity to pursue some other goal. This concept is known as *opportunity cost*—or the price you pay for giving up the resources you would need to do something else.[2]

People who have mastered the tracking lifeskill have an innate sense that the things they do are meaningful and worth achieving. The question is, however, whether a particular goal is worthwhile when compared to the goal one is giving up to achieve it.

Assessing Your Goals

The system I use to make this determination is one I think you will find helpful. It is derived from Benjamin Franklin's "T." Franklin—a great futurist in his day—believed that before you set about doing something, it is important to sit down and evaluate its benefits and drawbacks. Let's look at how this system helped me determine whether writing a book was a worthwhile goal.

In deciding whether or not a book would be worthwhile, I draw a large "T" on a sheet of paper (see Figure 3.1).

On the left side of the "T," I put a minus sign (-), and on the right side of the "T," I put a plus sign (+).

On the left side of the "T," I list all the negatives that might be incurred while writing a book, that is, the costs. First, writing a book takes a lot of time and effort. There are also monetary costs involved—including the cost of not engaging in activities that generate immediate income. "Time," "effort," and "money," then, are the three factors I list on the left.

My next step is to list the anticipated rewards of writing the book on the right side of the "T." As a result of writing this book, I anticipated accumulating more knowledge than I previously had. That knowledge would, in turn, enhance my expertise and ability to fulfill my purpose.

When people perceive a book to be helpful and well written, the author derives a certain amount of prestige. Since the books I write are an integral part of the work I do, they are helpful in generating more clients and useful as market-

FIGURE 3.1

✧

Is My Goal Worthwhile?

Goal: To write a book on indipreneurial lifeskills

–		+	
– 8	Time	Knowledge	+ 10
– 1	Effort	Prestige	+ 9
– 8	Money	Profits	+ 10
		Client base	+ 10
		Effective marketing tool	+ 10
– 17	Total	Total	+ 49

$$\text{Ratio} = \frac{49^+}{17^-} = 2.88^+ \text{ to } 1^-$$

ing tools. Therefore, I write down the following on the positive side: "knowledge," "prestige," "long-term profits," "increased client base," "effective marketing tool."

My next step is to assign a number for each entry on both sides of the "T." I rate each item on the left or negative side with -1 (for the smallest opportunity cost) to a -10 (for the greatest opportunity cost).

First, writing a book takes time. I rate this factor a -8 because I'm acutely aware that time is an exceedingly valuable resource. Still, I decide that I can schedule the necessary time without significantly hurting my other endeavors.

The next cost I need to evaluate is effort. I rate this a -1 because experience has taught me that when I'm enthusiastic about what I'm doing, any effort I expend tends to generate more energy than it depletes. Still, I know I must factor in effort as a cost—so I give it the lowest possible negative rating.

Money is the third cost I need to consider. As I stated, one of my concerns in this area is not being able to accept income-generating opportunities while I am in the process of writing the book. I can't be sure what this will amount to, but I am inclined to give it the high-negative rating of -8.

Moving to the plus or right side of the "T," I rate each item from +1 (for the minimum reward or least positive anticipated outcome) to +10 (for the maximum reward or most positive anticipated outcome).

Increasing my knowledge is something that can translate into all sorts of benefits in every area of my life. Therefore, I rate this factor a +10.

Since I value respect, prestige is very important to me—though somewhat less so than knowledge. Still, when people think highly of your work, the positive impact on your motivation and self-esteem cannot be overestimated. Therefore I rate prestige a +9.

Making long-term profits is clearly a +10. It provides the opportunity to reinvest in my work and to build my business.

To my way of thinking, it isn't the dollars per se that are important, but what they say about one's value in the world. If people are willing to pay more for your products and services, that is a sign that you are doing something right.

Increasing my client base also gets a +10—as does the book's usefulness as a marketing tool. Since the growth of my business is so intrinsically connected with the achievement of my mission, I place a primary value on all such factors.

Totaling the scores on both sides, I wind up with a minus score of 17 and a plus score of 49. I consider a 2.5:1 relationship between positives and negatives an indication that a goal is worth pursuing. Since my differential was almost 3:1, that was a clear sign for me to proceed with writing the book. Now I'd like you to try this exercise with one of your own goals.

SELF-EVALUATION EXERCISE: ARE YOU DOING SOMETHING WORTHWHILE?

✦ ✦ ✦

First, choose a goal. Then draw a "T" on a piece of blank paper. On the left side, list all the possible disadvantages of pursuing the goal. On the right side, list all of the possible advantages of pursuing the goal.

Now assign a number for each entry on both sides of the "T." Rate each item on the left or negative side with -1 (for the smallest opportunity cost) to a -10 (for the greatest opportunity cost).

Now move to the plus or right side of the T. Rate each item from +1 (for the minimum reward or least positive anticipated outcome) to +10 (for the maximum reward or most positive anticipated outcome).

Finally, total up the scores on both sides. Put the higher number over the lower number. Obviously, if your minuses are greater than your pluses, this is not a goal you should be pursuing. If, on the other hand, the plus-to-minus relationship is greater than 2.5:1, the goal you are evaluating is probably worth pursuing. If the differential is less than 2.5:1, you may want to reassess in the near future.

Four Motivational Tools to Keep You on Track

EMOTIONAL COMMITMENT While it is essential to be objective and logical about the worthiness of pursuing a particular goal, there must also be a strong passion if we are going to bring our efforts to fruition. The question comes down to this: *Are we doing what we are doing only because it seems to make good sense, or are we truly passionate about our desire to get what we're after?*

Tracking by definition requires a strong emotional identification with what you are doing. The distance from that ideal is, in essence, a measure of how far you need to travel before you reach the road for which you were uniquely designed. The closer we can get to traveling on that road, the easier it will be to maintain a high level of motivation.

If the field of motivational psychology has taught us anything, it's that people invariably perform better when they are driven by internal rather than external forces. One useful way to think about tracking is as an effort to match external realities with inner passions.

PERIPHERAL VISIONING There are many people and organizations who never realize their long-range goals because they don't have the strength of purpose to negotiate the hard road. In other cases, goals are not realized because their creators have not developed the visioning skills needed to respond to critical changes.

The old rules of success dictated that, once a goal is set, you put on blinders and go for it. Long-range goals were conceived as still photographs in the distance that you close in on incrementally. This singular approach may have been appropriate at one time, but it is not responsive to twenty-first-century realities.

In light of all the rapid social, economic, and technological changes going on around us, we cannot afford simply to focus our sights in a singular or narrow way. To do so is to risk missing opportunities on the periphery.

To stay on track, we need to engage in what we at The Center for the 21st Century call *peripheral visioning*. I'm not talking about some mysterious process. Here's what I am saying:

> Keep both eyes open not just to what is happening in front of you—but also to what is taking place on your flanks and your rear.

When people begin pursuing a dream, they often don't have a totally clear vision of their destination. As I have noted, part of the master planning process involves clarifying the steps that are needed to get you where you want to go. But that doesn't mean you have to know how all the pieces will fit before you start on the puzzle. Remember, the creative process rarely goes in a straight line.

At first, your vision may be fuzzy. Still, it would be a mistake to abandon it on that basis. If your gut tells you that you are on to something worthwhile, try to work through the ambiguity. Eventually, things will come into clearer focus, and you can adjust your vision accordingly.

Be aware also that fuzziness and ambiguity can kick in at any time. That's where bifocal visioning skills come in. Instead of thinking in a straight line, look around for alternative opportunities and solutions. As you close in on your long-range goals, keep adjusting your peripheral vision to accommodate changes. In terms of moving ahead on a day-to-day or week-to-week basis, it is important not to neglect that still photograph of your long-range goal that keeps getting closer as you accomplish those daily and weekly tasks. Just remember that most photographs aren't likely to stay unaltered for long in this rapidly changing world. That's why it's important to develop the kind of bifocal visioning that lets you deal with the moving picture while inching ever closer to that still photograph in the distance.

Risk taking I truly believe that it is impossible to win unless you are first willing to risk failure. Consider the following:

✦ A baseball player has no chance of hitting a home run unless he comes up to the plate and risks striking out.

✦ No company can successfully market a new product or service unless responsible people are prepared to absorb a loss.

✦ To achieve any worthwhile goal, an individual must recognize the possibility of falling on his face.

When people talk about being a winner, they are often looking for the quick fix. It certainly would be great if all our ideas became massively successful. For better or worse, though, most successful people have had to work hard for what they've achieved. Most have also experienced their share of setbacks in the process.

Have you noticed that organizations and people who make their mark in this world are constantly putting themselves on the line with new ideas and ventures? You will also note that perfect track records in business—and in life—are about as rare as 1.000 batting averages in baseball.

The playing fields on which most of us operate aren't nearly as public as those of a professional athlete or the CEO of a major corporation. When those folks strike out, millions know about it. The rest of us have a much easier time hiding our mistakes and foibles. It may surprise you to learn, however, that concealing your goals and visions can put you at a disadvantage.

Sharing your vision always involves a degree of risk, but the potential benefits make that gamble worthwhile. When you let others share your vision, you unleash a key motivating force. By giving other people the opportunity to see you fail, you strengthen your commitment to yourself. You also unleash a strong motivator that inspires you to work harder to achieve your goals.

I belong to a *motivational resource group* whose stated purpose is to share goals and give each other feedback. In Chapter Four, I will show you how to set up and utilize these and other resourcing groups.

Sharing your vision with others, whether in groups or on a one-to-one basis, opens you up to all sorts of informational and critical feedback. When I decided to write this book, I shared that vision with a wide range of people. In doing so, I made it a point to solicit responses that would further my goal.

If, for example, I talked to a writer or someone connected with book publishing, I would be most concerned with that individual's feelings about the viability of the book and what competing products might be on the market. If I talked to a business leader or a person at one of my lectures, I would try to get a feeling about the kind of vital information he or she felt was neglected elsewhere.

Perhaps even more important than feedback, letting others in on what we're trying to achieve helps reinforce our commitment. As the months passed and I was in different stages of making this book a reality, the people with whom I had shared my vision would inquire about my progress.

"How's the book coming along, Carolyn?" they would ask. "Are you finished writing it? When will it be in the stores? I'd like to get my hands on a copy."

At this point, you might be wondering what might have happened if I had been unable to see my vision through. Imagine my embarrassment at having to tell people that the book was never written or sold to a publisher. Wouldn't I have felt like a fool and a failure?

I can honestly answer that question with a resounding "no!" I would never claim that all my visions and goals have been realized. But, even in those instances, I wouldn't say that I failed.

While it's true that some of the things that you try may fail, that doesn't mean *you* are a failure. Mistakes and false starts are an integral part of winning. Ultimately, they can be as instrumental to your success as are fully realized achievements.

Although not realizing a vision should never be judged as personal failure, you want to do everything in your power to avoid those feelings. When something isn't working, you may be justified in deciding to abandon it and move on. At the same time, you want to be careful not to quit too soon.

When you are thinking of abandoning your mission or giving up the pursuit of a goal, ask yourself these eight questions:

EIGHT FACTORS TO CONSIDER BEFORE ABANDONING YOUR GOAL

1. Do I feel less passionate about this goal than when I started?

2. Have I devoted sufficient time and effort to my pursuit?

3. Have I thought out every available option for moving ahead?

4. Have I eliminated the possibility that the problems I am experiencing can be solved by altering or clarifying my original vision?

5. Have I taken the time to review each phase of the master planning process and make appropriate revisions?

6. Have I eliminated outside pressures that conspire to sap my original energy and enthusiasm?

7. Have I been as creative as possible in everything I do?

8. Have I exercised self-discipline and avoided procrastination?

If you can honestly answer "yes" to each of these questions, you may be justified in quitting a particular goal and going on to something else. Still, you must be careful never to quit simply because things are not going as smoothly as you hoped.

You've undoubtedly heard the saying: "When the going gets tough, the tough get going." In trying to achieve anything worthwhile, there are times when you grow frustrated and feel like giving up. I submit that, more often than not, this is when it is most important to persevere.

One of the many benefits of taking the hard road is that fertile new ground often lies immediately beyond the most difficult obstacle. You just have to be patient and persistent enough to work through those impasses and rough spots. These are times when you need to draw strength—from both your own internal resources and from others. That's why I want you to demonstrate trust in yourself by sharing your vision with others. And remember, even if you wind up falling on your face, you're going to be that much stronger when you get back on your feet.

BUILDING ENERGIZERS/ELIMINATING DEENERGIZERS People frequently ask what they should do when they feel unmotivated to act in their best interests. Oftentimes, they are mired in procrastination—which is really nothing more than an expression of denial and fear. Have you ever thought about what procrastinators are really afraid of?

Most procrastinators fear attacking a complicated problem that does not lend itself to a quick fix. Consequently, they never get around to doing what is necessary to realize their goals. We have a saying at The Center for the 21st Century that I think gets to the heart of the matter:

Fear is the passport to emotional and financial poverty.

To overcome the fear that causes us to procrastinate, we must program ourselves mentally to guide our bodies into gear so that we can move ahead. For people who find this to be a constant battle, it is especially important to build in *energizers* and eliminate *deenergizers*.

- ✧ Energizers are people, activities, and thoughts that energize and inspire us to move ahead. They can also be thought of as positive motivators.

- ✧ Deenergizers are people, activities, and thoughts that deenergize us and render us frustrated and fatigued. They can also be thought of as negative motivators.

One of the simplest ways to eliminate *deenergizers* is to establish *blockers*—that is, external or internal controls that keep distractions and energy drainers at bay. In terms of overcoming procrastination and getting things accomplished, one of the easiest *deenergizers* to block are interruptions.

Whenever I am working on a creative project, I make certain that I cannot be interrupted. During normal business hours, for example, I have my secretary take all phone calls. In essence, she is *blocking* me from potential interference. When I work at home, I can achieve the same result by disconnecting my phones or using the call-screening function of my answering machine.

Unfortunately, not all *deenergizers* can be blocked as easily as phone interruptions. Still, the same basic principle can be applied to more subtle and insidious *deenergizers*.

People who deenergize or sap us are often manipulative and controlling, and they can be tough to deal with. Things can become even more complicated and problematic when we sap ourselves. How, you may ask, do we do that? By allowing ourselves to be overwhelmed by negative thoughts or engaging in activities that distract us from our mission.

I've discovered that it takes approximately 15 *energizers* to counteract the effect of one *deenergizer*. That's why blocking these negative motivators is essential for tracking. At the same time, the simplest way to raise your level of motivation is to increase your internal and external *energizers*. There are two basic ways to do this: the first is pursuing pleasure or rewards and the second is avoiding pain or punishment. Consider the following case in point:

Marion was 25 pounds overweight and wanted to shed that surplus bulk so that she would look more attractive. Unfortunately, she loved to eat junk food and lacked the self-discipline to cut down. Marion often talked about going on a diet and occasionally took some tentative steps in that direction. But, ultimately, she could not sustain her resolve.

Let's look at Marion's situation in terms of *energizers* and *deenergizers*. There was no *energizer* or positive motivation to get rid of those extra pounds that could counteract her *deenergizer*—that is, an addiction to junk food. From Marion's dysfunctional perspective, the pain of being overweight wasn't as great as the pleasure of eating cookies and candy.

Then one day the equation changed for Marion. When she went for a physical, her doctor informed her that her cholesterol and blood pressure levels put her at risk for heart disease. He told Marion in no uncertain terms that she had to begin a low-fat diet immediately to take the excess weight off.

When Marion walked out of that doctor's office, she was no longer thinking about the choice of giving up fattening foods and fitting into a smaller-sized dress. All of a sudden the question came down to: "Do I want to stop eating junk or risk having a heart attack?"

At that point, the avoidance of pain became an *energizer* that was much more important to Marion than the need to eat junk food. Understandably, the motivation to avoid serious illness became far stronger than those that were driving Marion to have a slimmer shape.

Speaking of diets, have you noticed that several celebrities who took off significant amounts of weight subsequently became spokespersons for various diet programs? Statistics show that most dieters regain all the weight they lose within a year. Some public personalities, however, seem to have retained their svelte figures for a number of years. Do you think the thousands of dollars they received for appearing in weight loss commercials might have been an added *energizer* that kept them motivated to avoid overeating?

Let's move to another example of how *energizers* and *deenergizers* function as motivating tools:

Thirty-year-old John was the only one of three brothers not to have obtained a college degree. Although he got by in high school, John had never been a studious person. At the time he graduated, a number of his friends were making a good living building machinery for a large corporation that specialized in government defense contracts. John decided to take the same road. In John's area in California, defense work was a lucrative field for people with mechanical ability and a high school education. John had been doing well on his job. The work wasn't bad, and he earned more than enough to live a comfortable bachelor's life. Still, John wanted eventually to marry and have children, and this meant he would have to improve his financial prospects.

During his years on the job, John decided that engineering would be a field in which he could excel. This would mean going to college and pursuing an arduous course of study. John decided that he would make the commitment some time soon. Unfortunately, things kept getting in the way.

John loved to hang out with his friends. A group of them often went on weekend hunting and fishing trips. Although he could not articulate the exact words, John understood that these deenergizing activities were preventing him from pursuing his goal. Still, with all that was going on in his life, who had time for college?

At one point, John actually did register for two night courses, but he soon dropped them. Why couldn't John commit to his stated goal? Apparently, the reward was still not great enough—nor was the avoidance of anticipated pain. Suddenly, something happened thousands of miles away that would provide the spark John needed.

With the breakup of the former Soviet Union, the balance of military power in the world began to shift. The result was, among other things, a significant reduction in defense-related work. John's company was retooling, and many people were being laid off. More layoffs would certainly follow in the ensuing years. People with just slightly less seniority than John were starting to be let go. The writing on the wall couldn't have been clearer.

At last, John had the motivation he needed to get serious about college. The *energizer* in his life was twofold:

✧ He would be avoiding the substantial pain of being out of work and without marketable skills.

✧ At the same time, John could anticipate the rewards of having a more interesting career—as well as the financial means to support a family.

John is two years into his studies toward an engineering degree and is earning straight As. Even more important, John has gotten his life on track. In a sense, he was lucky. The *energizer* that turned things around for John came from the outside. Since you can't count on something like that happening, you have to work at creating your own *energizers*. By way of illustration, let's get back to a subject that's near and dear to my heart—losing weight.

Several months ago, I decided that I would like to lose ten pounds so that I could fit into a smaller-sized suit. I immediately recognized, however, that I lacked the necessary motivation to reach my goal. The reward was not great enough, nor was the avoidance of pain. Still, I did want to lose that weight.

One thing I know about myself is that, when I'm in a contest, I go all out to win. Although I always try to be an *optimizer*, my primary response style is that of a *controller*, and competitiveness is one of the characteristics that is bundled into that particular package. So, whenever I really need to lose weight, what I do is set up a contest with somebody to see which of us will be more successful. This gives me all the motivation I need: I have the pleasurable reward of winning a contest *and* losing the weight. At the same time, I avoid the pain of losing.

If I needed to increase my motivation even further, I could build even more *energizers* into this kind of situation. For example, I could set up the competition with someone who is even more set on winning than I am, or I could establish some kind of cash bonus for each pound lost.

Some people find such techniques gimmicky. Still, they can be effective. I believe it's important to make use of every *energizer* at your disposal. As long as you or nobody else is hurt in the process, I say use whatever works.

PRACTICAL EXERCISES FOR SUCCESSFUL MASTER PLANNING

✦ ✦ ✦

1. After some time for real introspection, write down your purpose in what you perceive to be the key areas of your life.

2. Select one purpose or mission that you would most like to accomplish within the next two years. Write it down.

3. Using the mission just selected, develop a perspective or blueprint of the purpose. Now write out that blueprint. In doing so, be sure the following questions are addressed:

 a. What will the completed product look like?

 b. What people, activities, special problems, and feelings will be involved?

4. What broad steps will it take to reach your goal or to accomplish your mission? In other words—what plans do you have? Write these down.

5. List the kinds of information you will require to create an effective plan.

6. Rank in order of priority your top three steps. Write these down.

7. Write down your top three goals. Be sure to establish criteria and an initial target date. For each goal, ask yourself the following questions:

 a. Is the goal attainable?

 b. Is the goal worthwhile?

 c. Can the goal be further divided into smaller, more manageable pieces?

8. Prepare brief written reports periodically to help measure your progress.

9. Use the following five-step exercise to help you increase motivation:

   a. Pick a goal.

   b. Make a list of your particular energizers and deenergizers.

   c. Write down the categories of pain you wish to avoid.

   d. Write down the kinds of rewards that you want to achieve.

   e. Using the kinds of techniques we've explored, try to invent your own rewards and pain-avoidance systems.

PHASE 2:
MEASURING

A former New York City mayor was constantly asking his constituency: "How am I doing?" In theory, the responses he received gave him a basis for determining if he was staying on track in terms of the goals he had promised to achieve.

For purposes of tracking, we as individuals need to ask ourselves how we are doing with respect to key aspects of our lives. To come up with realistic answers, we need self-evaluation tools by which we can measure our progress. Such measurement instruments provide accountability—if only to ourselves. These tools also furnish a means by which we can monitor our progress.

Peter Drucker, the distinguished management guru, has said: "If you can't measure it, you can't manage it." This principle holds for every aspect of business and personal management. It is important to set standards so that we will know if and when we are slipping off track.

Tools that measure tracking may not be exact from a scientific standpoint. Nevertheless, they are accurate in terms of letting you know where you stand at a given point, as well as how far you have progressed.

Throughout this chapter, we use a variety of self-evaluation tools to help you gauge where you are now and where you are heading in terms of pursuing specific goals. The evaluation tool that provides the most comprehensive measurement of how well a person is tracking is called the *life-quality index*.

The men and women who have completed this exercise have found it most helpful in pinpointing the areas of their lives that can most benefit from improved tracking skills. The exercise also highlights areas of strength, for which people sometimes do not give themselves sufficient credit. I think you will find it helpful to spend a little time completing this enlightening measurement tool.

The Life-Quality Index

Quality of life is an interesting concept—one that is used with respect to a wide range of issues. I mentioned earlier that one definition of tracking concerns a person's success at matching external realities with inner passions. Another way of phrasing this is the difference between what a person's life is as compared with what he or she would like it to be.

The *life-quality index* (see Figure 3.2) lets you make this assessment with respect to the following areas of life in which you set goals: (1) *spiritual,* (2) *personal,* (3) *family,* (4) *friends,* (5) *career,* (6) *financial,* (7) *civic,* and (8) *leisure.* Please note that, while these are the general areas of concern to most people, you need not make assessments in categories for which you have not set goals.

FIGURE 3.2
✧
Life-Quality Index

	Column 1 Imp	x	Column 2 Re	=	Column 3 Total Imp x Re
Spiritual	_____		_____		_____
Personal	_____		_____		_____
Family	_____		_____		_____
Friends	_____		_____		_____
Career	_____		_____		_____
Financial	_____		_____		_____
Civic	_____		_____		_____
Leisure	_____		_____		_____

Total Imp = _____

Total Score for Column 3 = _____

$$LQI = \frac{\text{Total Score for Col. 3}}{\text{Total Imp x 10}} \times 100 = \underline{\qquad}$$

Exercise:
CALCULATING YOUR LIFE-QUALITY INDEX

✦ ✦ ✦

Instructions To help you use this life-quality index (LQI), consider the preceding list of eight categories that tend to make up areas of our lives. In the figure, there are three columns. The first column is *Imp,* which stands for importance. *Re,* the second column, stands for reality, and concerns how things really are in your life right now. And the third column, *Total (Imp × Re),* represents your total score, obtained by multiplying the first column (*Imp*) by the second column (*Re*). To complete the exercise, rank each of the eight aspects from 1 to 10 with reference to the following:

1. *How important is that aspect of your life to you?* The way you rate this column indicates the importance of each aspect of your life on a scale of 1 to 10, with "1" being not important and "10" being very important. For example, in the area of family life a "1" would indicate that this aspect of life was of virtually no concern to you. A "10" would indicate that family matters were of primary concern. For illustrative purposes, let's assume this area warrants a rating of "10." This is your importance score, which goes in the first column.

2. *To what extent is that aspect of your life on track?* As you assess your family life, what are your current feelings? What is the reality in terms of how you are actually doing? Are you involved with your family in positive ways? Are you currently estranged from your family and experiencing pain in that area? Rate how your family life really is on a scale of 1 to 10, with "1" being low quality and "10" being high quality.

Let's assume that you rate yourself as operating on a "5" in terms of family. This is your reality (*Re*) score, which goes in the second column.

To determine your total (*Imp × Re*) score, multiply your importance (*Imp*) score by your reality (*Re*) score. In this case your total *Imp × Re* would be 50. A 10 for importance (*Imp*) score times 5 for reality (*Re*) equals a total of 50.

Repeat this process for each of the eight categories. When you have finished, compute the score as follows:

Scoring Add up all your importance (*Imp*) scores and put that total in the blank beside the words *Total Imp* in the table. Add up all your total *Imp* × *Re* scores and put that number in your blank beside the words *Total score for column 3*.

You are now ready to generate a life-quality index. Take the *Total Score for Column 3* and make that the numerator. Multiply the total *Imp* by 10 and make that the denominator. Then divide the numerator by the denominator.

For example, if my *Total Score for Column 3* is 590, and my *Total Imp* score is 70, I would multiply the *Total Imp* score by 10 and get a total of 700.

I would then compute my LQI by dividing 590 by 700, which gives me 0.84. Then I would multiply that number by 100, which would yield 84. This would mean that my LQI is 84 out of a possible 100. Another way of expressing this result is that I am 84 percent on track in my life. Even though that is a very good score, I may still want to review the individual categories to pinpoint opportunities for improvement.

In general, a differential of three points or more between the importance (*Imp*) and reality (*Re*) scores in any category requires careful monitoring—with an eye toward possibly resetting goals in that area.

In some cases, you may find that your reality exceeds the defined level of importance you set for yourself. You may, for example, rate your financial importance a 7 and the reality a 9. This means that this aspect of your life is really better than it needs to be. This may be a very positive development— so long as other aspects of your life are not out of balance.

If, for example, a positive financial index is offset by a negative family and spiritual index, this may be an indication that an individual is compensating for other areas where he is not doing very well. To have a good quality of life, we must constantly assess our aggregate score as well as those in each individual area of our lives. True mastery of the tracking lifeskill means addressing and finding satisfaction in all the key areas.

PHASE 3: FEEDBACK ANALYSIS

Measurement tools like the life-quality index give us access to a vital source of feedback about how well we are tracking. We receive a wide variety of feedback in the course of our lives. On the job, we may be subject to formal and informal performance reviews. In terms of our own well-being, we receive all sorts of physical and emotional feedback from our bodies. People we come across in our lives give us a great deal of feedback through body language as well as verbally.

On-track people know where to look for different kinds of feedback and are adept at making the best use of it. There are times when a seemingly minor suggestion or piece of information can spark a major breakthrough in your life. On other occasions, we may decide that a certain piece of feedback is not useful.

In some instances, feedback is given when we don't specifically ask for it. On the other hand, people respond to our explicit or implicit requests for input in a number of ways. At times, their silence or lack of response may constitute a vital piece of feedback.

All of us have asked for feedback, hoping to be told what we want to hear. Consider the following brief verbal exchange, and your feelings about how the participants solicited, offered, and received feedback:

"How do you like my new suit?" Bill asked Sally, certain that she would tell him he looked smashing.

"Frankly, I'm not crazy about it," Sally answered. "The pants are too tight and the color isn't particularly flattering."

Bill was disappointed in Sally's response—most people would be, at least initially. Still, positive reinforcement should not be the critical issue when one is soliciting feedback.

One of the characteristics of codependent family systems is that people say what others want to hear. A child in a codependent family tells a parent what he wants to hear to gain approval or avoid abuse. Likewise, a dysfunctional corporate CEO surrounds himself with "yes people" because he wishes to receive only positive feedback. You can be sure that all his ideas are confirmed by his codependent underlings as being great.

Which brings us back to Bill and Sally. The question remains: Did Sally do Bill a favor or a disservice by telling him that she didn't like his suit? Only Bill can ascertain that. First, he must decide whether Sally was offering an honest assessment. Is she someone who he perceives to be in his corner? Is she jealous of his position in the company?

Let's assume that Sally is well meaning in her criticism. That still doesn't mean Bill should necessarily take her feedback seriously. There are other things to consider: Does Sally know anything about clothes, or is she a poor dresser? Again, Bill must make this decision for himself. He has asked for and received a piece of feedback. What he does with it is up to him.

Since Bill knew the answer he desired, he was asking Sally a loaded question. Many of us do the same kind of thing in one way or another, and it's important to be aware of our tendencies.

When I solicit feedback, for example, I am often hoping to receive a favorable response along with a tangible piece of constructive criticism. Like most people, I don't like to be hit with a great deal of negativity. At the same time, I tend to be skeptical if the person I'm asking can't at least point out something that needs improvement. Let me give you two examples of the kind of feedback I prefer:

Question: "How does my dress look?

Answer: "Just great, Carolyn. I think the other earrings would set off the color even better.

Question: "How was that speech?

Answer: "I found it both informative and inspirational. I would have liked it even better if you would have distributed more handouts."

Admittedly, I don't always get responses that are balanced in this way. Ultimately, that's good. It's one thing to know what you would like to hear, and quite another to manipulate people to massage you in that way. "Yes people" might make you feel good for a moment. But they ultimately do not provide the kind of feedback you need to stay on track. More times than not, they are either concealing their real feelings or trying to undermine your success.

One of the valuable features of resourcing groups is the opportunity to test out our response patterns with people we trust. The way we solicit and use feedback are key issues for all of us. It is important to be sensitive, not only to your tendencies, but also to those of the person who is giving the feedback. The ultimate decision as to incorporating a given piece of feedback will depend on how you answer the following questions:

Five Questions to Ask When Assessing Feedback

1. Do you respect the person sharing the information or criticism?
2. What is your assessment of the person's honesty?

3. Do you believe that the person offering feedback has your best interests at heart?

4. Has the thrust of the feedback been reinforced by a number of sources who you consider reliable?

5. How do you assess your own gut feelings with respect to the feedback?

No matter what others may tell us, we must rely on our internal feedback system to provide much of the basis for decision making. We receive internal feedback in such forms as pleasure, pain, and energy level. We have made reference to the importance of gut feelings—which is a more colloquial way of talking about our internal feedback system. Let's see how this relates to tracking.

Simon was one of New York's top matrimonial attorneys. His client list included numerous celebrities, and his calendar was overflowing with appointments. All of Simon's colleagues agreed that they had never seen a more able attorney when it came to negotiating divorce settlements. In terms of the feedback he was receiving from the world, Simon's career could not have been more on track. Unfortunately, his gut was delivering a much different message.

In law school, Simon had been the picture of health. He had an athletic physique and never indulged in smoking or drinking. During his ten years as an attorney, however, Simon had gained 65 pounds. He had also started smoking cigarettes, and frequently ordered a couple of martinis with lunch and dinner.

Simon had also become a workaholic. Despite the protests of his wife, the couple had not taken a real vacation in over seven years.

"There never seemed to be time," Simon recalled. "I was always starting new cases even as I was wrapping up old ones. I guess you could say I was on a destructive treadmill."

Fortunately for Simon, he was required to take a physical examination for insurance purposes. His physician was quite disturbed with what he found. Although Simon was only 35, his physical condition was that of a much older man. Although he was in no immediate danger, Simon had developed an ulcer and his general health was poor. The physician was adamant that Simon lose weight, cut out cigarettes and alcohol, and take an extended vacation.

In spite of his doctor's admonitions, Simon still hated the thought of spending time away from work. "Somehow, I feared it wouldn't be here when I got back," he recalls. "As it turned out, my worries were unfounded. On the contrary, getting away from my grind was the first step in changing my life."

With the doctor's mandate strengthening her resolve, Simon's wife would not take no for an answer, and the couple planned a three-week vacation in Hawaii. After a week of total relaxation, Simon began to unwind. Only then did he realize how bad he felt.

"It began to dawn on me that I hated what my career had become," Simon recalled. "It's one thing to have the mental tools to do a good job, but your intestinal fortitude is another story.

"My own parents had gone through a very bitter divorce when I was young. As a matrimonial lawyer, I was spending my life watching estranged couples fighting over the most petty things while their children suffered the same pain I had gone through. Why, I wondered, should I keep punishing myself."

As Simon became more relaxed, he recalled a time several years earlier when he woke up in the middle of the night with a vision that he had to get out of this kind of work before it was too late. He chose to ignore this vital piece of internal feedback.

"I had climbed to the top of my field at a very young age," Simon reflects. "How could I just give that up because of a dream and some bad childhood memories?"

When Simon returned from his vacation, he attended an indipreneuring seminar. There he learned that his dream was his internal feedback system telling him that he needed to get off his present career and life-style track. Simon's poor health habits were other indications that immediate changes had to be made. During the course of that weekend seminar, Simon was able to connect further with his gut feelings. The choices he needed to make were now clear. He decided to start with his career.

"I always enjoyed copyright law—which was my second choice to matrimonial work when I became a practicing attorney," Simon recalls. "It's an interesting field that doesn't incur the same kind of angst. I knew there would be no phone calls in the middle of the night from wives or husbands being harassed by estranged spouses, no contentious battles over children who were being fought over like chattel, and no painful childhood memories."

Today, Simon is a successful copyright attorney. Although his income is less than half of what his matrimonial practice brought in, he is still quite comfortable. On the other hand, Simon has regained much of his former good health. He works a normal 40-hour workweek and takes several vacations a year. Most important, he feels good because his career—and his life—are on track.

What Is Your Internal Feedback System Telling You?

If, like Simon, your internal feedback system reveals that you are not on the right track, don't hesitate to do something about it. In Simon's case, the problem was the specific field of law and the way he approached it. As you evaluate your own career track, examine your feelings and comfort level with respect to the following areas:

✦ The field you are in

✦ The health of the company for which you work

✦ The corporate culture

✦ Your supervisor

✦ Your peers and coworkers

One of the techniques Simon used to get on track was the life-quality index we explored on pages 99–103. In reviewing that instrument, you will note that the assessments you make about the importance of the various life areas are subjective. They are, in effect, a reflection of your internal feedback system.

All of us have areas of dissatisfaction and pain. By pinpointing these internal signals and utilizing the tracking techniques we have been exploring, you can make those difficulties the basis for movement into areas that will bring you greater rewards *and* peace of mind.

As you work through the materials in the chapters that follow, you will find it useful to review the tracking techniques we've developed. Whatever you do in life, you always want to be certain that you are on the road for which you have been uniquely designed. This is what mastering the tracking lifeskill will enable you to do.

The following box reiterates some of the key points covered earlier. I urge you to come back to them—and to the more detailed materials in this chapter—whenever you need to get back on track. By doing so, you will ensure your arrival at that special place in life where you are truly happy and functioning at your best.

SEVEN TECHNIQUES FOR STAYING ON TRACK

✦ ✦ ✦

1. Establish a master plan that starts with a mission and works through the daily tasks needed to support it.
2. Set specific criteria and time frames to lend structure to your goals.
3. Avoid procrastination—which is nothing more than a devastating form of denial.
4. Identify and control your deenergizers.
5. Identify and augment your energizers.
6. Monitor your tracking in each major area of your life by using specific measurements and standards.
7. Commit to others—and to yourself—that you are determined to do whatever it takes to realize your mission.

ENDNOTES

1. Robert Moskowitz, *How to Organize Your Work and Your Life* (Garden City, NY: Dolphin/Doubleday, 1981).
2. The concept of opportunity cost is derived from the book by economist Leonard Silk, *Economics in Plain English* (New York: Touchstone/Simon & Schuster, 1978.)

CHAPTER 4

RESOURCING: MAKING THE MOST OF INFORMATION AND PEOPLE

To meet your career and personal needs, you must master the tracking lifeskill—which we have defined as the ability to maximize yourself as a resource. To facilitate those efforts, it is essential that you learn to make the most of the information and people at your disposal. This is accomplished through resourcing.

Mastering the resourcing lifeskill enables us to go out and find the means necessary to achieve our goals and solve our problems. There are three major categories of resources available to us:

1. Self
2. Information
3. People

ACTIVATING THE RESOURCING LIFESKILL

We have discussed the resourcing of self in the previous chapter on tracking. Our skill at resourcing people and information will go a long way in determining how successful we are at achieving the goals that we set in tracking.

When I talk about the importance of being resourceful, I am literally suggesting that you make your life as resource-*full* as possible. People rarely dispute this to be a wise course of action. The question they most commonly ask is: "How do you go about it?"

When I invite participants at my seminars and corporate lectures to talk about the ways in which they resource, the response is often one of bewilderment. Let me tell you why this is not at all surprising.

The schools most of us attended may have provided some limited opportunities to develop information-resourcing skills—but these are largely inadequate in terms of addressing today's and tomorrow's needs. I am happy to report, however, that we are currently working with a number of school systems to develop programs in these areas.

There is little doubt that the entire focus of education will have to undergo radical changes in the coming years. You can be sure that the lifeskills in this book will be an essential part of what your children and their children will learn in the classrooms of tomorrow.

Consider this forecast that was made in a special issue of *Time* entitled *The Year 2000 and Beyond:*

> The standard high school diploma will be replaced by a series of achievement goals. Advancement into college, a trade or a career will be based on attainment of those personal goals.[1]

This kind of educational system can be described as one that rewards *indipreneurship*. These are the values we emphasize in our lifeskills courses, in our corporate work—and in this book. It's great to know that people in future generations will be taught the indipreneurial skills they need to succeed, but how is that going to help us start addressing the needs we have today? We all want to excel in our careers and find fulfillment in our personal lives—and none of us has unlimited time.

Whenever I discuss the shortcomings in our formal education at workshops and lectures, I often get a response that goes something like this: "I agree that my educational background didn't adequately prepare me to meet my needs. Still, what am I supposed to do: Discard the diplomas and degrees it took me years to attain and start all over?"

In case you share these concerns, let me put your mind at ease. It is not my purpose to discount what you have already learned—whether in school or elsewhere. Quite the contrary. People often suffer a loss of self-esteem when things are going badly. During difficult periods, they develop a pattern of denigrating everything about their lives. Such individuals can be frequently heard making self-defeating statements like:

✧ My education has been a complete waste of time.

✧ All my choices have been ill advised.

✧ I'd like to throw away everything I've learned and start over again.

My approach to overcoming difficulties and moving ahead is to build on a person's or business's existing strengths. It is my strong belief that nothing you've learned or attempted in your life is without value. At the same time, it's a mistake to cling to a particular body of knowledge or method of problem solving as the only way just because it's all that you know. With respect to evaluating your resourcing needs, you must ask yourself the following:

✧ Are the things I am doing working for me?

✧ If the answer is yes, ask "What else can I do to achieve continuous improvement in the major areas of my life?"

✧ If the answer is no, ask: "What resources can I access that will give me the means to move ahead?"

If you feel that things are working well, you must continue to improve—or that positive condition will begin to deteriorate. If, on the other hand, things are not going well, you would be well advised to seek out a better approach. Since new learning will be required in either case, there is no point in labeling your previous education and experience as being good or bad. Whatever your present assessment, there are three fundamental but critical questions every individual and business needs to address:

1. Where are you now?
2. Where do you want to go?
3. What resources do you need to help you get there?

In my work, I use a paradigm for learning, behavior, and change that can be summarized as follows:

Before any sort of learning takes place, we start out in a state of relative ignorance. We may have some knowledge at that point—but not necessarily as much as we need to facilitate achievement of our goals. Our desire to attain more information is based on one of the two motivating forces we discussed in Chapter Three:

1. The avoidance of pain or punishment
2. The pursuit of pleasure or reward

Pain for organizations is often experienced during periods of high employee turnover or financial loss. Similarly, the most severe pain for individuals tends to occur during times of personal loss or career interruption.

Whatever its cause, the most productive way to look at pain is as a form of emotional intervention—an internal voice telling you that change is needed. Opening yourself up to emotional intervention gives you an opportunity to activate the change mechanism. Positive change can then be achieved through an ongoing process of continuous learning and adjustment. In a nutshell, the process works like this:

THE LEARNING PROCESS IN ACTION

✧ You experience pain or emotional intervention.

✧ As a result, you expose yourself to a new set of stimuli.

✧ Learning takes place.

✧ More adaptive and productive behaviors follow.

It's only fair to point out that the tangible results of what you have learned may not be immediately apparent. Keep in mind, though, that the increase in self-esteem generated by responding to emotional intervention is in itself a very positive result. And, as always, our focus is on long-term improvement rather than the quick fix.

As we have seen, many individuals and organizations continue to feel pain but choose to ignore it. Such behavior can be labeled as dysfunctional or unadaptive. Whatever you choose to call it, the important thing to understand is that this negative approach ultimately has disastrous results.

As we saw in Chapter Two, organizations that refuse to learn and change lose their best people. Many succumb to mergers, acquisitions, or outright bankruptcy. The same kind of thing eventually happens to people who refuse to open themselves to new stimuli. Their careers stagnate or fall apart. Oftentimes, they wind up experiencing profound depression that leads to personal and financial bankruptcy.

So where does all this leave us? Wherever you are now, I have no doubt that you have already acquired a good deal of valuable knowledge. We've all accomplished worthwhile things in at least some aspects of our lives. Nevertheless, there is always more to learn.

If things are working well, you want to perpetuate that success and lay the groundwork for achieving even greater rewards in the future. If, on the other hand, you find yourself at an impasse or in a state of pain, you want to utilize this emotional intervention as an opportunity for improvement.

In either case, the only way to get where you want to go is to maximize the resources that are waiting to be accessed. To do any less would amount to cheating yourself. So, without further ado, let's get this process into motion.

USING THE FOUR ESSENTIAL INFORMATION-RESOURCING TECHNIQUES

1. Researching
2. Discovering
3. Testing
4. Innovating

Researching

Researching is a structured process of accessing existing information. Before you begin, you obviously have to know what you want to find out—and this harks back to master planning. If, for example, you were thinking about starting a business, you might want to research the state of that particular industry, or the nature of the competition, or sources for venture capital.

Researching entails going to various sources to review whatever knowledge already exists. These may be in the form of print and electronic media such as books, trade and professional periodicals—even tapes of relevant television or radio programs. Researching is such a basic and important step, yet people often neglect it. As a result, goals are not achieved, dreams go unrealized.

In theory, many of us learned to research in school. I can remember being taken to my high school library and instructed on how to negotiate the various card catalogs. It was assumed that we would use these in the process of writing term papers. As it turned out, this technical information regarding library science did facilitate my schoolwork. But, even then, I had a sense that I wasn't being given the essential tools that would help me make the library a vital ally in achieving my goals. It wasn't until years after I completed my formal education that I learned how critical a lifeskill researching is.

Many of the people who attend my seminars want to access new skills or implement new ideas within the companies at which they work. Others are interested in launching their own business ventures. No matter where your interests lie, there is a whole world of informational resources just waiting to be accessed. And, for the most part, the costs involved are nominal.

Some valuable resources can be accessed with the help of new technologies. Still, you may be surprised to learn that you don't have to be a computer whiz—or even computer literate—to take advantage of them.

Those of you who know how to use a computer are probably aware of the many database services that are available. With the use of a modem, you can call one of these services over the telephone and retrieve on your computer all available information on a particular topic. But what if you don't have a computer and a modem: Does that mean you can't benefit from modern technology? Not at all.

Before I tell you how to solve that little dilemma, let me ask you a question: When was the last time you made use of your public library? Perhaps, like me, you learned to use the card catalog when you were in school. If you're like a lot of people, that one experience may have been enough to convince you that libraries were useless once your academic career was over. I respectfully submit that it's time to give the library another chance to be the fantastic resource it was designed to be.

If you haven't been to the library for a while, you're sure to notice some changes. For one thing, many of the old-fashioned card catalogs have been replaced by computerized data bases such as Infotrack. Not to worry. You don't need to know anything about computers to use these tools. Just walk into the local library in your area that maintains the largest reference section. Once you get there, here's what to do:

Ask for the reference librarian, and tell her what it is you're looking for. If she directs you to Infotrack, a card catalog, or some other system with which you have no familiarity, just tell her you need help. You will be amazed just how much assistance these resource-*full* women and men are able and willing to provide. The accompanying box provides some tips for helping them help you:

USING YOUR AREA LIBRARY'S RESOURCES

✦ No matter what subject interests you, there are sure to be relevant books and articles available. If your library does not have these publications, it may belong to an interlibrary system and can obtain them for you within a short time.

✦ Numerous trade and professional societies have useful career-related information. Most major libraries carry directories that list these. For example, trade associations are listed in the *Encyclopedia of Associations*. Information about many industries is available in Standard & Poor's industry surveys.

✦ Some information may be available only through computerized database services. But what if you don't own a computer, or can't afford to sign up with those services? Many major libraries now subscribe to such services and can access information for you for a very modest fee. All you have to do is ask.

✦ Once you get to know her, your reference librarian can become a vital research tool. Librarians are committed to helping people solve their research problems. At the same time, they are aware that most people don't take advantage of this resource, so they are especially appreciative of those who do.

In some cases, libraries may provide all the information you need. At other times, they will serve as the first stop in your quest for information. Let's see how this process worked for Bob, a 37-year-old accountant whose middle-management position had been eliminated in the wake of a massive corporate downsizing.

One month after he was laid off, Bob attended one of my seminars. Not wanting to rekindle the sense of false security he had as a corporate employee, Bob was considering starting his own financial planning consultancy.

"I know I could help people make positive financial decisions," Bob told the group. "In fact, these same skills have enabled me to save enough money to absorb the financial blow that seems to be devastating other people in my position.

"I've been building a diversified investment portfolio since I started working. I've also been putting dollars into a forced savings and retirement plan on a regular basis. Consequently, I now have enough money to explore some professional options. At the same time, I must admit that I am depressed over losing my job.

"I never realized how much I depended on my company for self-esteem and social validation. Frankly, I feel as if I've been cast adrift. Since I don't ever want to be in that position again, I'd like to set up my own business. But how do I start: by hanging out a sign that says *Bob's Financial-Planning Services* and waiting for the phone to ring?"

We helped Bob develop a customized researching plan. First, he was encouraged to seek out relevant books and articles on the subject at his local library. After he discussed his needs with the reference librarian, she gave him the names of several publications that listed local and national professional organizations in the financial planning field.

As helpful as a reference librarian can be, it is not her job to determine the goals of a particular researching project or determine the specific steps that may be involved. This is an aspect of resourcing each of us must do for ourselves—or in conjunction with a resourcing group. We worked with Bob in developing a list of relevant questions before he set foot into the library. Some of these included:

✧ What are the professional or licensing requirements needed to enter the field?

✧ What kind of office and support facilities are normally required?

✧ What are the typical start-up costs?

✧ What are some established ways of generating new clients?

✧ How much does someone entering the field typically earn in the first year—and after several years?

✧ Who are the potential competitors on the local level?

✧ What are successful people in the field doing right?

✧ What are they not doing that someone with vision can do?

These are general questions that pertain to a wide range of business ventures. Perhaps one reason people don't bother to ask them is that they don't realize how easily accessible the answers actually are.

When Bob sat down with his reference librarian, he explained the ultimate goal of his researching project: *To find out as much relevant information as possible about setting up a financial planning consultancy.*

Bob then showed the librarian his list of questions, which enabled her to direct him to the specific information he needed. The librarian suggested that Bob consult the Bureau of Labor Statistics to see if they had any relevant publications or information. She also happened to know of a local professional group of financial planners that was mentioned in a recent newspaper article.

Within a three-week period, Bob received preliminary answers to all his questions. At last report, he was still researching the situation, while considering several corporate offers.

"I'm not completely certain about where I'm going to land," he told me. "Whatever happens, I'll be going into the situation with my eyes wide open. This researching process has given me a new slant on decision making. For example, I plan to investigate any company I consider working for. It will be useful to know in advance how they treat their people. I'll also be researching their future financial prospects. Whether I land in the corporate world or strike out on my own, I intend to be spending a good deal of time at the library."

Early in the researching process, Bob confirmed that he had the professional and personal qualifications to become a financial planner. Your specific researching requirements will depend on your particular goals and how far you have to go to achieve them.

Should you need to acquire additional knowledge, it may be useful to take a course or seminar in a particular field or subject. Adult education and learning network courses now abound in areas as diverse as grant proposal writing, Chinese cooking, and coping with an aging parent. Some of these are given in schools. Others at people's homes or work spaces. Whatever the setting, the information provided can be tremendously rewarding.

Several years ago, I helped a client set up a small business marketing attractive, low-cost designer watches. I soon became aware that there was a potentially large demand for this product in Germany and several other Western European countries. My client had never been involved in exporting, but, as it happened, a local learning center was offering a one-day course in exporting to the European market. I immediately called my client and suggested that she register for the class.

Based on a forty-dollar investment and eight hours in an informal classroom setting, my client acquired sufficient information to start marketing a product line in several European countries. Last year, sales in these countries accounted for over 50 percent of her total revenues.

There are many intricate forms of research that are beyond the scope of our present discussion. Depending on your goals, you may have to develop related skills that are not in your present repertoire—or you may have to hire experts to do the research for you. If you are developing a product that is completely new and untested, for example, you may have to engage in some form of original research.

Keep in mind that one objective of your initial researching efforts is to pinpoint areas of further research that need to be done to achieve your goal. In some instances, this may lead you to conclude that the goal is not feasible—at least in its present form. On the other hand, your initial research may point the way to the next step in the process. In either case, the information you glean will help you decide which way to step on the track you have set for yourself.

RESEARCHING EXERCISE

✦ ✦ ✦

Think of something that you have wondered about but never were able to find out. Put aside some time to pursue the answer. Think of people, books, databases, directories, and so forth that will help you find what you are looking for. Maintain a written log of your progress.

Discovering

Discovering is, in a sense, on the opposite end of the creativity spectrum from researching. The process has been described by psychologists as the ability to go beyond the available information and develop a solution that is the product of your own mind. Have you ever asked yourself the following questions:

✧ How does a composer of music envision and realize the brilliant combination of sounds and rhythms that make up a symphony?

✧ How does a scientist envision and realize a formula that winds up curing a dread disease?

✧ How does an entrepreneur envision and realize a unique business concept that sets a standard of excellence that is years ahead of all competitors?

✧ Ludwig von Beethoven wrote his 9th Symphony—one of the revered landmarks of music history—despite the fact that he was totally deaf at the time.

✧ Jonas Salk developed a cure for polio—a disease that had crippled millions of young people—eclipsing the work of scores of other distinguished medical scientists.

✧ Bill Gates, CEO of Microsoft, is one of the most influential figures in the computer industry. Gates, who began programming computers at age 13, possesses a rare combination of technical genius and business acumen that enabled him to drop out of college and become a billionaire before he was out of his twenties.

To some extent, the talent that underlies such extraordinary acts of genius is beyond acquisition. Let's face it, most of us will not become a Beethoven, or a Salk, or a Gates. On the other hand, there are people with comparable innate talents who never even approach maximizing their gifts. As Robert J. Sternberg, IBM Professor of Psychology and Education at Yale, notes:

> There may be genetically determined limits to how well a particular [person] may think. But let's worry about those limits when we reach them, and so far [most of us] haven't.[2]

There are two questions each of us must ask ourselves:

1. Am I making the most of what I have?
2. Am I allowing myself the freedom to discover?

If the answer to these questions is "no," you must then ask yourself a third question:

3. What's stopping you from maximizing the genius within?

In too many cases, the answer lies in erroneous belief systems that are drummed into us from early childhood. "Not everyone can be a Beethoven," says David Henry Feldman, a developmental psychologist and the author of *Nature's Gambit*, a study of child prodigies. "But . . . all humans, by virtue of being dreamers and fantasizers, have a tendency to take liberties with the world as it exists. . . ."[3]

Too often, this tendency is squelched by a society that values predictability and control. Today, there is much rhetoric about the importance of creativity. Nevertheless, we continue to place children in groups and force them to conform the moment they enter school. The world of business perpetuates this attitude by rewarding conformity and tangible results while tacitly discouraging the kind of process-based resourcing that generates discovery.

Behavioral scientists have dispelled the notion that the ability to discover and innovate are inborn. Nor are these skills correlated with measurable levels of intelligence.

"There just isn't any correlation between creativity and IQ," says Dean Keith Simonton, a psychology professor at the University of California and author of *Genius, Creativity and Leadership*. "The average college graduate has an IQ of about 120, and that is high enough to write novels, do scientific research or any other kind of creative work."[4]

Simonton believes that one reason people stop trying to discover and create is that they made an effort and failed. Here again, they have been erroneously taught that highly creative people always succeed. But, in fact, the opposite is true.

"Great geniuses make tons of mistakes," observes Simonton. "They generate lots of ideas and accept being wrong. They have a kind of internal fortress that allows them to fail and just keep going. . . . Thomas Edison held almost 1,000 patents, but most of them are not only forgotten, they weren't worth much to begin with."[5]

All of us have an untapped potential for discovery and creativity. But, too often, these are stifled by a society that demands conformity—not only in what we do, but in the way we think and view the world. As a result, we lose confidence in our own perceptions and process and fall into the trap of perceiving the world in terms of rigidly defined categories.

Ellen Langer, the Harvard psychologist who wrote the book *Mindfulness*, and her colleagues have been researching the creative process since the mid-1970s. They believe that we restrict ourselves to a kind of mental automatic pilot to accomplish routine or repetitive tasks. Langer calls this state of passive learning and robotic conformity *mindlessness*.[6]

On one level, this kind of narrow mind-set helps us filter out the complexities that can overwhelm us. Too often, however, it causes us to stifle our potential for discovery and independent action. The consequences of such mindlessness include stunted potential, a narrow self-image, and learned helplessness. To avoid these stifling traps, Langer suggests that we think in terms of alternatives rather than absolutes.

As children, we are taught to see the world in rigid, mutually exclusive categories. Accordingly, we are told: "This is a fork, which is used for eating." "This is a pen—which is used for writing."

Langer suggests that it would be more useful to explain such objects in a more flexible or conditional way: "This *could* be a fork. This *could* be a pen." The most common objection to this kind of teaching is that it might confuse a child and make his everyday decisions more complex. However, as Langer points out, we are living in a world that is conditional—not absolute—so why not teach skills that address life as it really is?

Just as every object has more than one use, every problem has multiple solutions. But, before you can discover what those possibilities are, you must start tearing down some walls and implementing some changes.

THE FIVE-STEP DISCOVERY PROCESS

1. Don't be afraid to unleash the creativity within you. The first step in activating the processes that enable you to discover and create is to remember that, for the most part, these are skills that can be accessed rather than innate talents with which you are born.

It is one thing to admire and learn from a Beethoven or Bill Gates, but comparing yourself to them can be frustrating. Maybe it would be more helpful to look at the massive successes of all the minimal talents who discovered how to make mountains out of molehills.

There is undoubtedly a kind of genius to that kind of optimizing of potential. However, this genius is the result of lifeskills that any of us can learn. There are always more people underachieving than overachieving—whether in school, in business, in science, or in the arts. In a sense, though, overachieving is a misnomer. A far more accurate description would be, *someone who is using more of his or her potential for discovery and innovation than most people.*

The first step in optimizing your potential for discovery and creativity is to purge yourself of all those negative and restrictive messages imposed on you by parents, teachers, and others who told you that only a few geniuses are capable of greatness. They may have been well intended, but they were dead wrong.

As we saw in our discussion on tracking, it is important that you find those areas where your potential for discovery is most likely to thrive. It is doubtful that Beethoven could have discovered a life-saving vaccine, just as it's unlikely that Bill Gates could have composed the 9th Symphony. On the other hand, it is clear that most endeavors don't require such a high degree of specialization—or innate genius.

   2. Tune into your internal response system. When the composer Johann Sebastian Bach was asked how he discovered his musical ideas, he answered: "The problem is not finding them, it's not stepping on them when you get up in the morning."[7]

All of us receive numerous internal messages that can lead to the discovery of problem-solving solutions—be they in music, business, or the personal realm. Unfortunately, as Bach noted, we often squander or ignore these gifts from our unconscious.

As we have discussed in Chapter Three, success in any area of life requires that you trust and rely on gut feelings. To recognize and interpret these feelings, you must consciously cultivate a relationship with your unconscious mind. From the perspective of problem solving and discovery, unconscious messages and gut feelings are often experienced as intuitions.

Intuition has been defined as "a perception that spontaneously occurs without conscious deliberation."[8] Intuitive thoughts often follow intense concentration on a particular problem, although they may also inexplicably occur while we are thinking about something else. When I describe a person as being intuitive, I'm talking about someone who can use these inner feelings to spark discovery.

Intuition often happens immediately before going to sleep and just after awakening. Sometimes, the solution to a problem may come in the form of a dream that you recall in the morning. But the process can take place at any time. To take full advantage of these windows into your unconscious, it's a good idea to always keep a pen and paper or a small cassette recorder close by.

Like all internal messages, intuitions may not have logical explanations at the time they enter our awareness. Skeptics will argue that intuitions don't make sense and should, therefore, not be taken seriously. While it's true that some intuitions can lead us down blind alleys, they are, nevertheless, an invaluable informational resource that deserves as much consideration as information gleaned through logic.

3. Emphasize process rather than tangible results. I believe that many of our schools emphasize linear, results-oriented logic rather than the kind of process-based intuition needed for discovery. Most of our standardized tests—including those that measure IQ—are multiple-choice instruments that seek to extract one right answer. Typically, we are given four possible answers to each question and are told to select the correct one. This way of testing might be expeditious, but fostering this kind of literal approach can only have a detrimental effect on critical thinking and the discovery process.

The vast majority of women and men in this culture are products of this one-right-answer kind of learning. They (we) are now the professionals, managers, business owners, and workers of this world. If we are to reach our potential—as human beings, as organizations, and as a society—we must break down this linear, results-oriented mind-set. Instead, we must keep our eyes and ears open—and start using our hearts and guts as well as our minds.

Activating the discovery process requires the ability to *focus*. This entails concentrating on what you are doing while remaining watchful for ideas or inspirations that can pop up at any time. Discovery tends to come about when you can get your mind and body into a state of *flow*. Some people use various forms of meditation and other forms of deep relaxation to achieve this.

When you relax and allow the discovery process to take over, you will eventually develop *insight* into your problem. At that point, the proverbial light bulb in your head goes off and you have what is sometimes called an "Aha!" experience.

Before you can properly focus and move into a state of flow, you must first rephrase the question from: "What is the right answer?" to "What are the possibilities waiting to be unearthed?" As Robert J. Sternberg, IBM Professor of Psychology and Education at Yale, points out:

> In critical thinking problems, there are [often] no right answers. And even when there are, *it is the thought process that counts*. Ultimately, [individuals] who think well will be in a position to generate good answers, whereas [those] who generate good answers don't always think well.[9]

Sternberg argues that glib, one-dimensional answers no longer suffice. "The key," he says, "is to learn to seek deep and complex solutions for deep and complex problems." Sternberg also stresses that people must teach themselves how to think critically—and to inspire those around us to do the same.

As managers, educators, and parents, it is up to us to "provide every means possible to enable this self-instruction to take place. To the extent that we are able to influence others, we must serve as teachers and facilitators even as we simultaneously recognize ourselves as learners."[10]

4. Have the courage to embrace uncertainty. By now, it should be clear that discovery cannot take place if one insists on working in an atmosphere where everything is strictly controlled and predictable. On the contrary, discovery is a process that tends to raise more questions than it answers.

When explorers like Columbus set out on their adventures, they weren't certain as to what they would discover.

Apparently, Columbus was seeking a route to the Far East, not the area that later became known as the Americas. The ability to discover—to break new ground in any endeavor—requires a willingness to forge ahead in the face of uncertainty. That takes courage, confidence, and vision.

> Studies indicate that intuitive thinkers tend to be unconventional and comfortable in their unconventionality. They are confident and self-sufficient, and do not base their identities on membership in social groups. . . . They enjoy taking risks and are willing to expose themselves to criticism and challenge. . . . They describe themselves as independent, foresighted, confident and spontaneous.[11]

It is not coincidental that these characterizations of intuitive thinkers are much like those we use to describe *indipreneurs*. The time has come to recognize that discovery and critical thinking are not warm and fuzzy concepts of use only to creative artists and research scientists. They are hard-edge skills that have everything to do with gaining a competitive advantage and improving the bottom line.

Today, individuals and companies must respond quickly to all sorts of change and turbulence. Consequently, the real value of such critical thinking skills as discovery and innovation is finally being acknowledged. And, as we have noted, improving these skills is important to each of us—even as we attempt to inspire those whom we influence to make similar strides.

From a motivational perspective, discovery is more likely to take place when group members have a role in the designing of a problem. Under such circumstances, "the problem becomes 'theirs' and in some ways the ownership of the solution is theirs as well."[12] But how do managers and other organizational leaders create an atmosphere that inspires discovery?

Ellen Langer believes that one of the most powerful qualities a manager can have in this regard is a degree of uncertainty:

> If a manager is confident but uncertain—confident that the job will get done but without being certain of exactly the best way of doing it—employees are likely to have more room to be creative, alert and self-starting. When working for confident but uncertain leaders, we are less likely to feign knowledge or hide mistakes, practices that can be costly to a company. Instead, we are likely to think, "If he's not sure, I guess I don't have to be right 100 percent of the time," and risk taking becomes less risky. . . . Admission of uncertainty leads to a search for more information, and with more information there may be more options.[13]

5. Make the most of creative rest. What do you do when you find yourself at an impasse in trying to solve a problem? Do you keep pushing ahead until you reach the point of mind-boggling frustration? If so, you may be doing yourself more harm than good. Psychologists Robert and Marilyn Harris Kriegel believe that there are times when it's best "to turn your attention to something completely different that will let your mind wander. When you do that, your conscious mind, or 'front burner,' lets go of the puzzle while your subconscious mind [or 'back burner'] takes over."[14]

This kind of back-burner thinking has also been called *creative rest*. Eugene Raudsepp, president of Princeton Creative Research, Inc., and author of *How Creative Are You?* refers to the process as *incubation*. Whatever you call it, the idea is to stop one thought process consciously and "do something else for a while so that the solution to the first problem has time to take shape and reach maturity."[15]

Raudsepp is among those researchers who believe that incubation is a regenerative process during which our subconscious or intuitive mind is still working on the problem even while we are engaged in something completely different. "All we see of [the process] is that one day we have an unsolvable problem that just keeps getting worse, and the next day it is solved."

How do you maximize your back-burner thinking skills? Raudsepp suggests that you first gather all the information and data pertaining to your project. Then spend some time going over the material—but don't consciously try to come up with a solution. Then put it aside and do something totally unrelated. Some people find walking or jogging to be a productive back-burner activity. Others like playing a musical instrument or drawing—or watching a baseball game. Just choose an alternate activity that relaxes and rejuvenates you—and then get back to the problem at hand. More often than not, you'll find that things will start falling into place.

In a high-pressure corporate setting, it may be difficult to stop what you're doing to engage in creative rest. Nevertheless, a growing number of forward-looking leaders are recognizing the value of making creative rest part of a flexible work environment. Even if you can't find time in the middle of a busy workday, there are other times when incubation seems to work especially well.

"A good way to start incubating is while you're asleep," says Raudsepp. "Think about your problem for 20 minutes before you go to bed. The next morning you may wake up with some good ideas."

The incubation process works equally well before you pursue any kind of relaxing activity. If you're going to jog, for example, try mulling the problem over just prior to starting your run. If you're going to have dinner with a friend, try reviewing the problem in your mind just one more time before leaving work. The key is to find one or more incubating activities that work well for you. You might also want to experiment with different lengths of break time at varying hours of the day. In any case, the next time you feel stuck, try giving it a rest!

Discovery Exercise

✦ ✦ ✦

To activate the discovery process, we must have an open mind and let answers unfold as they may. Otherwise, we will not recognize when we have hit upon something significant. This can be frightening to people who are accustomed to the kind of structure that has already determined the correct answers even before questions are asked.

Children are always discovering new things—because society has not yet had a chance to restrict their minds. There are few things as beautiful as watching a little child make new discoveries and have what we call "Aha!" experiences. To emulate this in our own lives, we must allow the child inside us to surface. This is the object of the following exercise:

Set aside a long weekend. Embark on an unstructured trip to an unspecified destination. Make no plans, save the general direction and the number of miles your car can travel, so that you can arrive back home on schedule. Keep an open mind. Make notes on what you see, how you feel, your level of energy. After you return, think about the relationships between what you've observed and problems you were contemplating before you left. Write down any insights and discoveries you might have made.

Testing

Once you've made a discovery, you'll need to test it out. *Testing* asks the question: "Will what I've discovered work?" The exact nature of the testing process depends on the particular endeavor. In the case of the creative arts, for example, there are no objective measurements. The creator alone determines whether her discovery meets the necessary criteria.

Imagine that you are a composer who has just discovered what you believe to be a great melody for the second movement of your symphony. At that point, you can test it out by playing it in context with the rest of the musical piece. You might also play the piece for a trusted colleague or mentor and ask for feedback. Perhaps you will conclude that the melody needs a bit of refinement—or even a complete revision. Whatever the case, your decision is not subject to any sort of objective measurement.

Scientists are obliged to engage in far more rigorous and objective testing procedures. A medical researcher may believe that he has discovered a vaccine that can cure a particular disease. But, unlike a musical composer, his belief is not enough to justify implementation. Before that vaccine can be used on humans, it must be tested on experimental animals or special groups of people who are willing to assume a risk. It can take years before such a product is approved for general use.

There are, of course, many testing grounds that fall in between the complete subjectivity of a creative artist and the stringent objective validation required by a medical scientist. Psychotherapy and business provide two useful examples.

Psychiatrists have medical degrees and, thus, know a great deal about scientific experimentation. Yet those who practice psychotherapy base many of their practices on theories and methodologies that have little or no strictly scientific support.

A person suffering from a neurotic disorder may be helped by a psychiatrist that has a neo-Freudian orientation. A second person suffering from the same disorder may achieve better results from a practitioner who takes an existential approach. In fact, it is generally agreed that a psychiatrist's medical and scientific training may have little or nothing to do with how effective he or she is in helping people.

In a sense, a psychotherapist's testing methods closely resemble those of an artist. The particular theory she uses to help people overcome their problems tends to be the one in which she is trained and feels most comfortable with. If that method seems to be working, the therapist will continue to use it. If it is not working, she may or may not be able to shift to a more effective method.

As in psychotherapy, the testing methods used by many businesses are also somewhere in that middle ground between total subjectivity and objective validation. Corporations spend millions of dollars in research that is supposed to be scientific. But apparently human behavior is too quirky to be predictable by market researchers or anyone else.

Computers were the innovations of a corporation called Univac. They chose not to invest heavily in this product because their very expensive and supposedly scientific market research showed that in the year 2000 there would only be 1,000 computers in use. IBM did not engage in extensive market research and did invest heavily in computers. The rest, as they say, is history.[16]

Unless you are involved in medical research or some other scientific field, I wouldn't be overly concerned with developing tests that supposedly meet strict standards of objectivity. In most endeavors, the key question is: Will it work for you? As you will see later in this chapter, a notoriously unscientific resource—human beings—often provides the most critical testing ground.

Innovating

Innovating is the culmination of *researching, discovering,* and *testing*. There is an old Native American saying: "Do not follow where the path may lead, but go where there is no path and leave a trail." When you innovate, you are following the spirit of that timeless concept.

Innovating can be viewed as taking the discovery process a step farther. The light bulb in your mind or the "Aha!" experience that characterizes discovery is still just an idea at that point. Once it has met the criteria set in *testing*, you are ready to innovate—that is, to put your discovery into action. There are three basic ways to innovate:

*T*HREE ROUTES TO INNOVATIVE PROBLEM SOLVING

1. Invent something new.

2. Create new combinations.

3. Find new uses for existing products or services.

1. Invent something new. Every so often, somebody invents a new product or service that didn't exist before. There was Thomas Edison and his light bulb, Alexander Graham Bell and his telephone, and so on. Scientists and inventors will continue working to create products to improve the quality of our lives. But it's important to keep in mind that many important innovations were created by people who had no particular scientific or technical talent.

Federal Express was the idea of Fred Smith, a college student who recognized a need in the marketplace that wasn't being fulfilled. People—and especially businesses—often needed to have their letters and packages delivered to faraway places the next day. The post office was not providing such service—and neither was anyone else. The student suggested in an economics paper that such a service would be useful to the public—and highly profitable to the person who got it off the ground.

The teacher who was grading the paper gave it a mediocre grade. What a ridiculous idea. Imagine trying to beat the post office at its own game. I assume you know how the story turned out. Federal Express has set the standard for next-day delivery, and the post office is still struggling to close the gap.

There are a couple of very important lessons here. The first is never to be discouraged by so-called experts who happen to be in a power position with respect to you. Should you come up with an ingenious idea, that person may not have the vision to recognize its merit. That's why you should never be discouraged if you believe you are on to something worthwhile.

The second lesson is to never be intimidated by venerable institutions—especially those that are part of massive bureaucracies. On the contrary, the post office is a great example of what can happen to an institution that has no competitors to worry about.

Federal Express has been computerized for years. Virtually anyone with a credit card can set up an account. Shortly after your order is placed, a representative arrives at your office or home to pick up your letter or package. You are assured that your shipment will arrive before a certain hour. Once that hour has passed, you can call an 800 number and be given prompt information about the status of your package: when it was delivered and who signed for it.

It is worth noting that, as of this writing, the post office still is not offering many of these services. Meanwhile, Federal Express finds itself with lots of competition in the next-day shipping business—some of whom have started offering comparable services at a lower price. As with most products and services, however, the innovator tends to hold a *positioning* advantage—particularly when its company name has come to be used as a general descriptive term.[17]

2. *Create new combinations.* Have you ever heard the saying, "There is nothing new under the sun"? In a sense, that's true. It is worth noting that Beethoven used the same 12 notes that are available to everyone else to compose his

9th symphony. Let's look at a somewhat less esoteric example of innovating by creatively combining existing resources.

Back at the 1903 Worlds Fair in St. Louis, there was an ice cream vendor in one booth and a waffle vendor in an adjacent booth. The waffles had not been selling and the vendor felt that something needed to be done. So he went home, ironed his waffles, coned them up, and made the following proposal to the ice cream vendor in the next booth—whose sales were also less than earth shattering.

"Why don't we take your ice cream and place it into these coned waffles?" That's how the ice cream cone was invented.

I mentioned earlier that I helped a client set up a company that markets watches on a worldwide basis. When she first went into business, the watches were being marketed with standard-issue bands. Naturally, the buyer could always purchase another band that he found more suitable. Business was fair—but not great—until we had the idea of contacting several watchband companies that specialized in unusual designs my client found attractive.

Admittedly, these designer watches haven't made as much of a splash as the ice cream cone. Nevertheless, this new synthesis opened up a wide variety of new markets and outlets for these products. My client's little business has grown dramatically, and she has been able to delegate the day-to-day operation to others.

3. *Find new uses for old products or services.* There is something ecologically appealing about recycling things that are already in existence that might otherwise go to waste. When Levi Strauss arrived in San Francisco in 1850, he brought bolts of cloth from which he intended to make tents. Unfortunately, there was no demand for tents.

One day, a prospector mentioned that what he and others like him needed were strong pants that could hold up during the long days and weeks of digging. Strauss took the prospector's advice and used the tent cloth to make pants. To increase their strength, he used the same kind of rivets on the pockets that are used to hold tents together. Almost a century and a half later, Levi Strauss remains the world's leading manufacturer of blue jeans.[18]

I believe that people and business squander many opportunities for innovation. The problem harks back to the kind of one-right-answer teaching that is still the hallmark of many of our schools. We are helping a number of school systems reshape their methods and invent new courses to enable students to become more innovative in all aspects of their lives.

The nonproductive teaching methods that still characterize many of our schools are also stunting innovation in the workplace. Part of the problem has to do with a misplaced reverence for authority. Just as a teacher in school is deemed to be right by virtue of her position at the head of the class, it is too often assumed that those in power in a corporate setting know more than their charges.

Psychologist Ellen Langer is one of a growing group of researchers who have found that this kind of rigid and defensive thinking serves only to smother innovation. She stresses the importance of managers being open to questions that cannot be addressed with easy answers.

Langer laments over the many innovative ideas that have been turned into dead ends by mindless statements like: *Do it because I say so,* or empty retorts like, *What if we let everybody do that?* or *We've never done it that way.*

What difference does it make if an authority figure wants something done, if doing that thing leads to a negative result? Who cares if it's never been done *that* way—especially if *that* way is the best and most innovative way to get things done?[19]

These are vital questions for all organizations and individuals. If we are going to maximize our ability to create and innovate, we must first break free of the myths that perpetuate this misplaced and destructive dependence on rigid rules of authority. Instead, we must strive to create conditions for ourselves and others that nurture commitment and support innovation.

INNOVATION EXERCISE

✦ ✦ ✦

Think of a problem to which you would like to find a new solution. Use one or more of the following methods to achieve that objective:

1. Create a completely new innovation for an idea or product that would address that problem.

2. Think of a product, service, or idea that can be improved or enhanced. Write down exactly how you would go about it.

3. Think of two or more products that can be combined or synthesized into something new. Or formulate a new idea from two or more existing ideas. Write down and/or illustrate your product/idea.

MAKING PEOPLE YOUR MOST ESSENTIAL RESOURCE

As we noted at the beginning of this chapter, there are three major categories of resources: self, information, and people. In a sense, the divisions between these categories are cosmetic. You will recall, for example, that in discussing the library as a key informational resourcing tool, we mentioned the importance of developing a relationship with the librarian. In effect, he is a people resource who opens the door to informational resources.

The same principle applies to many other aspects of resourcing. If you decide to take a course to improve your informational base, your teacher or professor is potentially more valuable than any book or informational concept in the syllabus. Think back to the high school and college courses that have had the greatest impact on your life. Chances are they're the ones that were taught by the most memorable teachers.

Most people receive no formal training in accessing people as resources, yet few skills are more critical. Al Reis and Jack Trout, the authors of *Horse Sense*, believe that success in life is based more on what others can do for you than on what you can do for yourself.[20]

In my view, it's not a question of choosing between yourself and others. Nevertheless, there is no doubt that who you know can be every bit as important as what you know. And, as we've seen, what you know often comes from who you know. Show me a successful woman or man, and I'll show you someone who knows how to take full advantage of human resources.

Selecting the Resourcing Group That Best Meets Your Needs

In my book *Strategies 2000*, I noted that a survey of self-made millionaires by Georgia State University marketing professor Thomas Stanley revealed that these individuals had only one thing in common: a very thick Rolodex. I also observed that Henry Ford, who began his career as a poor, illiterate businessman, eventually became one of this country's wealthiest men. "His greatest achievements came after he began associating with Thomas Edison, Harvey Firestone, John Burroughs and Luther Burbank."[21]

The world is full of examples of successful people who are adept at utilizing human resources to realize their potential. Many of these individuals have no special gifts, nor do they have access to any information that is unavailable to the rest of us. What they have mostly is the *indipreneurial* spirit to ask for feedback, motivation, and support.

Why don't more of us make better use of the people at our disposal? Perhaps one reason is that the very idea of *using* others is repugnant to some of us. Yet numerous studies have shown that people who give of themselves often reap more psychic benefits than the recipients of that giving. [22]

Then there are people who will tell you that they can get along on their own and, therefore, don't need the help of others. I find it ironic that many of these same individuals are content to accept help passively when it comes in the form of entitlements.

When you reach out for people, there's always a certain amount of risk involved. I submit, however, that it has become far riskier to depend on corporations and other institutions to address these needs. Dr. Adele Scheele has observed that people who take full advantage of human resources "demonstrate their willingness to participate in a positive human system." She finds that this kind of participation works best when people "invest wholeheartedly in the process.

"You need to appreciate other people's time . . . to care about their work. You need to value people's stories and experiences, for they are the stuff of life itself, and can lead to some of your own most rewarding experiences."[23]

Resource-connector groups often focus around a particular goal. As you will see, it is often possible to fill more than one need through these groups. But, in general, resourcing groups are designed specifically to address the following needs:

✦ Social

✦ Career/professional

✦ Role modeling/mentoring

✦ Motivational/self-esteem

✦ Shared interests

✦ Spiritual

Let's take a look at the reasons why resourcing groups are so important. As we approach the new century, a growing number of men and women find themselves increasingly isolated. In our high-tech world, more and more of us are becoming telecommuters working from home in isolation from others. As these technologies become more accessible and pervasive, corporations are finding that it is cost- and time-efficient for many of their people to work at home and communicate through computer terminals and fax machines.

This kind of arrangement can be desirable for those of us who seek to spend more time with our families and less time commuting. Still, it tends to create a situation that is isolating in a number of ways. When we work in an organizational environment, there are many natural opportunities for socializing. Those of us who work in more solitary settings need to seek out positive social situations.

A group of writers in New York have a regular luncheon meeting every Wednesday at an upper West Side restaurant. While there is a core group of people that attends regularly, the meeting is open to anyone who wishes to participate.

"The group serves a variety of purposes," says Katherine, a health and fitness writer who has become a regular attendee. "It provides a forum where people in the same business can exchange ideas and contacts. We talk about everything from publishers and agents to computer software and dealing with writer's block. I've received a good deal of useful advice and support from other writers—and I like sharing what I know with others. Beyond that, I look forward to these Wednesday meetings as a way to break up my week and an opportunity to meet with others."

As you can see, this informal resourcing group fulfills several of the needs on our list. Initially, the group was set up to address a social need for people who spend much of their time alone. As it turns out, it also provides a good context for career and professional resources.

At times, the group serves a role-modeling or mentoring function in that it provides a context for aspiring writers to meet experienced authors who in some cases have penned best-sellers. It also serves a motivational function for writers who may be having a problem selling a proposal or difficulties working. Katherine talks about the motivation and boost to her self-esteem she has received from two other participants in the group.

"I've become very close with two other regulars in the group. We often call one another or meet on an informal basis to exchange ideas and give each other feedback. I recently hit a dry spell during which I felt tapped out of ideas. My two friends helped me in a number of ways. One shared a similar experience and told me how he used creative rest to get through the impasse. The other is simply so upbeat about my work that just talking to her is inspirational."

In case you're wondering how this writers' group started, it was the brainchild of three friends who met regularly for lunch on Wednesdays. These writers found the meetings so helpful that they shared the experience with others. Soon, the group began expanding. Five years later, the Wednesday meetings can have anywhere from 8 to 30 attendees. But, as you've seen, the benefits of the group go far beyond the weekly meetings.

No matter what your professional interests or personal needs might be, setting up or joining a resourcing group is not a difficult matter. Today, there are groups for career changers, divorced parents with children, overeaters, Scrabble players, and almost anything else you can imagine. Your librarian can direct you to some of these, and you can take it from there—or you can start your own.

Several years ago, Paul decided that he wanted to change careers. After practicing law for five years, he had grown disillusioned with the field. "I found law school intellectually stimulating and rewarding, but I just couldn't stand the politics of actually being a lawyer. I thought I might be more comfortable in some kind of research field, but I needed support and information."

After reading several books on career changing, Paul decided to place an ad in a local paper asking for people with similar needs to join him in a discussion group. He procured a room at a local community college for the initial meeting.

"I was amazed when twenty people showed up for that first meeting. After we hashed out our ideas, about ten expressed an interest in meeting on a weekly basis. For the next year and a half, we had regular meetings at the home of a member who was kind enough to offer his large living room. Each week, a different member was asked to run the meeting. The results were somewhat erratic—but most of us received a good deal of help.

"People talked about their needs, shared contacts and information. At the end of the meetings, each member would commit to doing certain goal-oriented things during the following week. Then, at the next meeting, everyone would report on what they actually accomplished. Frankly, it was embarrassing to admit you did nothing, so most of us would follow through.

"People within the group eventually developed closer relationships with one another and these were extremely helpful. For example, if I was having a problem following through, there were one or two people I would always call to lift my spirits and lend encouragement. We also did some unusual things for each other.

"One of our members had a job interview and was uncertain about using an ex-employer as a reference. How could she be sure he would say good things about her? Suddenly, I hit on a solution. I would call the ex-employer up and say I was considering hiring this person. I would simply ask if he had been happy with her work. His answer would determine whether or not my friend would benefit from listing him as a reference."

AN OBJECT LESSON IN SETTING UP YOUR OWN THINKTANK

Aside from addressing specific needs, resource connectors can serve a more general ongoing function in your professional or personal life. Let me share with you how I've activated this process for myself.

Several years ago, I became aware that I didn't have the time to keep up with all the information that was important to me. I decided to address that need by forming a *thinktank*.

Now, the dictionary defines a thinktank as, "A research institute or other organization of scholars, social or physical scientists . . . [who are] employed by government or large corporations to solve complex problems or predict future developments."[24] So what, you may be wondering, does that have to do with me?

Obviously, I'm not a government—or even a large corporation. What I am is an *indipreneur* whose need to solve problems and predict the future is every bit as critical as those large entities. Furthermore, it's not my style to depend on institutions of any kind to do my predicting and problem solving for me. So I decided to start my own brain trust or thinktank.

I proceeded to discuss my idea with Juanell Teague, a professional colleague who shared my concerns. She agreed that it was impossible to keep up with the many vital areas of knowledge that determine which way the world is headed—and she wanted to join me in setting up a resourcing group.

The first thing we did was decide which disciplines were to be represented in the thinktank. Then, we proceeded to target people in our geographic area who could meet with us on a once-a-month basis. We tried to find individuals who had different styles of thinking, people who would give us a local, national, and global perspective. When we decided whom we wanted, we contacted each of them personally.

At present, we have one person representing each of the following disciplines: finance, the environment, health care, publishing and communications, entrepreneurship, public school education and adult education, computers and technology, family issues, innovation and creativity, ethnic and gender diversity, aging, and transportation.

When the group initially got together, we spent the first two or three meetings coming up with a mission statement, so that we would all be in sync with what we wanted to accomplish as a group. Our stated mission is:

> To produce position papers, articles, and seminars on various socioeconomic issues. Methods used to obtain results will be research and review of literature, original studies, and assimilation of results through cooperation of the group members. The approach will evolve from the affective as well as the intellectual dimension influencing all age groups and life

stages. Projected byproducts of group work will be: mono-graphs, books, and radio and television spots.

When we first formed our thinktank, we really had no structure or firm agenda for how we would go about realizing our mission. What we did have was a diverse body of women and men who wanted to get together to exchange ideas. Since we were essentially breaking new ground, we decided to give the structure of the group as much time as it needed to unfold.

At first, some of the members were uncomfortable with the lack of structure. They had never been in a group that was given such a free rein. The whole idea was scary at first, but the benefits of allowing something to evolve in unforeseen ways is something none of us anticipated.

Most group members were accustomed to working with the kind of deadlines that we discussed in Chapter Three. It wasn't easy for us simply to allow things to develop at their own pace. This process required time, patience, and the willingness to let go of some traditional notions of how things are supposed to get done. Yet all the while, we continued to move ahead with confidence that the answers would somehow make themselves known—which they did.

During the first few months, we all benefited from the free exchange of information and resources contributed by the members. In time, the group decided that it would be beneficial to concentrate on a number of specific projects. One of our current ventures involves working with a local high school in developing a curriculum that will prepare students to succeed in our changing world.

Donating our services in this way was not something that we originally planned. But, as we continue to evolve, all sorts of exciting and unexpected opportunities continue to come our way.

The group has more than satisfied my original goal of keeping abreast of vital information that determines which way the world is headed. But, as is so often the case, the process has provided a more important lesson than the information itself.

Like most businesses, I operate with time lines and deadlines—and I'm not about to denigrate their importance. Nevertheless, the evolution of our thinktank has helped me anticipate what I consider to be a twenty-first-century innovation.

I believe that, in the future, businesses and individuals will have to recognize that the time lines that emerged in the twentieth century require some serious revision. Giving people the freedom to innovate in collaborative groups—as well as on their own—is something all corporations will need to consider. Implementing this process may well mean suspending conventional notions of time management and goal setting.

For those of you who are serious about becoming *indipreneurs*, and truly want to innovate, I strongly suggest that you consider setting up your own thinktank. The accompanying box details the six basic steps involved:

HOW TO START YOUR OWN THINKTANK

1. Determine the particular issues on which you want to focus. Consider enlisting a partner early on to help you put the group together from the start.

2. Select potential members from diverse disciplines and backgrounds who you would like to participate. Try to select men and women with different styles of communicating and thinking. This will create an ambiance that is both challenging and diversified.

3. Call each of those people and meet with them individually or in small groups.

4. Decide on a meeting place and time. Make sure each potential member is able to commit to attending on a regular basis. Once the group gets rolling, it is important to set up criteria for attendance. In our group, members cannot miss more than three meetings a year—or they will give up their place to someone else.

5. During the first three to four meetings, start developing a mission statement. It is important to determine what you want to accomplish as a group—but remember the importance of remaining flexible.

6. Select one or more projects for the group to work on that further its mission.

USING FOCUS GROUPS TO TEST-MARKET YOUR IDEAS

Focus groups are typically brought together to concentrate on specific issues that have been predetermined before the group has been assembled. Such groups are particularly useful to people and businesses looking for ways to measure the potential marketability of a product, service, or business idea.

Let's say that we wish to know how people 55 years of age and older feel about cosmetic surgery. One way to glean that information is to identify and assemble a cross section of men and women in that age group and ask them to come to a neutral place.

At that point, a moderator will pose relevant questions to the group and record the various responses. Sometimes, the sponsoring organization will have representatives sitting behind a one-way mirror. These representatives may, from time to time, ask the moderator to pose additional questions to the group.

Organizations that make frequent use of focus groups would like to think they are objective, but this is not the case. Nevertheless, such groups can provide a good deal of valuable feedback and information.

It is relatively easy to set up a focus group to test market your idea. You can invite people to participate on a one-time basis. If you choose, you can offer to pay them a modest amount, or you can offer to serve on a focus group they assemble. The people you select can be known to you. Just be sure that they are qualified and predisposed to give you the kind of feedback you're looking for.

Les is a commercial artist who creates cover art for books and compact disks. He often mixes abstract and semiabstract images with photographs and other representational materials. To make sure that he is getting his ideas across, Les sometimes invites a focus group of three to five people to his studio. For the most part, the people he invites do not have any training in the visual arts.

Les shows the artwork to the group, and then asks them to write down what the images mean—as well as their qualitative responses. Afterward, he asks the participants to read and discuss their responses.

"These focus groups have really helped me to see my work through other people's eyes. There are times when I think the message I'm communicating is obvious, yet nobody in the group seems to get it. On a number of occasions, I've been able to implement relatively minor changes that have made my work more accessible without compromising my artistic statement."

TEN WAYS TO ADDRESS NEEDS AND PROBLEMS THROUGH CREATIVE RESOURCING

1. Make reading a habit. Constantly read broad-based periodicals like *Business Week, Newsweek, Time,* and *The Wall Street Journal.* Read professional journals, newspapers, and other resources that pertain to your career. I also find it useful to subscribe to lesser known newsletters and publications. One of my favorites is a newsletter called *Challenges,* which is put out by the Council on Competitiveness (900 17th Street N.W., Suite 1050, Washington, DC 20006).

Always read with an open mind. Make it a point to write down your insights and take all the time you need to absorb the material. When the late President John F. Kennedy was in high school, he did not receive particularly good grades. Nevertheless, he was described by his classmates as being the most analytical, well-informed boy among his peers. When a friend asked how he was able to retain so much more information than his classmates, the future president responded as follows:

"I'll pick up an article, I'll read it and then I'll force myself to lay it down for about half an hour and go through the total article in my mind, bringing to memory as much as I possibly can and then analyzing the article, and then attacking it and tearing it down."[25]

2. Make it a practice to clip relevant newspaper and magazine articles. Organize them in a filing system under the appropriate category. When you come across an article that might be helpful or of interest to one of your resource contacts, send it to that person along with a thoughtful note.

3. Write articles for your local newspaper and submit article ideas to magazines. Getting a byline is a great way to demonstrate your expertise and increase your visibility.

Developing ideas for articles in your area of interest gives you a multitude of opportunities to sharpen your resourcing lifeskills. One good way to enrich your writing—while developing new insights and expanding your resources—is to interview experts in the field. Most people enjoy seeing their name in print and are willing to speak to people who present themselves in a professional manner.

4. Learn to identify your needs and seek people and information to help you fill those needs. Many people are unaware or in denial with respect to what their needs are. Consequently, those needs are never met.

5. Keep a Rolodex of people with whom you can network. Set a goal of eventually gathering 1,000 or more names of people to whom you can turn for various kinds of information, feedback and help.

Studies have shown that the average person is probably no more than seven steps away from reaching any person he or she desires to contact. Increasing your people resources can reduce that distance even further.

6. Socialize on a regular basis. Socialize with professional colleagues in your field as well as with those who can bring different interests and insights into your repertoire of information. Don't ever hesitate to mix business with pleasure. Let me relate an amusing anecdote with respect to that point.

Some years ago, an aspiring singer-songwriter was having an enjoyable dinner with a top entertainment lawyer who was well known for his quirky personality. In the course of the meal, the two discussed a variety of personal and professional matters. When the check arrived, the lawyer insisted on paying.

"Are you going to list this as a business deduction on your income tax?" the writer asked.

"Certainly," the lawyer responded coyly. "But do they have to know that we *like* talking business?"

7. *Develop a panel of experts upon whom you can call in your professional and personal life.* A knowledgeable attorney, a skilled accountant, and a trusted family physician are essentials. These and other experts should be interviewed in person. Remember, you are retaining them to work for you—even though some of them may charge for their time during an initial interview.

The best way to contact experts is through personal and professional referrals. A number of attorneys we have interviewed say that they generally won't charge for an initial interview if the person is referred by an existing client or professional colleague. If you can't obtain firsthand referrals, try contacting professional associations such as the local Bar Association.

8. *During the next 30 days, start or join one or more of the sorts of resourcing groups discussed in this chapter.* Start by assessing your most immediate need—be it some aspect of your career or personal life or a hobby you would enjoy pursuing.

One interesting exercise that some of our seminar participants find helpful is becoming part of a group that is involved in an activity that is substantially different from the kinds of things you usually do. Arnold, a civil engineer who had never done anything artistic or associated with people who were engaged in such activities, decided to take a course in furniture design.

"Almost everyone with whom I associated was an engineer, a scientist, or involved with computers. As much as I wanted to try my hand at something artistic, I found it refreshing and enlightening to be around people who were unlike most of my colleagues and friends."

Arnold enjoyed furniture design so much that he decided to take it up professionally. After two years, Arnold found it difficult to make a living—and resumed his engineering career. Still, he has no regrets.

"I consider those two years to be among the most important of my adult life. I felt as if I was growing stale—in terms of both my career and my personal perspective. Trying my hand at something completely different has given me a new and much broader view of the world. I have also made some important friendships that I expect will last for a long time."

9. *Conduct some original research in an area of interest.* You can do this on your own or in conjunction with a thinktank group that you initiate.

10. *Always listen with an open mind.* Consider every person you meet as a source of learning. In fact, each man and woman you meet really does have something valuable to share—but you have to be open.

Each of us has expectations, preconceptions, and prejudices that cause us to filter out important information—simply because something doesn't fit into our existing schemata. Note the ways in which others are closed minded, and think about the impact this might be having on them. Make a special effort to unearth such tendencies within yourself—and set a goal to eliminate as many of these self-imposed limitations as possible.

ENDNOTES

1. Michael D. Lemonick, "Tomorrow's Lesson: Learn or Perish," *Time,* special issue, Fall 1992, *The Year 2000 and Beyond.*

2. Robert J. Sternberg is quoted in his "Teaching Critical Thinking: Eight Easy Ways to Fail Before You Begin," *Phi Delta Kappan,* November 1987.

3. David Henry Feldman is cited in Lesley Dormen and Peter Edidin, "Original Spin," *Psychology Today,* July/August, 1989.

4. Dean Keith Simonton quote is cited in Dormen and Edidin, "Original Spin."

5. Ibid.

6. Ellen Langer, *Mindfulness* (Reading, MA: Addison-Wesley, 1989).

7. Bach quote is cited in P. Goldberg, *The Intuitive Edge* (Los Angeles: Tarcher, 1983).

8. The Random House College Dictionary (New York: Random House, 1990).

9. Sternberg is quoted in his "Teaching Critical Thinking."

10. Ibid.

11. This description of intuitive thinkers is cited in M. R. Wescott, *Toward a Contemporary Psychology of Intuition* (New York: Holt, Rinehart and Winston, 1968).

12. The quote regarding group participation in the discovery process appears in William J. Stewart, "Stimulating Intuitive Thinking Through Problem Solving," *The Clearing House,* December 1985.

13. Langer, *Mindfulness.*

14. The Kreigels' quote is from Marilyn Harris and Robert Kreigel, "How to Master Backburner Thinking," *Working Woman,* January 1988.

15. The Raudsepp quote is cited in Mark Golin, "Take a Break and Incubate," *Prevention,* September 1987.

16. Univac's failure to invest in computers is mentioned in Al Ries and Jack Trout, *Horse Sense* (New York: McGraw-Hill, 1991).

17. Fred Smith's idea regarding Federal Express was cited in "People Behind the Wonders," *Reader's Digest*, July 1987, and condensed from John M. Ketteringham and P. R. Nayak, *Breakthrough* (New York: Rawson, 1986).

18. The Levi Strauss story is detailed in Ries and Trout, *Horse Sense*.

19. Langer, *Mindfulness*.

20. Ries and Trout, *Horse Sense*.

21. Carolyn Corbin, *Strategies 2000*, rev. ed. (Austin, TX: Eakin Press, 1991).

22. The benefits of doing good for others is well documented in Alan Luks, with Peggy Payne, *The Healing Power of Doing Good: The Health and Spiritual Benefits of Helping Others* (New York: Fawcett, 1992).

23. Adele Scheele, *Skills for Success* (New York: Ballantine, 1979).

24. *The Random House College Dictionary.*

25. John F. Kennedy is quoted in Nigel Hamilton, *JFK: Reckless Youth* (New York: Random House, 1992).

CHAPTER 5

FUTURING:
ENVISIONING
TOMORROW

Between now and the early years of the twenty-first century, you can expect to be bombarded by all sorts of predictions. Some of these will be the result of research—or at least the products of serious thinkers. Other prognostications will be off the cuff or completely frivolous. In any case, a new century marks a milestone on every level, and you can hardly blame people for wanting to scope things out in advance.

As someone whose professional life revolves around helping organizations and individuals deal with change, I am vitally interested in anticipating what the future holds. It should come as no surprise, then, that I have my own ideas about what to expect in the new century. And, while I do share some of these in the course of our discussion, it is not my purpose to add to the glut of predictions and prognostications. Instead, I want to focus on giving you a methodology for anticipating and optimizing the future.

To deal effectively with the difficulties we face today and to prepare for the predictable uncertainties that can befall us at any time, we must sharpen our futuring skills. That's why my primary goal in this chapter is to help you become your own futurist.

In case you're a bit unsure about what "being your own futurist" means, let me put your mind at rest. We're not going to be gazing into crystal balls or pulling any rabbits out of hats. Our focus will be on developing the skills to address such important questions as:

1. What are the predictable uncertainties I'm likely to face?

2. How well prepared am I to respond to those eventualities?

3. What kinds of proactive plans can I make?

As we explore these issues, you will note that there is a strong linkage between futuring and the tracking and researching techniques we've been discussing. This is not a coincidence. Although the five indipreneurial lifeskills are covered in separate chapters, there is a tremendous amount of overlap and synergism between them. I'll have a lot more to say about the synergism between the various lifeskills in subsequent chapters.

We are now ready to start exploring the essential futuring skills and techniques. But, first, I'd like to share eight basic steps you can start taking today to sharpen your futuring abilities.

BECOMING YOUR OWN FUTURIST NOW

1. To develop a broad knowledge of futurism, consider join-ing the World Future Society and reading its bimonthly publication The Futurist.[1]

2. Read books, articles, and research materials by leading futurists. Many of these publications can be obtained through the World Future Society or in area bookstores. Leading popular futurists include Alvin Toffler, Marvin Cetron, Faith Popcorn, and John Naisbitt and Patricia Aberdeen—coau-thors of the *Megatrends* books.

3. Whenever you read an article or view a topical TV pro-gram, make it a habit to ask yourself the following questions:

✧ How might those particular events influence or alter some aspect of my future?

✧ What subsequent events might it set off?

4. Keep your mind-set in a proactive mode. Always stay on the alert for problems to solve—keeping in mind that many of today's problems are tomorrow's opportunities.

5. Try to develop effective ways to cope with fear and anxiety in facing the predictable uncertainties. These include career interruption, illness or disability, property loss, raising and educating children, coping with aging parents, divorce or death of a spouse, and retirement.

Just as actors and musicians are trained to *use* their stage fright to enhance the emotional intensity of their perfor-mance, your future success hinges on your ability to use anxiety and fear to spur you toward positive action and innovation. No matter how great your fears, it's important not to let them overwhelm you. Instead, try to use them to create optimism and hope for the future. We will be talking more about this in Chapter Six.

6. *Select an area on which you would like to become an expert.* This can be something that pertains to your career, a hobby or some aspect of your personal life. Look at that area of interest as a system. Then proceed as follows:

✦ Identify and define all the discrete topics or variables that interrelate in that system. Approach each topic as a special area of interest.

✦ When you come across any information on any of those topics, keep a record of it—whether on computer disk, hard copy, or videotape or audiotape in a separate file.

✦ Look for as many connections as you can find between the topics that comprise your chosen area.

7. *Read everything that you can possibly get your hands on about the topics that you have selected in your specialty.*

8. *Talk to as wide a range of people as you can about your specialty and invite their feedback.* Form a focus group or thinktank or some other resourcing group that will keep you informed and updated.

MASTERING THE FOUR-PART FUTURING SKILLS CLUSTER

1. Consequential thinking
2. Critical thinking
3. Creative thinking
4. Observational thinking

You'll notice that the four skills listed have an important concept in common: *thinking*. If you *think* about it, you'll realize why this is so. Thinking is a mental rehearsal for action. When we describe a person as unthinking, we are saying that he is reactive—that he reacts on impulse without bothering to reason or analyze situations. People who do that are responding to present circumstances without engaging in any sort of futuring.

When you think futuristically, you lay the groundwork for such action-oriented processes as decision making and problem solving. While these processes are not quite the same as thinking, I find that people who need to improve in these areas can do so by sharpening their thinking skills. Helping people do that has become an important part of our work at The Center for the 21st Century.

Thinking Versus Thoughtlessness

Have you ever looked back at a mistake you made earlier in your life and said: "I just wasn't thinking"? That's quite different from the feeling you get when, after trying your best, you make a decision that doesn't pan out or come up with a solution to a problem that's less than optimal.

As we saw in our discussion of *tracking*, there's a big difference between having some of your efforts fail and experiencing yourself as a failure. Remember, mistakes and false starts can be as instrumental to your success as fully realized achievements. The critical difference between interpreting a setback as a personal failure or a positive learning experience depends on the way you answer the following question: *Have I done everything in my power to succeed?*

If your decisions and solutions to problems are based on impulse or fear, your only honest answer is "no." While you have every right to still hope for the best, there is no rational basis for expecting things to turn out the way you'd like. Under the circumstances, you have effectively relegated your prospects for the future to a game of chance. Now I'm going to change the scenario:

Let's assume that you've used the *master planning* techniques we discussed in Chapter Three and the thinking skills we are about to explore to make a decision that doesn't pan out. You may still experience feelings of disappointment and loss, but it's far less likely that you'll blame yourself or feel like a failure. Instead of remorse, you'll understand that this apparent setback has provided a valuable learning experience. Perhaps even more important, you'll have the lifeskills to generate more productive solutions and build a better future. And the engine that puts this process into action is futuristic thinking.

To maximize your thinking skills, you must be adept at the four kinds of thinking listed on page 162. Once these skills are accessed, you'll be better able to formulate connections between seemingly diverse events. At the same time, your ability to recognize the potential consequences of your actions in advance will enable you to make more productive choices.

As you continue to sharpen your thinking skills, you'll find that you have an in-depth understanding of your problems and a far greater role in shaping your future. But, before any of that can happen, you must begin to own up to and recognize the effect your past and present actions have in determining your future.

Consequential Thinking

Consequential thinking is not a new notion. Most of you have probably heard the saying: *every action has a reaction*. These words are often used in everyday conversation. But, in fact, they express a basic principle in physics and chemistry. The

Bible teaches us that *you reap what you sow*. As far as I know, this may be the oldest known reference to consequential thinking. A more contemporary but lesser known version of this idea is expressed in a popular song by The Band: "Just be careful what you do, it all comes back on you."[2]

With all these admonitions to heed the cause-and-effect relationship that is intrinsic to all our actions, there is a remarkable lack of consequential thinking—in business, in government, and in the conduct of individuals from every strata of our society.

How often do we read or hear about corporations that dump hazardous waste into the surrounding waters because they seek an inexpensive means of disposal? This method may, in fact, save the company money this year and next— but what about the future? Such thoughtless dumping fouls the waters and destroys the ecological balance. In addition, it often destroys the local economy—and can eventually bankrupt the offending company.

The leaders of companies that act in such thoughtless ways will claim that they are only trying to protect the bottom line. But, in reality, they are very much like the substance abusers who readily throw away the future in favor of a quick fix. While such business leaders may not be inflicting imme-diate physical damage upon themselves, they are contribut-ing to the creation of a future that will put their families, their companies—as well as themselves—in peril. Let's consider another example that highlights the importance of conse-quential thinking.

Craig was a "C" student who had been classified as an academic underachiever since his freshman year. The young man was bored in school, and he made no bones about it. He wasn't a disciplinary problem, but he often daydreamed in class and did just enough homework to get by. Still, a number of his teachers recognized Craig as being a young man of superior intelligence—an observation that was confirmed by Craig's performance on every intelligence test he had taken since the third grade. Craig also scored in the eighty-fifth percentile on his college entrance examinations, which excited his parents. Nevertheless, he simply did not want to attend college.

At the insistence of his parents, Craig reluctantly attended one of my lifeskills seminars. From the start, the young man made it clear that, as far as he was concerned, there were many more exciting things he could be doing with his time.

"There's no law that says everyone must go to college," Craig told the group. "I don't know what my parents are so upset about."

"What would you do if you didn't continue your education?" I asked.

"I'd get a job and earn some bucks. Then, instead of spending my nights in the library doing homework, I could go on dates and hang out with my friends."

"Okay," I countered. "But what about the future?"

"What about it?" Craig responded, testily. "I'm too young to worry about what's going to happen ten years down the road."

At that point, a 29-year-old man named John expressed a desire to speak directly to Craig.

"Twelve years ago, I was in exactly the same position as you," John told Craig. "My parents were pushing me to go to college, but that was the last thing on my mind. Instead, I got a job as a laborer. I didn't mind the work and the pay seemed good at the time. But then things started to change.

"When I was 23, I got married. My wife had a good job as a secretary, and we were making enough to go to concerts and ball games and take nice vacations. We eventually put some money down on a little house, and things seemed to really be shaping up.

"Three years later my wife had twin boys and quit her job. Suddenly the money I was making was barely enough to make ends meet. Then one of the boys contracted a serious illness, and I found out that I didn't have adequate medical coverage.

"Now I had to take a second job, but even that wasn't enough. We were getting further and further into debt, and I was getting depressed. Around that time, I ran into a couple of my high school friends at a local coffee shop. They had both gone to college and were now attorneys—partners in the same firm. I know it's useless to envy others, but I couldn't help thinking how shortsighted it was of me not to take advantage of the educational opportunities that were available."

Last year, John enrolled in night school and plans to become an accountant, but it's going to take at least six years for him to graduate. Meanwhile, his family continues to struggle.

"Fortunately, my son is fully recovered from his health problems," John continued. "On the downside, we had to sell the house and move into a two-bedroom apartment in order to cut expenses. Eventually, I'll have the professional skills I need to build a secure future. By then I'll be in my late thirties. I sometimes get depressed thinking about how much more I could be giving my family—and how much better I'd feel about myself—if I hadn't been so shortsighted.

"It's your life, Craig," John said in conclusion. "But take it from someone who knows: Hanging out with your friends may seem important now, but it gets tiring pretty soon. Before you throw away your opportunities, ask yourself how sure you are that the things that seem so exciting now will have the same meaning when you're older."

Craig seemed visibly moved by John's story. As the youngest participant in the group, he would have a chance to hear many other tales of regret that resulted from a lack of consequential thinking. To help Craig clarify his options and develop his futuring skills, I asked him to envision—or *scenario*—how the potential outcomes of going and not going to college might be different. The seminar participants joined me in posing the following questions:

✧ How do you envision your life if you choose to attend college?

✧ What do you picture your life as a college graduate being like in 10 years? In 20 years?

✧ How do you envision your life if you decide to not attend college?

✧ What do you picture your life as being without a college degree in 10 years? In 20 years?

✧ Are there any needs and goals that might be important to you later in life that don't matter now?

✧ What possible effects can ignoring those needs and goals have on your future?

When the seminar was over, Craig was still not ready to say that he would definitely attend college. But it was clear that he had started considering the questions posed by the group. Whatever this young man ultimately chooses, he left that seminar with a greater realization that the decisions he makes today may have serious consequences tomorrow. He understands too that the question is not what he wants versus what his parents want. The essential questions for Craig—and for all of us—are:

✧ What are the consequences if I choose option A?

✧ What are the consequences if I choose option B?

Consequential-Thinking Exercise

✦ ✦ ✦

Select a current problem or dilemma in your life that is presenting you with two mutually exclusive choices. Using the example given, envision the different consequences of taking either choice. You might also find it instructive to try this exercise with a choice you made earlier in your life. If you do this, compare the actual consequences of the choice you made with the outcome you envision had you selected the other option.

Critical Thinking

Critical thinking is the process of standing back from a situation and establishing its positives and negatives. While this futuring skill is closely akin to consequential thinking, there are some subtle differences.

When we think consequentially, we are projecting how we might feel about the ramifications of choosing one action over another. When we think critically, we are trying to avoid value judgments and opinions. While it's no small task for human beings to be objective, developing skills in this direction is essential if we are going to differentiate the way things are from the way we would like them to be.

Here's a basic critical-thinking exercise I've developed that is currently being used in a number of school systems:

Imagine that a person is standing on the corner. The traffic light is red, but the driver of an oncoming car fails to stop. What are the positives of that action? What are the negatives of that action? Can you make any other observations about that action?

I find that this and similar exercises help young children start thinking critically—without opinions or judgments. Let's now consider a somewhat more sophisticated example:

Allen, a middle manager at a company that had retained my services, had been informed by Frances, one of the five people he supervises, that—based on her research—a method he implemented would be costly and ineffective. Allen told Frances that he appreciated the feedback. He then proceeded to reevaluate his method and concluded that she was right. There was, indeed, a glitch in the method—and it appeared to be irreparable. Allen realized that his pet project would have to be scrapped, but he felt conflicted about a number of things.

It may not have been her intention, but Frances had put Allen in a precarious position. If he revealed his mistake to his superiors, Allen feared he would be reprimanded in some way or not allowed to pursue self-generated projects in the future. At the same time, he envisioned Frances becoming a hero and eventually taking over his job. If, on the other hand, he ignored this new information, Allen realized that much time and additional resources would be wasted.

"Who is more important?" Allen asked himself. "Me or the guys who run this company?" At some point, Allen even considered finding a pretense for firing Frances to conceal his miscalculation.

To say the least, Allen was not thinking critically. Instead he was engaging in what Drs. Ed Stephens and Ona Robinson call "cover-your-rear thinking." Stephens and Robinson are principals in On Step, a corporate consulting firm, and coauthors of the book, *Compelled to Compete*. They describe cover-up thinking as an approach to problem solving that is "grounded in concerns about missing deadlines, losing face, being judged a failure and covering one's tracks.

"Instead of being guided by a genuine desire to broaden the base of understanding and to work with others in cogenerating useful solutions, the cover-up thinker is driven by a need to control—and a fear of being controlled by others. These feelings often lead to such defensive or vindictive tactics as concealment, espionage and fraud."[3]

Stephens and Robinson point out that, in the long run, such strategies invariably corrupt the person using them as well as the systems affected by that person. In the case at hand, Allen understood that his decision would affect his position in the organization, the productivity and cost-effectiveness of his department, as well as Frances's standing in the company. Until Allen could start thinking critically, however, he had no chance of finding the best and most appropriate solution to his problem.

One of the reasons my services were retained by this firm was that a disturbing number of talented managers were defecting to the competition. It turned out that there was a dysfunction in the company that was contributing to Allen's problem. The CEO had surrounded himself with "yes people" who told him what he wanted to hear—and the same kind of dishonesty and codependence had wended its way through the organization.

Fortunately for Frances, she hadn't been around long enough to become corrupted by the prevailing politics. She simply communicated things the way she saw them. Frances's light bulb skills had enabled her to recognize that Allen's method was faulty. Furthermore, her abilities were unencumbered by dysfunctional thoughts about covering her rear. Once Frances made her discovery, she rightfully assumed that she had an obligation to her company—and herself—to share all relevant conclusions with others in the department.

I was able to help Allen objectively evaluate the negatives and positives of revealing and concealing his error. Shortly thereafter, he disclosed the problems in his method to the supervisor and credited Frances with making the discovery. In the process of utilizing both critical and consequential thinking, Allen came to some important conclusions about the corporate culture and his future.

"I still don't know what the fallout from all this is going to be," Allen told me, "but that's not the most important thing. If I'm going to be happy and productive in the future, I just can't allow myself to drown in a sea of confusion and ambivalence. If the leaders of this company can't accept my mistakes, I'll have to go elsewhere."

CRITICAL-THINKING EXERCISE

✦ ✦ ✦

Try to put yourself in Allen's position. Write down the positives and negatives of being forthcoming about your mistakes versus concealing them. Also make a note of any observations you think may be relevant to the situation. You might also find it instructive to consider the following questions:

✦ What effects could Allen's decision have on the long-term future of his career—whether in his present corporation or elsewhere?

✦ What are the likely personal ramifications of Allen's decision?

✦ Now put yourself in Frances's position. What effect might Allen's responses and the ensuing consequences have on your own future in the organization?

Creative Thinking

Creative thinking is a process that is in many ways synonymous with futuring. To say that a light bulb has gone off in a creator's mind is tantamount to saying that he has found a way to link the present with the future. As we noted in our discussion on *discovery* and *innovation,* all of us have a great deal of untapped potential for creative thinking. But, if our ideas are going to bear fruit, they need nurturing and time to develop.

Every good idea starts with a problem—whether in art, business or any other endeavor. The composer who is trying to find the right musical passage to complete a symphonic movement uses creative thinking to solve that problem. The same is true of the medical researcher who is attempting to eliminate a negative side effect in developing a vaccine. Creative thinking is the tool that enables us to solve problems in our careers and personal lives. As I see it, today's problems are the seeds of innovations that will flower in the future.

In Chapter Four, we explored some ideas about activating your creative powers. From a problem-solving perspective, those energies can be directed in three ways:

1. Pursue a particular solution—and take that as far as you can.

2. Experiment with a variety of solutions and combinations.

3. Find a new problem, and match it with an existing solution.

In the late 1960s, while "fooling around" with a new group of pressure-sensitive adhesives, a chemist at 3M named Spencer Silver developed a new material. The stuff was sticky—but not strong enough to create a lasting bond between two surfaces. Nevertheless, Silver believed he was on to something. For over five years, he tried to convince colleagues at 3M to help him find an application for his new product—but his efforts were in vain. Nobody could think of a use for an adhesive that wasn't very good at adhering. Still, Silver was not discouraged.

3M is a corporation that prides itself on nurturing creativity, so nobody was about to tell Silver to stop wasting his time. As long as he continued to complete the work assigned to him, he was permitted to continue pursuing his dream. Silver kept knocking on doors, hoping to find someone with a problem that matched his solution. That person turned out to be a chemical engineer named Arthur Fry—who also happened to sing in a church choir.

Fry often used small slips of paper to mark his place in the book of hymns. Since the paper had no adhesive, the little pieces would always wind up somewhere on the floor—and Fry would have to scuffle to find his place. Suddenly, the light bulb flashed in Fry's head in the form of a slip of paper with a bit of Silver's adhesive on the top. That light bulb would eventually become Post-its^{TM}, those little yellow pads of semiadhesive stickers that are so useful for highlighting and indexing books and reports.

Arthur Fry now assumed Silver's mantle of trying to convince the powers at 3M that a new innovation was waiting to adhere itself to their grasp. The company's mechanical engineers felt that it would be difficult to apply the adhesive uniformly to paper, but Fry would not be dissuaded. He proceeded to set up a small machine in his basement that proved the product was both reliable and effective.

At last, 3M put Post-its^{TM} into production and tested the product in its own offices. Employees loved the sticky yellow slips, but the company's marketing department was still not impressed. The results of a four-city marketing test were not great enough for upper management to sit up and take notice. But a new link in the creative chain was about to emerge: Geoff Nicholson, Arthur Fry's supervisor.

Nicholson believed in the product, but he understood that Post-its^{TM} were something you had to use to appreciate fully. Since Nicholson was not sufficiently high up on the chain of command, he enlisted *his* boss, Joseph Ramsey, to help him. Ramsey wasn't particularly enamored with Post-its^{TM}, but he believed in Nicholson. The two spent days going to clients' offices and asking people to try the product. Once Ramsey had a firsthand opportunity to see the way people reacted, he knew that 3M had a winner.[4]

This case is instructive for a number of reasons. It shows what can happen when a company encourages—or at least does not discourage—creative thinking and indipreneurship on the part of its members. From an organizational standpoint, we see how creative process can manifest itself as a positive chain reaction among individuals who are allowed to challenge the values and opinions of higher-ups. From an individual perspective, it is important to recognize that creative thinking can flourish only when fear of failure is not an issue. As Drs. Stephens and Robinson observe:

"Creative thinking sometimes yields immediate results. It is more common, however, for the process to require time-consuming trial and error. In either case, creativity must be nurtured by an attitude that treats mistakes and false starts with respect rather than with a sense of loss, shame or fear that time is running out."[5]

Observational Thinking

Observational thinking is a futuring process that enables us to stand back and observe people, events and other happenings. At that point, we are better equipped to make connections and decisions based on these observations. One of the best ways to become a good observational thinker is to exercise the researching techniques we discussed in Chapter Four. Let me share a personal example.

A number of years ago, I became interested in people in their twenties—their values, their problems, and what they were thinking. I soon learned that print and TV reporters had labeled this group the 20-something generation—and were churning out all sorts of pieces about them. Many of the articles stressed the impact people in their twenties would have in the workplace and the ways in which they differed from members of the so-called "baby-boom generation."

I began my observational thinking by cutting out as many of those articles as I could find. I also informed the other members of my thinktank of my interest and asked them to clip articles and share any information they came across.

Several months after beginning my observational thinking and making connections between the various data I had accumulated, I felt I was ready to make some decisions.

Based on my observations and the connections they generated, I decided that the 20-something generation will exert a great influence on shaping the world's future. While it is likely that our next few presidents will be baby boomers, I concluded that the shape of the world during the first part of the new century would be most affected by the thoughts and values of women and men who are now in their twenties.

If you want to start developing a picture of what America will look like in the future, I urge you to look at people in their twenties. The same is true of Russia, Japan, and Germany. To determine how these nations are going to fare in the new century, keep your eye on the 20-something crowd.

Based on my observations and the resulting connections I made about the potential influence of people in their twenties, I was ready to activate fully my futuring skills. By incorporating my consequential, critical, and creative thinking processes, I was able to use the product of my observations to make some specific decisions about creating businesses, about exporting, about hiring people, and about the state of the world.

The key to making effective use of the four types of thinking is to discipline yourself to be thought-*full*. Remember, when you react to events without using thinking, you are acting in a thought-less manner. With that in mind, I would suggest three basic steps to becoming an effective futurist:

1. Discipline yourself to always be thought-*full*.
2. Determine which one or combination of the four types of thinking a situation involves.
3. Proceed with confidence.

People sometimes resist thinking because they fear the processes will be too time consuming. While it's true that effective thinking requires a long-term commitment, a specific piece of critical or consequential thinking can sometimes take five minutes or less. In any case, when you're looking at an ongoing process that will affect every aspect of your future, the amount of time involved should not be the most important consideration. The idea is to make thought-*full-* ness a part of everything you do. I'd now like to share five critical futuring techniques that will help you do just that.

ACCESSING THE FIVE ESSENTIAL TWENTY-FIRST-CENTURY FUTURING TECHNIQUES

1. Environmental scanning
2. Trend tracking
3. Cross-impact analysis
4. Preferability-plausibility analysis
5. Creating scenarios

Futuring Technique 1: Environmental Scanning

Environmental scanning is the review, research, and screening of informational resources to draw some broad conclusions. The environmental-scanning process involves three steps:

STEP 1: DEFINE THE SUBJECTS FOR WHICH YOU WANT TO SCAN INFORMATION In our company, for instance, we scan for information on these five broad topics:

1. Shifting power of the United States among all nations
2. Changing global demographics
3. The direction in which technology is moving in the world
4. General trends in business and the economy
5. Shifts in the practices and values of institutions

Since these are such wide-ranging issues, we have broken them down into some 188 subtopics. My researchers and I are constantly scanning for information on each of these subtopics.

STEP 2: DEFINE THE RESOURCES THAT YOU ARE GOING TO USE IN YOUR SCANNING These resources should be as varied as possible. At The Center for the 21st Century, we use professional journals, business publications, newspapers, and magazines. In addition, we read every book on those topics that we can find, we listen to news reports around the world, and we solicit feedback from trade and professional associations.

STEP 3: DEVELOP A SPECIFIC RESEARCHING PLAN In our company, we enlist a loose network of professionals to help us in our scan of specific areas. These can be paid researchers, as well as friends who glean information from various informational sources and report back to us.

Once articles are clipped or information is recorded in some fashion, summaries are written up, filed, and cross-referenced. Then, as the need exists, we start to make connections concerning all the happenings in these particular areas. Remember, no matter how modest your researching budget, you can adapt these steps to meet your needs.

Futuring Technique 2:
Trend Tracking

Trends are directions or tendencies that we discern in the course of observational thinking. The term *trend tracking* describes the ongoing process of observing these tendencies. While my study of the 20-something generation is a useful example of this technique, the ongoing movements of this group is only one of many trends that I track.

For example, I have observed in recent years that a growing number of baby boomers have started simplifying their lives. This is due to corporate downsizing, stress in the workplace, and the desire to spend more time with family and friends—among other factors.

I am interested in tracking this trend for a number of reasons—not the least of which is that I myself am a baby boomer. Many of the people I deal with in my work are also members of this group. So are many of the men and women who occupy the highest elected offices. Whether or not you care about the movements of this or any other specific group is not the point. What is important is that you have the tools to spot and track those emerging trends that will have a bearing on your future.

As you read magazines and books and listen to various news reports, you will begin to observe that certain things tend to recur. Should you decide these things are of interest, you might start clipping articles. As your stack of articles continues to grow, you'll see definite trends beginning to emerge. This is exactly what happened when I started tracking trends among both baby boomers and people in their twenties.

Whatever trends you decide to track, it's important to talk with a variety of people who can impart relevant information. Ask these individuals for feedback on key issues—in terms of both the future in general and the particular trends you are following. In utilizing your human and informational resources, look for common threads and connections between events. This will help you come to conclusions that are broad based and useful for futuring.

Back in the late 1980s, it was my observation that many corporations were operating in a chaotic fashion. The term "chaos" was not being used to describe companies that were experiencing certain problems. However, there were numerous references to such problems as excessive bureaucracy, widespread employee dissatisfaction, and a growing incidence of substance abuse in the workplace.

In addition to clipping articles on these subjects, I began to share my observations with people who could give me a wide range of feedback. I also launched my own survey of a cross section of corporations. Once I had pinpointed the specific characteristics that constituted corporate chaos, I was able to use that information to help my clients become more effective in planning for the future.

As we discussed in Chapter Two, companies often experience chaos when they initiate change—even when that change is based on increased profitability and growth. By working with management to recognize and anticipate the kinds of chaos they are likely to encounter, we can often prevent problems before they occur. This technique can be used in a similar fashion to address a wide variety of personal, business, or career-related issues.

---

*T*REND-TRACKING EXERCISE

✦ ✦ ✦

Pick a trend that holds a particular interest for you, and try to pursue it by writing an article. Even if you've never been published, many local newspapers will run your piece—though the fee is likely to be small or nonexistent. In any case, generating immediate dollars should not be a primary goal in this exercise.

Writing an article is a good way to focus in on your topic. It also helps you reach people who can give you valuable feedback and information. Don't be afraid to reach out to the top people in your field of interest—even if you have to call them several times. Some of these busy and powerful men and women may refuse to see you, but many others will enjoy becoming a part of your project. Don't be discouraged if you can't land an assignment before you start. You can always submit the article once it is completed. And even if it never gets published, you'll have greatly advanced your trend-tracking skills while making valuable contacts for the future.

Futuring Technique 3: Cross-Impact Analysis

Cross-impact analysis determines the impact of one variable—such as an event or activity—upon another. One helpful way to visualize this is by setting up a chart like that in Figure 5.1

On the left side of your graph or chart, list each variable, event, or activity. Then, make a list of the same variables, events or activities along the top of the chart. The next step is to take each entity separately and determine the impact one has upon the other, using the following system of scoring:

-2 for the most negative impact

-1 for a moderately negative impact

0 for a neutral or undetermined impact

+1 for a moderately positive impact

+2 for the most positive impact

Note: The setting up of variables and application of the scoring system is demonstrated in the discussion on pages 188–190.

FIGURE 5.1
✧
Cross-Impact Analysis

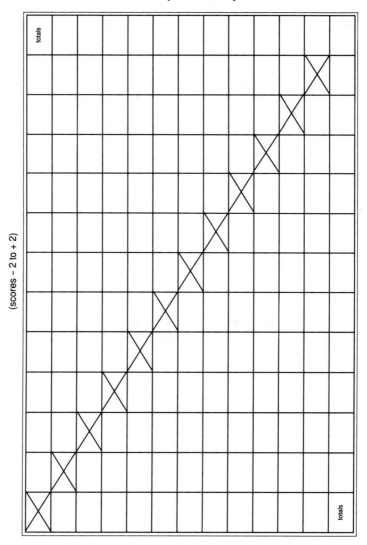

Futuring Technique 4:
Plausibility-Preferability Analysis

Based on the skills and techniques we have discussed, we can design a list of activities or trends for which we would like to evaluate the probability of occurrence. While this is not a scientific analysis designed to compute statistical probability, it is a useful qualitative method of predicting the likelihood that something will happen. This technique is investigated and demonstrated in the case study that follows this discussion (see Figure 5.2).

I start out by listing the trends or actions I want to measure on the left of my chart. Then I make a column headed *plausibility*. This is the estimated likelihood or believability that a given event will occur—based on the futuring I have done to this point. I rate each variable from 1 to 10—based on the projected likelihood of that event actually happening.

A rating of "1" would indicate my feeling that the occurrence of this event was not really plausible or believable. A rating of "10" would indicate my utmost belief that this event will occur.

To the right of that, I next set up a *preferability* column, which I also rate on a scale from 1 to 10. This is a subjective value of an occurrence's desirability—that takes into consideration my personal point of view as well as that of society. Preferability also involves outside forces that impact on the probability of something taking place.

Once I've given a preferability rating to each variable, I go down each line and multiply my *plausibility* score by my *preferability* score. This yields a total score that takes both probability and desirability into consideration. By combining these two variables, I am able get a sense of how much energy and resources I wish to put into the pursuit of a particular scenario.

FIGURE 5.2
✧
Artwatches, Inc.
Cross-Impact Analysis

(scores −2 to +2)

	retail down	mass hi-lo end	overseas markets	Western fad	niche markets	independent contractors	Western market	too few salespeople	no competition	not price competitive	lower volume sold	totals
retail down	✕	+2	+1	−2	−1	−2	−2	−2	−2	−2	−2	−12
mass hi-lo end	0	✕	+1	−1	+2	0	0	0	+2	−2	−2	0
overseas markets	−2	0	✕	+2	+2	+2	+2	−2	+2	+2	+2	+10
Western fad	+2	+1	+2	✕	+2	+2	+2	+2	+2	+1	+1	+17
niche markets	0	+2	+2	+2	✕	0	+2	−2	+2	−2	+1	+7
independent contractors	−2	−2	+2	+2	+2	✕	+2	−2	+2	−1	−1	+2
Western market	+2	0	+2	+2	+2	+2	✕	−2	+2	−1	−1	+8
too few salespeople	−2	−2	−2	−2	+2	0	−2	✕	−2	−2	−2	−14
no competition	+2	+2	+2	+2	+2	+2	+2	0	✕	−2	−2	+10
not price competitive	−2	−2	−2	−2	−1	−2	0	−2	−1	✕	−2	−16
lower volume sold	−2	−2	+2	+2	+2	−2	0	−2	0	−2	✕	−4
totals	−4	−1	+10	+5	+14	+2	+6	−12	+7	−11	−8	

After I compute my totals and enter them into the next column, I rank each of these. The highest total score would receive a rank of "1." The next highest total would receive a rank of "2," and so on.

Futuring Technique 5: Creating Scenarios

Creating scenarios is a way of developing various narratives and assessing the potential outcomes of each. This is an inclusive technique that brings together all the skills and methods we have explored in this chapter.

Scenarios can be expressed in short paragraphs, or they can be quite lengthy—containing charts, graphs, and summary boxes. In creating scenarios for any impacting trend or key issue, you will want to use at least two—but no more than five—alternative scenarios. Each scenario should take into account different directions or implications based on the assumptions that are used.

I now want to take you through a problem in futuring that utilizes the five techniques we've discussed.

A CASE STUDY IN FUTURING TECHNIQUES

Artwatches, Inc. is a wholesaler of low-cost designer watches that sell through independent contractors to retail markets, stores, and catalogs. The company had been marketing 11 different designs and wanted to add one or more additional designs. The problem was to determine which new watch designs would be most marketable.

The owner of this small business—who happens to be a client—did not have a budget to undertake an extensive market survey. I agreed to help her implement the futuring techniques we've been exploring to select and launch the company's new designs into the marketplace.

STEP 1: ENVIRONMENTAL SCANNING To develop a big-picture analysis, we scanned and identified the total environment or system in which the watches existed. This system or environment included the following factors:

✧ The potential markets for the watches

✧ The salespeople who sold the watches

✧ The organization's operations department

✧ The manufacturing company that produced the watches

✧ The designers of the watches

✧ The administration of such related services as billing and shipping

✧ The final products, that is, the actual watches themselves

After engaging in a good deal of observational and critical thinking, we concluded that, irrespective of whether new watch designs were introduced, all but three of the foregoing factors would remain fairly stable. The key variables for this company were:

1. The potential markets for the watches
2. The salespeople who sold the watches
3. The final products, that is, the watches

Since these were the only variables that were subject to change—depending on what products we introduced—we limited our environmental scanning to these three topics. We started reading all sorts of publications that would give us information about trends in retail marketing. We were interested in things like the kinds of products that were selling and how they were priced. We also scanned for information on foreign markets.

In terms of evaluating our sales force, we scanned for information on employment trends. At the time, there had been a number of downsizings and layoffs in the area. Consequently, there were likely to be additional salespeople willing to work as independent reps.

In terms of the watches themselves, we looked at various styles that were likely to be popular during the upcoming seasons. Country designs, such as guitars, log cabins, and quilts, and Western designs, such as boots, saddles, and longhorn cattle, seemed promising. Our research indicated that country music and Western-style fashions were experiencing growth—both here and abroad. We also considered watches with animal, nature, and Southwestern themes—such as Native American designs and a Santa Fe Pueblo look. In addition, we felt that creating customized designs for clients might also be a viable option.

STEP 2: TREND TRACKING We noted that, in general, retail markets were experiencing a downturn. We also observed that cost cutting was a popular marketing device that discount stores like Wal-Mart and K-Mart were using to drive out many smaller retail operations.

It appeared as if there were different niches around the country where specific designs could be successful. In general, mass markets were giving way to niche markets. At the time, overseas markets were good for some American products.

In terms of trends pertaining to salespeople, we found that our needs would be best served by adding independent contractors rather than salaried employees. Many of the salespeople we identified were trained for the Western market—which would be a good match for the way the market seemed to be heading that particular year. However, if

Artwatches, Inc. decided to concentrate on other markets, salespeople with a different orientation might have to be added. We also concluded that, in general, our existing sales force was generating fewer sales per person than had been the case a few years earlier.

As far as tracking product trends, we emphasized shopping the competition more than reading articles. We visited a wide variety of stores to see what was available. We found that there was little competition with the projected Artwatches product line. The closest competitor in terms of design was a fashion watch that sold at a higher price. However, it appeared that our pricing had to come down somewhat to be successful in its niche.

STEP 3: CROSS-IMPACT ANALYSIS Figure 5.3 lists some of the trends that we came up with in our trend tracking and environmental scanning. Those same trends are also listed across the top. To determine the impact of one trend on another, we assigned values ranging from "-2" (the most negative impact) to "+2" (the most positive impact). A rating of "0" indicates no impact or that no firm decision could be made at the time.

Once we assigned values to the lines across and down, we were able to pinpoint the trends that most highly impacted one another. This cross-impact analysis led us to the following conclusions shown in Figure 5.3.

The totals on the right side indicate that overseas markets have a tremendously positive impact. The Western fad is an important trend that has great impact and should be addressed. The Western market as a life style—as opposed to a fad—also has a high impact.

Our cross-impact analysis pointed out two negative situations that needed to be addressed: (1) the organization had salespeople whose volumes had been dropping, which meant that additional staff would probably need to be added

FIGURE 5.3
✧

Artwatches, Inc.
Plausibility/Preferability Analysis

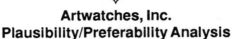

	Plausibility [1] (1–10)	Preferability [2] (1–10)	Total [3]	Rank
Design for overseas markets	10	6	60	2
Design for domestic markets	10	10	100	1
Niche markets:	10	7	70	3
Country	8	6	48	3.3
Southwestern	2	8	16	
Western	8	7	56	3.2
Nature	7	2	14	
Animals	7	5	35	
Custom designs	8	9	72	3.1
Massmarket	5	10	50	4

1. Plausibility can be defined as Reasonableness.
2. Preferability can be defined as Desirability.
3. Total = Plausibility x Preferability.

and/or additional reward systems implemented, and (2) a negative impact was being created because the watches were not sufficiently price competitive. The emergence of these two negative trends can be seen along the bottom of the chart. In addition, we can see the following positive trends:

✧ Positive impact in terms of no direct competition
✧ Positive impact in terms of niching the market

✧ A positive impact in terms of Western life-style markets in addition to the present Western fad

STEP 4: PLAUSIBILITY-PREFERABILITY ANALYSIS As Figure 5.3 indicates, we looked at the plausibility and preferability of marketing various designs in different locales. We evaluated designs for overseas markets, for domestic markets, for niche markets, and for mass markets. In the niche markets, we looked at country, Southwestern, Western, animals, nature, and custom designs.

We found the overseas market to be very plausible—thus the 10 score. But because of the complications involved in exporting, it was not as preferable and was assigned a "6." The total score for overseas markets was 60.

The domestic market was found to be equally plausible and much more preferable than the overseas market. The total score of this combination was 100 (10 × 10).

Our next step was to evaluate the niche markets. Niching received a "10" for plausibility. But because there were so many different trends, each one could only absorb a limited volume of sales. Therefore, it rated only a "7" in terms of preferability—for a total of 70.

In evaluating mass market potential, we had to consider that this approach was probably no longer the best way to market this kind of product. Therefore, it only rated a "5" for plausibility. On the other hand, the mass-marketing approach rated a "10" on preferability because we determined that the easiest course would be to design one or two items that could be sold in quantity. Still, the 50 (5 × 10) rating did not create much excitement.

In reviewing the various niche designs, we find that the same assessment applies to each one. In every case, domestic markets outrank overseas markets. It is also clear that niche markets outrank the mass markets and that the three styles of designs that we want to concentrate on are custom, Western, and country.

STEP 5: CREATING SCENARIOS From all the information we have gleaned, we are now in a position to create multiple scenarios. We are going to consider three alternatives that Artwatches, Inc. considered. I should also point out that, in most instances, the chances of any single, specific scenario coming true are less than that of effectively solving a problem by blending various aspects of the different scenarios.

Alternative scenario 1 assumes that the economy will remain the same or improve. Artwatches, Inc. will create a new watch design for the domestic market. In addition, designs will be created for overseas markets. The new design will be Western, to take advantage of the popularity of that look as a life style—both in the United States and abroad.

To increase sales in a sagging domestic market, the company will continue to recruit independent salespeople, work on the wholesale price schedule, and introduce a greater sales-reward system. A larger sales force will increase volume, which will in turn help the company receive a better price break from manufacturers.

Because niche markets are clearly established and easily identified, a country life styles line will also be introduced. Salespeople to serve that niche will be recruited.

Alternative scenario 2 assumes that the economy will get worse. Artwatches, Inc. will create a new watch for both the domestic and overseas markets. The design will be Western, as in scenario 1. The company will continue to recruit salespeople for the Western line, as well as independent contractors who specialize in country life styles.

Since the market is projected to go down instead of up, the company will work more aggressively with manufacturers to cut the cost of the watch. Recruitment of salespeople will also be more aggressive in attempt to improve—or at least maintain—current levels of volume.

Alternative scenario 3 assumes that the company will put most of its resources into marketing custom-designed watches for special groups. This approach can be handled by the current sales force. There will be no need to pursue overseas markets.

Because volume sales per design will increase and new salespeople will not have to be recruited and trained, per item profits will be higher. Furthermore, the purchase price will be of lesser consequence to the end buyer than would be the case in either scenarios 1 or 2. Another advantage to this alternative is that its success does not hinge on any major upswing or downturn in the economy. However, total company design costs will be higher.

FOUR EXERCISES FOR STRENGTHENING THE FUTURING LIFESKILL

FUTURING EXERCISE 1 Begin searching actively for trends in your industry. Correlate how your particular business or the organization for which you work will fare as these trends continue to evolve over the next decade. Once you have identified these trends, ask yourself how they might impact you or your organization in the future. List three actions that you might take as a result of your findings.

Once you have identified between three and five major trends, you can use the futuring techniques in this chapter as the basis for problem solving and decision making.

FUTURING EXERCISE 2 Utilize the data you gathered in the previous exercise to construct a cross-impact analysis similar to the one in the Artwatches, Inc. example. After you have scored your analysis, write down as many conclusions about the future as you are able to glean.

FUTURING EXERCISE 3 Draw a plausibility-preferability chart concerning three major directions that your business or company will take in the future. From this chart, determine the most probable direction that your business or company will take.

FUTURING EXERCISE 4 Construct a scenario that will answer the following questions:

1. What will your business or job look like in the year 2000?

2. What additional education or training will you need to be effective at that job or business?

3. Are your skills likely to become more or less valuable to you and/or your company by the year 2000?

4. How can you maximize the monetary and psychic compensation you will be able to demand in the future?

ENDNOTES

1. *The Futurist* can be obtained through World Future Society, 7910 Woodmont Avenue, Suite 450, Bethesda, MD 20814.

2. The Band quote is from the song "To Kingdom Come," by J. R. Robertson, recorded on the album *Music from Big Pink*, 1971.

3. The Stephens-Robinson quote is cited in Edward Stephens and Ona Robinson, *Compelled to Compete,* Corporate Training Workbook (New York: On Step, 1991).

4. The 3M story was cited in "People Behind the Wonders," *Reader's Digest,* July 1987, condensed from John M. Ketteringham and P. R. Nayak, *Breakthrough* (New York: Rawson, 1986).

5. Stephens and Robinson, *Compelled to Compete.*

CHAPTER 6

OPTIMIZING: STRIVING TO MAKE IT BETTER

ACTIVATING THE OPTIMIZING LIFESKILL

Accessing the lifeskills we've discussed thus far will provide you with many of the tools you need to shape your future. Still, it's important to recognize that even the most innovative methods can take you just so far if they exist in a vacuum.

Any kind of change—but especially those involving adversity—can test us in ways that no specific methodology can adequately address. These are times when we can be easily derailed by fear and uncertainty—unless we possess an underlying belief that we have a particular purpose in life that is linked to something greater than ourselves.

I happen to be a person who believes in God, and this belief helps me put adversity and setbacks into a larger perspective. While it is not my intent to persuade others to believe as I do, I think it's important for each of us to reflect on the spiritual side of our nature. After all, there would be no purpose in learning the lifeskills in this book if you did not believe that they were going to lead to something better. And, in my view, that implicit belief amounts to an expression of faith.

While faith is not something that lends itself to objective analysis, there have been a number of studies describing the impact of a person's faith on countering adversity. Harvard cardiologist Herbert Benson is among those researchers who have found that spirituality promotes better physical and mental health.[1]

This is not to say that one needs to be religious to make effective use of the methods in this book. Nevertheless, the whole idea of working toward positive change implies some degree of faith or hope in the future.

Tolstoy wrote that faith is "that by which men live." And a more modern author, the late Isaac Bashevis Singer, once remarked: "The belief in God is as necessary as air or water. . . . The power that takes care of you, and the farthest star, all this is God."

Whatever your beliefs, I would encourage you to search for those feelings and memories that make you feel connected with your internal core, and with the rhythms of the universe. It is this sense of connectedness that validates our efforts and gives us confidence that things can and will get better. This is what *optimizing* is all about: hard-edge methods backed up by the belief that there is something better on the other side. As we approach the new century, the ability to optimize is perhaps more important now than at any time in the past.

We live in an age of unparalleled rapid change. While these turbulent shifts create a good deal of anxiety, I see them as birth pangs for a whole new set of opportunities. Everywhere you turn, there are drastic changes taking place—in our economy, in our way of life, and in our prospects for the future.

Today, individuals and organizations are at a critical crossroad. We've been presented with a unique chance to reevaluate ourselves and our relationships. But, to take advantage of this window of opportunity, we must recognize the need for hope and optimism. That recognition is, in effect, the first step in activating the optimizing lifeskill. The next step entails using that recognition as the impetus for positive action. Let me illustrate how this works.

The economic recession that started in the late 1980s and hit with full force in the early 1990s generated a great deal of pain. At the time, it wasn't uncommon to read stories about 200 people—including college graduates—lining up around the block to interview for $7-an-hour jobs. Yet, in the midst of all this hardship, there were those who were thriving.

During this downturn, people often asked how I was faring. "I refuse to participate in recessions," I often remarked. "Instead, I use them as opportunities for innovation and change."

People were sometimes troubled by what seemed like a glib response to a serious problem. Perhaps they believed I was unsympathetic to all those who were hurting. In fact, that was not the case. I felt a great deal of empathy with individuals and organizations who were not adequately prepared to deal with this adversity. At the same time, I understood that much of their pain could have been avoided.

I believe that you don't have to be a victim if you choose not to be. Most people become victims because of a lack of planning—or because they fall prey to their own nonproductive response patterns. No matter how grim a situation appears to be, there are always opportunities to do something innovative. However, it is up to us to recognize and take advantage of new venues that become available.

When there is a downturn in the economy, it's up to us to find other ways to market our products and exhibit our talents. It is well known, for example, that Bernard Baruch and Joseph Kennedy were able to anticipate and profit during the Great Depression of the 1930s. Still, it's not necessary to be a world-renowned financier to take advantage of a bad economy—or, for that matter, any apparent setback. Take the case of Emily Koltnow.

Emily had been gainfully employed in the fashion industry for almost 25 years. In the course of her career in this fickle industry, this New York–based fashion designer had been fired six times. As most job-hunting books advise, she tried not to take it personally and sought out greener pastures—that is, another better and, she hoped, more secure job in the same industry. But, when she was fired for the seventh time, Emily decided that enough was enough. First, she formed a woman's discussion group in an attempt to obtain support and direction. Shortly thereafter, Emily decided to go into a business that specialized in what she knew best: getting fired.

Emily proceeded to set up a six-week workshop called Women in Networking (WIN) to help fired or soon-to-be-fired women turn this setback into a golden opportunity. Emily Koltnow's first-year revenues were in the low six-figure range. Shortly thereafter, she landed a book deal. The title of her highly successful publication is, *Congratulations! You've Been Fired.*[2]

You too can prosper during a setback if you remain optimistic and make the proper investments. I'm not necessarily talking about investing money. Organizations can invest in their people by inspiring them to be more creative. As individuals, we can invest in ourselves by improving our lifeskills so that we can maximize our opportunities in both good and bad times. We've talked a great deal about embracing the hard road. This is an important part of optimizing. You may not always have quick solutions for difficult problems. Still, if you can remain optimistic, while directing your energies toward making positive changes, things *will* ultimately work out in your favor.

As I've indicated, I believe that there are important lessons to be learned from every setback—lessons that can be turned into the seeds of opportunity. Now, skeptics may say that the reason I see things this way is I'm an optimist. But what about pessimists who always see the glass as being half empty rather than half full? While it may be true that optimism, for some people, is an automatic reaction, it is a skill that anybody can learn.

Psychologist Martin Seligman, author of *Learned Optimism*, believes that pessimism—and even many instances of clinical depression—are "the result of mistaken inferences we make from the tragedies and setbacks we all experience in the course of a life." Seligman's in-depth research indicates that ". . . the defining characteristic of pessimists is that they tend to believe bad events will last a long time, will undermine everything they do, and are their own fault."

Optimists, on the other hand, are described by Seligman as people who interpret the same kinds of downturns and misfortunes "in the opposite way. They tend to believe defeat is just temporary [and] that its causes are confined to this one case. The optimists . . . are unfazed by defeat. Confronted by a bad situation, they perceive it as a challenge and try harder."[3]

Seligman is correct in describing optimism as a group of cognitive skills. As the word implies, the ability to remain optimistic is a key to becoming an optimizer. However, as you are about to discover, the optimizing lifeskill goes well beyond a person's ability to see the glass as being half full rather than half empty.

HOW DO YOU RESPOND?

Just as people differ in terms of the optimism and pessimism they bring to a situation, there are vast differences in the way we respond to day-to-day situations. The following questionnaire is adapted from one I use in my seminars and consulting work. By completing the questions and making the appropriate evaluations, you'll become more aware of your particular response patterns—and those of the people with whom you come in contact.

To get the most out of this exercise, take the time to complete the questions before reading the rest of this chapter. It normally takes about 20 minutes to answer and score the questions.

---

*S*ELF-AWARENESS EXERCISE: *IDENTIFYING YOUR PERSONAL STYLE*

✦ ✦ ✦

The purpose of this self-evaluation instrument is to help you assess the way you respond to a wide range of situations that can come up at work or in a social or family context. Take as much time as you need to answer the questions, but don't agonize over your answers. This is not a test. There are no right or wrong answers, but please don't look at Figures 6.1 and 6.2 until you complete the questions.

As you read the questions, you may feel that none of the alternatives is an exact description of what you would do. Just try to picture yourself in the situation that is being described, and select the answer that best fits. Please don't try to "psych out" the questions by trying to give what seems like the most socially acceptable

FIGURE 6.1a
✧
Sample Response Profile

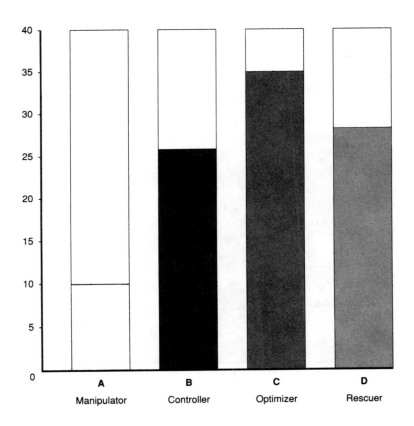

FIGURE 6.1b
✧
Your Response Profile

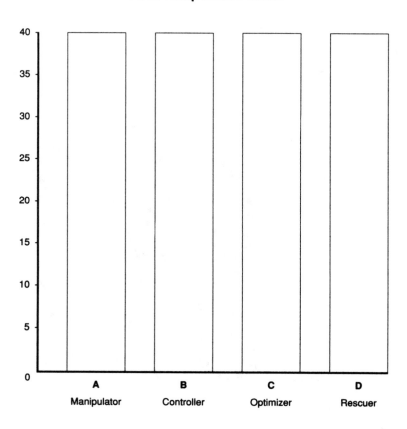

FIGURE 6.2

✧

Optimizing Lifeskill Index

	Entitlement	
Low		High

	Optimizer		**Controller**	
High	Expects: Double win		Expects: Others to follow his/her rules	**High**
	Emotional State: Love/Peace/Happiness		Emotional State: Anger	
	MO: Proact		MO: Attack	
	Reward: Equality of outcome, mutuality, sharing		Reward: Conquering, overcoming "perceived" enemy	

Self-Esteem (left, High to Low) / Self-Esteem (right, High to Low)

	Rescuer		**Manipulator**	
Low	Expects: Too much of self		Expects: Too much of others	**Low**
	Emotional State: Guilt/Frustration		Emotional State: Depression/Hurt	
	MO: React		MO: Ambush	
	Reward: "Thank you", attention		Reward: Subversive conquest	

Low		High
	Entitlement	

answers. You'll get the most out of this exercise by responding as honestly as possible.

Instructions   There are ten partially completed sentences in this questionnaire. Each is followed by four alternative ways of completing the scenario. You are to respond as follows:

Put a "4" in the blank after that statement that best describes you.

Put a "3" in the blank following the statement that gives the next-to-best description of how you would respond.

Put a "2" after the statement that you deem to be next to least descriptive of your response.

Put a "1" in the blank after the statement that least describes your response.

Note: You must use the numbers 4, 3, 2, and 1 each time and must use them only once to respond to each question:

1. When I am angry at someone—

   a. I tell the person what others think and say about him/her and how that person's behavior disturbs others. ____

   b. I attack the person head-on because he/she is disturbing me. ____

   c. I approach the person as objectively as possible to discuss how I feel and why I feel that way. ____

   d. I hold my feelings inside hoping that the situation will blow over. ____

2. When I must offer criticism to a peer—

   a. I try to find someone else to do it because I believe other people will be better at it than I am. ____

   b. I tell my peer the problem as bluntly as possible. ____

   c. I criticize the *behavior*—being careful not to criticize the *person.* ____

   d. I feel guilty that I must criticize my peer because, after all, everyone makes mistakes. ____

3. When I perceive that someone needs help in an area in which I am an expert—

   a. I don't offer to help because I'm usually too busy with my own work. ____

   b. I either take over or tell the person specifically how to do it and become somewhat irritated if the individual doesn't follow my instructions. ____

   c. I offer to help, facilitate, or teach the person how to do the task so that next time he/she can do it alone. ____

  d. I take over the project because I know I can do it more easily and quickly than the other person. ____

4. When I must ask a favor of an important person—

  a. I butter the person up with compliments, then ask the favor. ____

  b. I ask directly for what I want. After all, I deserve it and intend to get it. ____

  c. I ask directly for what I want, realizing that the person has the right to turn me down. ____

  d. I dread approaching the person, feeling that if he/she turns me down it will be because of something I did wrong. ____

5. When someone shows anger toward me—

  a. I get a hurt look on my face and either try to blame someone else or make the person who is angry at me feel guilty. ____

  b. I become very defensive and attack the person back. ____

  c. I assume the responsibility—if I am to blame—and work at rectifying the situation. ____

  d. I feel extremely guilty and apologize, apologize, and apologize. ____

6. When I must ask someone for something I want,—

  a. I generally try to find someone else to do the asking for me—feeling that the other person will have more persuasive ability than I. ____

  b. I ask directly for what I want because I feel I deserve it. ____

  c. I ask for what I want knowing the person has the right to say *no* to my request. ____

  d. I am hesitant and nervous because if the person turns down my request I'll feel extremely rejected. ____

7. When I have a need and my friends do not respond as I want them to—

  a. I feel extremely hurt because I really need and want their help. After all, I depend on them. ____

    b. I feel extremely angry and vow that the next time one of them needs something, I'll remember this incident. ___

    c. I feel that once I identify my need, I can freely ask my friends for help, and I will accept the validity of their response—whatever it is. ___

    d. I feel extremely hurt because I always try to anticipate their needs and be there for them, but most of the time they are not tuned in to my needs and aren't there for me. ___

8. When someone imposes on me—

    a. I usually tell them I can't help them and feel no obligation. ___

    b. I become very angry and tell them that this is an imposition. ___

    c. I explain to the person that it is an imposition and brainstorm with the individual to come up with other means to accomplish the request. ___

    d. I allow the person to impose upon me, do what that person requests, and then complain about their inconsiderate behavior to others while never confronting them. ___

9. When I invite someone to dinner, and the waiter spills a beverage on the person's outfit that severely stains his/her clothes—

    a. I really don't worry about it because the person has enough money to have the garment cleaned or buy a new one. I'm just glad that my garment wasn't soiled because I'd need to go to the trouble of getting it cleaned. ___

    b. I become very angry and verbally abusive toward the waiter for ruining my evening. ___

    c. I understand that accidents happen and ask to see the manager about compensation for the stained garment. ___

    d. I feel extremely guilty for having brought the person to this place for dinner and allow myself to feel totally at fault. I internally scold myself for always messing up and apologize profusely. ___

10. When a peer buys a beautiful new car and I cannot afford one right now—

    a. I look at it longingly and hope to borrow it sometime for my own use. ____

    b. I feel jealous that they have a new car and I don't because I work harder than they do and, therefore, deserve better than I get from life. ____

    c. I feel happy for that person, and hope soon to be able to afford such luxuries myself. ____

    d. I feel frustrated and become resentful of people along the way whom I've helped and who haven't repaid me. This resentment toward people who use me builds until I feel on the verge of exploding. ____

Scoring Separately total the numbers in each of your "a," "b," "c," and "d" responses for statements 1–10. Place those totals in the following blanks:

    a.   ____ (Maximum 40)
    b.   ____ (Maximum 40)
    c.   ____ (Maximum 40)
    d.   ____ (Maximum 40)

    Total score = 100

Note: No category should exceed a total of 40. When all categories are added, they should equal a score of 100. If these numbers do not check out, review your responses. Make certain that you have used 4, 3, 2, and 1 for each statement and only once per statement.

YOUR RESPONSE PROFILE

Plot your score for each category by shading in each of the boxes to indicate your scores in each category. If, for example, your scores were as follows—a = 10, b = 26, c = 36, and d = 28—your graph would look like that in Figures 6.1(a) and (b).

Using the foregoing example as a model, indicate your own score by shading in the areas to reflect your totals in each category. The response pattern we characterize as manipulating is represented by the set of responses designated by "a," controlling by "b," optimizing by "c," and rescuing by "d."

The section shaded to the highest level indicates your dominant response style. Your second highest score is your backup, or alternative, profile.

A 3- to 5-point score difference means that there is really very little difference in profile dominance. A 10-point spread among scores indicates that you do have significant attitude differentiation and that specific profiles do dominate. In general, the closer your scores are to one another, the greater the blend of response characteristics.

Visualizing the Four Basic Response Styles

Figure 6.2 plots the four response styles and their characteristics as expressed in a 2 × 2—or four-square—matrix. The horizontal plane represents the degree of entitlement, while the vertical plane represents the degree of self-esteem inherent in each response style.

People whose responses fall on the left-hand side do not possess feelings of entitlement. Such individuals believe they must earn their way and expect that nothing will be handed to them. People whose responses fall on the right-hand side of the matrix have a high degree of entitlement. They are women and men who feel that other people, organizations, and/or government institutions ought to be giving them something that's rightfully theirs.

People whose responses fall at the bottom of the matrix have very little of the kind of self-esteem that supports indipreneurship. People whose response patterns fall at the top of our 2 × 2 matrix possess a high degree of this quality.

Once you have assessed your particular patterns, you will be in a much better position to strengthen your responses to a wide variety of personal and work-related situations. You will also develop greater insight into the patterns of people with whom you come in contact. The responses on the self-evaluation exercises reveal a great deal about the effect feelings such as guilt, helplessness, chronic confusion, personalization, and optimism have on one's self-esteem and coping tools. Taken together, these tendencies are indicative of a person's general response style. As we've indicated, these fall into one of the following four categories: controlling, manipulating, rescuing, and optimizing.

In this context, we are using these terms descriptively as characteristic of personal style. Identifying yourself and others as controllers, manipulators, rescuers, or optimizers can serve as a useful shortcut for recognizing and countering the self-defeating attitudes and behaviors that lead to corporate codependence. At the same time, it's important to remember that no categories can adequately define the sum total of a person.

All of us, at one time or another, find ourselves acting out behaviors that are associated with controllers, manipulators, and rescuers. Once you become aware of your particular tendencies, and recognize their positive or negative effects, you will be in a far better position to begin shifting from controlling, manipulating, and rescuing into the optimizing mode.

EXPLORING YOUR AUTOMATIC RESPONSE PATTERNS

The Controller Profile

Controllers expect others to follow their rules. Because people often disappoint controllers by their lack of compliance, this type of person is prone to frustration and anger.

The typical controller is a highly competitive individual who sees life in win-lose terms and relationships in dominant-submissive terms. Controllers have a high degree of entitlement—that is, a feeling that things are due them. They also have relatively high self-esteem, although this is sometimes inflated by the individual's artificial sense of self-importance. As a result, controllers often come across as arrogant.

Our research into these response styles indicates that many controllers are deprived of affection during their formative years. This may be due to birth order—or what psychiatrist Martha Friedman calls one's standing in the "family Olympics."[4] On the other hand, some controllers received so much attention as children that, as adults, their expectations in this area cannot be met. Whatever the reason, controllers seem to feel isolated and deprived of affection. Consequently, they have problems sustaining positive long-term relationships.

Controllers often have trouble seeing themselves realistically. They have a great deal invested in believing that people enjoy being in their power. Some rescuers and manipulators actually do enjoy being dominated by controllers. However, most people who are not firmly entrenched in those categories find that controllers sap their energy and limit their potential.

The Manipulator Profile

Manipulators are sometimes mistaken for controllers, but there are a number of important differences. This person, typically, has a high degree of entitlement but relatively low self-esteem. Because manipulators have a low opinion of themselves, they have trouble asking for what they want or directly confronting problems. Manipulators believe that the only way to accomplish their mission is by using indirect tactics such as guilt and deceit to maneuver others to do their bidding.

Our research indicates that, in some way, manipulators were deprived of affirmation during their formative years. Consequently, people in this square generally do not have good self-esteem.

Since it is virtually impossible for anyone to meet a manipulator's needs, this type of person often goes through life feeling hurt or depressed. Manipulators frequently turn to addictive behaviors—such as overeating or substance abuse—to camouflage these feelings. Unless this type of individual recognizes such destructive patterns and attempts to change, he or she will have an especially hard time overcoming corporate codependence.

The Rescuer Profile

Rescuers have relatively low self-esteem coupled with a low degree of entitlement. Because they believe that all of life's rewards must be earned, rescuers expend a lot of energy trying to please others. This type of person tends to be easily intimidated. He or she goes through life burdened by guilt and frustration. Many rescuers emerged from childhood feeling deprived of unconditional acceptance. They interpreted this to mean that, since they aren't worthy, the only way to get approval is to perform.

Rescuers tend to be reactors who feel controlled by circumstances. They are subject to health problems—particularly those related to stress. What do rescuers hope to gain in return for their tireless efforts on behalf of others? Acceptance, attention, and affection are the immediate rewards they're after, but these strenuous campaigns on the part of the rescuer almost always prove insufficient.

The Optimizer Profile

The optimizer has high self-esteem, and can deal with others on a win-win basis. Optimizers look for mutuality and sharing in relationships. They don't have to exert manipulative behavior, nor do they feel an undue need to receive praise or attention. Optimizers know how to ask for what they want, and how to say no when they feel unable to fulfill the needs of others.

Optimizers tend to be proactive. They look optimistically to the future—and do not obsess about the past. Optimizers are far more interested in the quality of outcome than in the approval of others. Consequently, they don't feel the need to accommodate, manipulate, or control. Optimizers often describe their childhood as being a happy time. Apparently, they learned early to ask for what they want, and to say no when necessary.

Optimizing is, by definition, the most productive way of negotiating life's problems. Optimizers don't dwell on their mistakes, nor do they view adversity in terms of guilt or victimization. These individuals have a realistic and positive outlook on life and tend to have relatively few stress-related health problems.

Perhaps the best definition of an optimizer is someone who has learned to declare emotional independence from controlling, manipulating, and rescuing behaviors. The good news is that optimizing is a lifeskill everyone can learn, regardless of their present tendencies. Here are some of the skills that are helpful in making that transition.

MASTERING THE FOUR-PHASE OPTIMIZING SKILLS CLUSTER

Skill 1: Negotiating

The term *negotiation* can set off visions of high-powered lawyers controlling and manipulating each other in an attempt to prevail. This is *not* what we're forwarding as an optimizing skill. Today, one often hears the expression: "Everything is a negotiation." To the extent that we are dealing with other people, that's certainly true.

Whether you're making vacation plans with your spouse, hashing out an idea with a colleague, or asking your boss for a raise, you need negotiating skills to optimize the situation. I'm not talking here about circumstances that can be characterized as one hand washing the other. What I look for in an optimized negotiation is a pooling of mutual interests. In their book, *Getting to Yes*, Roger Fisher and William Ury suggest the following ways to negotiate and resolve conflicts:[5]

✧ Separate personalities from problems.

✧ Focus on common interests, not polarized positions.

✧ Explore as many options as possible in attempting to reach mutually acceptable solutions.

✧ Use objective criteria—not subjective feelings—to make determinations.

At The Center for the 21st Century, we've expanded these principles into a five-step process that focuses on optimizing the outcome for both parties to a negotiation.

Step 1: *Know what you want*—and know your limits in terms of how much you are ready to give away to get that.

Step 2: *Find out what the other person wants*—and his or her limits.

Step 3: *Focus on the issues at hand*—never resort to personal attacks. If you must attack something, attack issues.

Step 4: *Always deal from strength*—as much as possible, stay away from tactics like bluffing and browbeating. Despite all the chicanery and tricks some books suggest, a negotiation that furthers optimizing is characterized by people who say: "Here is what I want and here are my limits. What do you want and what are your limits? Now, let's work from there."

Step 5: *As much as possible, try never to walk out of a negotiation*—on the other hand, you should never want anything so badly that you can't walk away. Once you enter a situation ready to accept unreasonable terms, you'll be defeated before you begin. I'm not talking here about the kind of defeat one suffers in a competitive game. What I'm more concerned about is relinquishing your needs—and, therefore, the possibility of optimizing. Remember, the essence of any good negotiation is a double win.

Skill 2: Fostering Mutuality

Fostering mutuality is, in essence, an extension of the negotiating process. If you and I are to have a satisfactory relationship, nothing can be all mine—or all yours. Mutuality means that some kind of synergism exists in terms of how we view our relationship and common goals.

Many well-intended people fall down in this area because they have blindspots in how they perceive themselves and others. These limitations are often a function of a person's response style. Thus a controller who is not aware of his tendencies may perceive himself as being a leader. In a fashion that typifies controllers, such individuals view their role as one requiring them to dictate what others do. It never occurs to this type of person that others want their leaders to be empowerers and good listeners.

For there to be a mutuality of goals and relationships, we need to recognize our own expectations, needs, and values—as well as those of others. Then, we must ask ourselves the following questions:

✦ Am I being realistic?

✦ Am I too perfectionistic?

✧ Do I have blindspots that others are afraid to point out?

✧ Am I asking more from others than I'm willing to give?

Fostering mutuality does not mean that you become selfless. To the contrary, people who act in their self-interest recognize the need to work with others toward a common mission. That's a lot different, however, from being selfish, which implies a covetous and thoughtless individual who cannot see beyond his or her own needs. Indeed, it is this type of destructively competitive person who creates dysfunctions and who winds up sapping an organization's competitive strength.

Skill 3: Empathizing

Empathizing involves respecting and supporting others. A key part of this entails meeting others on *their* turf. This can be difficult, particularly when the other person has needs and a response style that are different from yours. You've probably heard the expression: *walk a mile in my shoes.* That's really what empathizing is all about—projecting yourself into another's circumstances and getting a feel for how that person responds.

When you empathize, it's not simply a matter of asking: "What would I do if I were in that person's situation?" In many instances, your particular personality and values would lead you to a far different conclusion. Empathizing means considering a person's strengths, weaknesses, sensitivities, and dominant response style and then asking yourself: "Based on all I know about this individual, how can I best help her?"

One of my good friends—let's call her Sam—likes to solve her problems without engaging in much discussion. I, on the other hand, am someone who likes to bring things that are troubling me out into the open and try to enlist others in helping me resolve them.

A few years ago, Sam's mother became critically ill and had to have emergency bypass surgery. My first inclination was to immediately rush to the hospital to be with her. Fortunately, my husband urged me to call first. When I spoke with Sam, she politely asked me not to come—and told me that she preferred to deal with this difficult situation alone. I learned that Sam is someone who prefers sorting out her options and making some decisions before she sees other people.

I stored that piece of information about Sam's personality. Now, when she's having a problem, I make it a point to call first and offer my support. She knows she can count on me to come if needed. At the same time, I know that she is likely to require a good deal of space and time to mull things over on her own, so I never push.

Because Sam and I are such good friends, she is able to empathize with my very different style of handling problems. I've asked her to come at once, should I be hit with a serious illness or a family tragedy. I want the support of my good friend as soon as possible, so there's no need to call first. Unlike Sam, I generally don't require time to sort things out before I see people.

The empathy Sam and I have for one another has greatly enriched our friendship. This same kind of empathy is equally important in business and workplace relationships. Activating this skill requires five simple steps:

             ———————————

1. Always show regard for where other people are coming from.

2. Be open about communicating your feelings, needs, desires, and values.

3. Recognize other people's parameters and how they differ from your own.

4. Use that recognition to respect and support the other person on his or her turf.

5. Never allow anyone to misinterpret your empathy as a sign that you are willing to let them violate your own boundaries.

Skill 4: Enlisting Others

Enlist *others* to buy into your vision. Whenever I think about this skill, the late Martin Luther King's "I have a dream" speech comes to mind. Millions of people bought into this vision of civil rights and equality, and today the man is honored with a holiday.

Before you can convince others to buy into your vision, you must be attuned to their dreams, goals, and ambitions. Then, if their dreams and visions are yours as well, the potential for optimizing is considerable. Obviously, leaders like Dr. King have exceptional talent for inspiring others to visualize a dream. They are also able to outline the practical steps it will take to go forward.

A more recent example of someone who was able to get millions of people to buy into a vision was H. Ross Perot during the 1992 presidential campaign. Despite dropping out of the race at a critical time and making what conventional politicians considered serious tactical errors, Perot received nearly one out of five votes—the most by an independent candidate since Teddy Roosevelt in 1912.

Why was Ross Perot so successful? He heard the heartbeat of a people who wanted to take back their government and start making decisions for themselves. The desire to push the government in a new direction was something that millions of Americans were thinking about. There was widespread dissatisfaction with both major party candidates.

Seemingly out of nowhere, Ross Perot came along and put that vision into words and pictures that the whole nation could understand.

Obviously, the man has ability. He is one of the most successful entrepreneurs in the world. He also has the money to buy television time to get his message across. On the other hand, there are lots of rich and capable businessmen, but only one who was able to enlist millions of people to follow his vision. And, while he did not win the election, the man has left a profound legacy on the American political system. Ross Perot's success provides a useful object lesson on how to inspire others to buy into your vision. I've broken this lifeskill down into a four-step process.

Step 1: *Recognize the dreams of others.* Perot recognized that the American people wanted freedom, a better life for their children, reduced debt, and prospects for a more secure retirement.

Step 2: *Share that dream.* Perot managed to convince average people that their dreams were also his dreams—and that his motives were unselfish. When the man said: "I'm doing this for your children—and for my children," people believed him.

Step 3: *Communicate your vision.* Perot was brilliant in packaging and articulating his dream. Recognizing that politicians often use doubletalk and complex answers to mask their intentions, Perot was a master of simplicity. And, while he might not have possessed the public-speaking skills of a Martin Luther King—or a Bill Clinton—he managed to get his message across with feeling and energy.

Step 4: *Once you've succeeded in getting others to support you, harness that energy and use it to make your vision a reality.*

Perot's great talent wasn't just in recognizing a widespread desire for change on the part of the American people.

He was actually able to organize this mass of raw, untapped energy into a synergistic, results-oriented team.

I'm not suggesting that everyone has the talent—or, for that matter, the need—to enlist millions of people to buy into a vision. Nevertheless, you can use similar techniques to inspire those around you to work toward a common mission. This is true in every area of life—and particularly in the workplace.

In his book, *The Winds of Turbulence,* former Braniff and Southwest Airlines CEO Howard Putnam summarized the importance of visionary leadership this way:

"Vision is a complex attribute. Within it are contained such intangibles as hope, faith, desire, ambition, and dreams—as well as the practical talents to bring these intangibles to fruition.

"A visionary possesses imagination, creativity, and curiosity. Vision is the spark for commitments and promises that construct the future. A visionary must have the courage to provide unwavering direction—the kind that fosters steady forward movement."[6]

CHANGING RESPONSE STYLES

As you consider the optimizing lifeskills cluster in relation to your particular personal response style, you may recognize the need for change. As was noted earlier, pain is often the motivating force that causes us to change. We must be careful, however, to make certain that the changes we make move us closer to the optimizing mode.

I have noticed, for example, that rescuers who manage to get out of a painful or abusive marriage sometimes seek to be more controlling and are less trusting in subsequent relationships. In the same way, people who are in pain because the corporation they trusted laid them off frequently interpret that experience in counterproductive ways. Instead of recognizing the need to optimize and become more indipreneurial, some people become mad at the world, or look for a new situation that fosters more codependence.

Significant pain can also cause a person to become more entrenched in his or her current stylistic scheme. I was recently working with a manipulator who felt victimized because his boss took credit for an innovation he had originated. Instead of looking for ways to optimize the situation, this individual responded by becoming even more defensive and manipulative.

Let me ask you a question: Why sink further into the quicksand of your nonproductive tendencies or shift to another equally destructive response style when you can use pain to catapult you into more productive ways of responding?

Moving from Rescuer to Optimizer

When Sandra's 75-year-old widowed father, Jack, had a stroke, he lost a good deal of mobility on his right side. Jack had always been an energetic and self-sufficient man. But since the stroke, he had become depressed. Furthermore, he was unhappy with the 24-hour care Sandra had hired to assist him.

"Why can't you look after me yourself?" Jack demanded. "When you were little, your mother and I sacrificed to give you everything you needed. Is it too much to expect you to do the same? It's a shame a man's own daughter can't care for him when he becomes too old and sick to look after himself."

"Dad," Sandra replied, tearfully. "You're not making things easy for me. But, since you're so upset, I guess I'll have to make it my business to come and see you for at least a few hours every day. Will that be okay?"

Over the next few months, Sandra went through all sorts of guilt and turmoil over the situation with her father. She would spend hours traveling across town to his apartment to make sure his hired caregivers were doing their job. As far as Sandra could tell, these caregivers seemed competent and considerate enough. Nevertheless, Jack was unhappy.

"These people don't do anything I ask," he complained. "They won't prepare my food the way I like it. Then again, if my own daughter doesn't care about me, why should a stranger?"

Sandra's situation was starting to overwhelm her. Her husband was growing resentful of the time she was spending with her father. He accused her of neglecting their 9-year-old son, and he had a point. Before her Dad's stroke, Sandra had been doing well in her part-time job selling residential real estate. Now, her commissions had fallen off drastically.

Three months went by, and things continued to deteriorate. Jack's complaints that Sandra wasn't devoting enough time to him had grown more bitter. Lately, she and her husband had been arguing almost every night, and Sandra feared that her marriage was in trouble. She had also decided to quit her job—at least for the time being.

Sandra's health was also starting to show signs of excessive stress. She was unable to sleep and was suffering from a number of digestive problems. As hard as she was trying to please everyone, nobody's needs were being met.

Sandra is typical of people who allow themselves to be maneuvered into playing the role of *rescuer* by someone who assumes the *manipulator* role. Jack, in his desperation, was using guilt to manipulate his daughter into devoting her full attention to playing rescuer. While situations like this can be heart-rending, Sandra had to learn that nobody could force her to give in to her guilt, unless she allowed it.

After Sandra discussed her problem during one of my seminars, she and three other participants were encouraged to set up a self-esteem resourcing group. By engaging in dialogues—both with herself and the group—Sandra learned how to move from a *rescuing* to an *optimizing* approach to resolving the difficulties with her father. Before she could make this shift, Sandra had to step back and reframe her dilemma in the following way:

> Why am I allowing my father's condition to destroy my life? My response to this circumstance is ruining my health, wrecking my marriage and hindering my career. Beyond that, I'm no longer able to spend any quality time with my father. I've got to face the fact that I've been sacrificing the welfare of all concerned in a futile attempt to address my guilt.

To optimize this situation, the key question Sandra needed to ask herself was:

> What is the solution that best serves my interests—as well as the interests of all parties?

In playing the role of *rescuer*, Sandra felt compelled to sacrifice her own needs for the sake of her ailing father. The key shift in her thinking came when she recognized that the only way to ensure the welfare of her father, husband, and son was to protect her own physical and emotional health.

Sandra's self-esteem resourcing group helped her understand that, despite her guilt and confusion, she had made some positive and appropriate decisions in finding competent care for her Dad. Sandra's one critical mistake was attempting to assuage her guilt by promising to spend every day with her father. Before Sandra could optimize this situation, she had to identify her rescuing tendencies, come to grips with her needs and boundaries, and explain them to her father. Here's how that conversation went:

"I want you to know that I love you," Sandra began, "and I appreciate everything you've done for me. But I have a family to care for as well as a career. I also have to look after my own health, or I won't be of much use to anybody else.

"I've brought in some qualified people to help with your care. If they don't do a good job, we can hire someone else. I'll be coming over to see you as much as possible, though it won't be every day. I hope you'll try to help me make this work."

The lifeskills Sandra learned as a result of optimizing this one problem have had a positive impact on her marriage, her health, and her job productivity. Although her father still wants Sandra to visit him more often, their relationship is no longer encumbered by guilt and manipulation. Sandra has seen to that!

Moving from Controller to Optimizer

As someone who possesses many controlling tendencies, I am, perhaps, most acutely aware of the problems people in this square encounter. In my own business, for example, I continue to fight a compunction to do everything myself. Like many controllers, I tend to become uncomfortable because others don't do things exactly as I would. In fact, that's true: each person has his or her own style and way of doing things.

It took some time for me to allow the people who work with me to enjoy the independence they need to be productive and happy. Letting go of that control wasn't easy at first. However, the positive results of moving to a more optimizing mode is all the motivation I need to avoid backsliding.

As I mentioned earlier, controllers also have strong feelings of entitlement, as well as a propensity for anger when they feel they've been wronged. That's exactly how Bob felt after getting laid off from his middle-management job.

Aside from being extremely angry, Bob was baffled. He had given his best, and felt he deserved to keep this job. From an objective standpoint, Bob's feelings were not without justification. He had, in fact, upheld his end of the contract in rendering good service to his corporation, and his firing was not due to any fault on his part. Nevertheless, the company was undergoing extensive restructuring, and many people were let go.

Bob was so enraged that his rules of fairness had been violated, he was unable to look for another job for three months. In evaluating his response to this setback, Bob eventually recognized that, in the final analysis, his sense of entitlement was not well founded. To begin optimizing this situation, Bob had to engage in the following dialogue—both with himself and with the members of the support group I encouraged him to join:

"In the business world, people are let go during recessionary periods. I can't deny that I feel upset and violated by the way my company treated me. Still, I have to ask myself if focusing on my disappointment and loss of control is going to get me anywhere. Obviously, the answer is no!"

Before he was able to optimize the situation, Bob had to understand that, although life is often unfair, the only productive thing one can do is to move ahead. The fact that Bob did a superior job for his company is really beside the point. Optimizers understand that giving one's best is most beneficial to the giver. And, while it is important to not let others exploit us—it's unrealistic to expect others to conform to our rules of fairness.

Before you can optimize, you must develop an inner certainty that there eventually will be a positive outcome or result. Rather than concentrating on feelings of entitlement and fairness, the optimizer is constantly striving for that positive result. To a great extent, Bob has succeeded in shifting his behavior in that direction. He is currently exploring a variety of job possibilities and business opportunities.

"I've come to understand that, in today's climate, it's unrealistic to expect companies to reward good work with job security," he recently told me. "I still don't like what was done to me, but I'm no longer angry. In the long run, I think getting fired will prove to be a growth experience."

Moving from Manipulator to Optimizer

Since manipulators often feel emotionally or physically abandoned, they have a need for affirmation that others can never fulfill. Because they have a high degree of entitlement, manipulators expect others to behave in specific ways. Underneath those unrealistic expectations, manipulators often lack the self-confidence and self-esteem to go after what they want. Instead, they walk around feeling that "this is what I deserve." Rather than trying to fulfill themselves, manipulators tend to rely on others to do the work—or to give them things that they believe are rightfully theirs.

Henry was an engineer who worked for a large corporation. His good friend, John, was his supervisor. Five years earlier, John had brought Henry into the organization. Things had gone smoothly enough—until Henry had to select one of the seven people in his department for a promotion.

John found himself in an awkward position. Lisa, another manager in the department, was the candidate he felt most deserved the promotion. Henry, who had been on the job longer, was his second choice. Henry viewed things somewhat differently. In Henry's mind, he sincerely believed he was the more deserving. He had always done a good job, plus he had seniority—not to speak of his long-standing social relationship with John.

When the time came to make a decision, John selected Lisa for the promotion, and Henry was devastated. It wasn't so much that he badly wanted a raise in salary or the prestige of a higher position. What bothered Henry most was the feeling that John betrayed him. By the time Henry spoke to me, he had tabulated every favor he had done for John during their years of friendship—both in and out of the workplace. He had already made it clear to John that he expected to be compensated for services rendered.

"I really deserve that promotion," Henry confided. "I'm sure the only reason I didn't get it is that John and I are friends and he didn't want to appear to be playing favorites. If anything, our relationship should work in my favor—not against me."

In trying to help optimize this situation, I asked Henry to ponder the following questions:

✧ To what extent do I feel that my personal relationship with John entitles me to this promotion?

✧ Am I trying to manipulate John into feeling guilty about promoting someone else?

✧ Am I certain that I am the more qualified candidate?

If Henry concluded that he was actually the best person for the job, I would have suggested that he engage in a face-to-face negotiation with John in an attempt to resolve the issue. In doing so, it would be up to Henry to present objective reasons to show why he was entitled to the promotion. As it turned out, however, Henry came to the realization that Lisa was, indeed, the most deserving candidate. This was a good first step in moving toward the optimizer square.

In dealing with similar situations in the future, I encouraged Henry to reflect upon the following questions—both in his self-talk and in the context of a self-esteem resourcing group:

✧ To what extent do I depend on others to compensate me for past hurts?

✧ Am I allowing an inflated sense of entitlement to mask my insecurities and feelings of inadequacy?

✧ Do I truly believe that I deserve more than I'm getting out of life?

---

*P*RACTICAL EXERCISES FOR STRENGTHENING THE OPTIMIZING LIFESKILL

✦ ✦ ✦

1. Take some time to reflect upon the following:

   a. Which of the response styles best characterizes you?

   b. Are you satisfied with that pattern of responses?

   c. Can you pinpoint specific events in your life that contributed to the development of this pattern?

2. If you are not an optimizer, what changes do you need to make to move into this square? List these changes.

3. Think of something you really want. Think of someone who possesses the power to help you get what you want. Using the principles developed in our discussion, make an active effort to negotiate the result.

4. Write down the name of someone with whom you might share more empathy. This person can be a peer at work or a boss, a good friend, a spouse, or a significant other in your life.

Think of a specific situation involving that person and you. Then write a paragraph that incorporates that person's traits and characteristics. How do you feel that person would want to be treated in the particular situation you have described? How is that different from what you would want from him or her under similar circumstances? Discuss how far you would be willing to go to meet that person on his or her terms without violating your boundaries.

5. Make a conscious effort to tune into the wants and needs of others. As you listen and observe the way different people express themselves, see if you can make connections and find commonalities in their dreams and desires. Then consider creating an organization or group where you would become the leader who creates and communicates a vision you share with these individuals. Using the principles we discussed in the section that begins on page 217, make a list of the steps you would take to make that vision a reality.

ENDNOTES

1. Herbert Benson's research on the benefits of spirituality is cited in Stephen Kieslin and George Harris, "The Prayer War," *Psychology Today,* October 1989.

2. Emily Koltnow's story is the basis of her book, *Congratulations! You've Been Fired* (New York: Fawcett Books, 1990).

3. The differences between optimists and pessimists are quoted from Martin E. P. Seligman, *Learned Optimism* (New York: Alfred A. Knopf, 1991).

4. The concept of family Olympics is discussed in Martha Friedman, *Overcoming the Fear of Success* (New York: Warner Books, 1980).

5. Principles of win-win negotiations are detailed in Roger Fisher and William Ury, *Getting to Yes: Negotiating Agreement Without Giving In* (New York: Penguin Books, 1983).

6. The discussion of the importance of visionary leadership is taken from Howard Putnam and Gene Busnar, *The Winds of Turbulence: A CEO's Reflections on Surviving and Thriving on the Cutting Edge of Corporate Crisis* (New York: Harper Business, 1991).

CHAPTER 7

BALANCING:
CREATING HARMONY
IN YOUR LIFE

Balance has emerged as one of the hot topics of the 1990s—with respect to both individuals and organizations. There is much talk, for example, about balancing career ambitions with personal and family life.

"Many parents who have overworked in recent years now want to change," Patricia Aburdene and John Naisbitt remarked in their 1992 book *Megatrends for Women*. These authors call taking time off work to spend time with family "the status symbol of the 1990's." In observing that many people would gladly sacrifice a day's pay for a day off, Aburdene and Naisbitt note that, "corporations that recognize [this] need . . . and how much it improves people's work will attract the best people and improve productivity."[1]

As it happens, I cited this same trend in the 1986 edition of my book, *Strategies 2000*. It was my observation that a growing number of men and women were beginning to feel somewhat less obsessed with career success. There was a sense that real fulfillment lay outside the workplace, and this caused people to ask themselves why they should give their all to the corporations for which they worked. My futuring indicated that the emphasis on career and corporate loyalty would continue to decrease—particularly among baby boomers who account for over 50 percent of the work force.

"Baby boomers who were once workaholics have come to realize that there are more important things in life," I wrote at the time. "These men and women, who are now in their thirties and forties, have always been self-dependent and oriented toward self-fulfillment. As more of them face the demands of child rearing, total devotion to careers and jobs will decline. Money and career advancement [will] still [be] important issues, but quality time spent with families and pursuing other interests (will be) perceived as being more important."[2]

On the surface, striking a balance between time spent working and time devoted to other pursuits is primarily a question of time management. But, as we shall see, the issue of balance cuts a lot deeper.

In his book, *The 7 Habits of Highly Effective People*, Stephen R. Covey talks about balance in terms of "four dimensions of our nature: the physical, the spiritual, the mental and the social/emotional." Covey correctly points out that these dimensions exist in organizations as well as individuals:

"In an organization, the physical dimension is expressed in economic terms. The mental or psychological dimension deals with recognition, development, and use of talent. The social/emotional dimension has to do with human relations and how people are treated. And the spiritual dimension deals with finding meaning through personal contribution and through organizational integrity."[3]

Covey and I are also in agreement that if an individual or organization neglects any of these dimensions, all the other parts—as well as the whole—will be negatively impacted. At the same time, growth or improvement in any area is likely to have a synergistic effect on everything else. As Covey puts it: "The things you do to sharpen the saw in any one dimension have (a) positive impact [on the] other dimensions because they are so highly interrelated."

I must say that, in all the reading I've done on the topic of balance, I find little with which to disagree. Like Covey, others writing on this subject make three irrefutable points:

1. Every person possesses different dimensions or sides.
2. A balanced individual must devote time and energy to each of these areas.
3. The time and energy a person apportions to one area impacts his or her overall balance.

You will note that these observations all refer to behaviors—which are simply reflections of what we are within. As is the case with all of the lifeskills, however, balance has more to do with what's going on inside. Behavioral issues may be important, but they are ultimately the by-products of deeper feelings and values. It is from this internal life that our priorities, passions, and character spring.

Accessing the Balancing Lifeskill

The counterproductive rescuing, controlling, and manipulative behaviors described in Chapter Six are often symptomatic of an internal imbalance. I like to describe people who fall into those categories as ego driven, by which I mean that they have a compulsion to demonstrate their value through performance. Some psychologists use the term *outer directed* to describe this need—and that is a useful way of visualizing what's taking place.

Sticking to the same terminology, optimizers can be viewed as *inner-directed* people who do not have to perform to prove their worth. These women and men are at peace with themselves—physically, emotionally, and spiritually. Because optimizers are sure of who they are, they know how to act in their self-interest without acting selfishly. When all is said and done, it is the ability to optimize that keeps all systems in balance.

As I see it, ego-driven people are trying to fill an empty, bottomless internal hole to cover a perceived flaw or lack of self-esteem. As was discussed in Chapter Six, these tendencies sometimes come about when one is an adult. More often than not, though, such behaviors can be traced back to childhood.

Most people do not achieve balance during the first 20 years of life. As children, we develop a fragmented or incomplete conception of what we want. Unfortunately, too many of us never fill those blank spaces. Instead, we walk around with an imbalance of what Dr. Ona Robinson, a New York–based psychotherapist and corporate consultant, calls screams and whispers.

"Have you ever thought of how many outside pressures are blaring in your ears?" Dr. Robinson asks. "Aside from the high-powered voice of a consumer-oriented, competitive society that keeps you longing for more, there is your mother's voice, your father's voice—not to speak of the voices of your friends and coworkers.

"At times, these screaming voices can exert a positive influence on our lives. But, far too often, they combine to form a deafening chorus that drowns out our most basic wants and needs. Meanwhile, buried beneath all that volume, there are far more subtle voices trying to point us in the direction where happiness lies: These are our whispers."[4]

Dr. Robinson concludes that, before we can achieve a meaningful balance that reflects inner freedom, we have to do two things:

1. Challenge the screaming pressures.
2. Pay attention to the whispering desires.[5]

In a sense, the pain caused by a profound imbalance in our lives can be thought of as a scream that's trying to tell us it's time to stop and reevaluate. Once we make that reevaluation, we can begin to restructure our internal balance system.

At The Center for the 21st Century, we use the terms *systemic homeostasis* to describe a state of balance and *systemic turbulence* to describe an unbalanced state. Let's explore the balancing lifeskill with respect to the various systems that come into play.

As individuals, each of us is a system unto ourselves. In the course of day-to-day living, we interact with many other systems. The people with whom we interact in the workplace are one system. There are also friends and family systems. Those of us who exercise our faith through an organized religion are part of yet another system. Each of us is also a citizen of our community, our nation, and ultimately the world. Those of us who are in touch with our spiritual center may also feel connected to a higher power or part of some other nonmaterial system.

When our interactions with even one of these systems becomes dysfunctional, problems are inevitable. If, for example, we become addicted—whether to work, another person, or a substance—all our systems can become unbalanced. When people talk about feeling splintered or out of control, they are, in effect, saying that they are in a state of *disintegration*. Balancing is the vehicle that enables an individual or organization to achieve a state of *integrity*.

SELF-EVALUATION EXERCISE:
HOW BALANCED IS YOUR LIFE?

✦ ✦ ✦

Instructions   To get an overall assessment of your present state of balance, take a few minutes to respond to the following questions with a yes or no answer.

1. Do you typically spend fewer than 60 hours per week on work and work-related activities?

2. Are you generally satisfied with your career and/or workplace conditions?

3. Would you say that your career-related expectations are realistic?

4. Do you meet with peers in your field at least once a month to discuss and compare problems, solutions, and issues?

5. Do you feed yourself intellectually on a regular basis through reading, attending classes, and availing yourself of other mind-building activities?

6. Do you plan at least two family days per month for leisure time or for enjoying special projects together?

7. Do you consider yourself someone who is able to communicate your personal boundaries to others?

8. Are you able to forgive people for real or imagined transgressions against you?

9. Do you have a multiplicity of friends on whom you can call for support in various areas of your life?

10. Would you describe one or more of the key relationships in your life as being troubled?

11. Are you relatively comfortable communicating with both males and females—as well as people of all ages, races, and religions?

12. Do you spend at least 30 minutes per day alone (not necessarily in one block of time) relaxing, meditating, and/or praying and feeding your mind with positive thoughts?

13. Do you reserve a minimum of 4 hours per week for play or an interesting hobby?

14. Do you engage in some sort of physical exercise at least three times per week?

15. Do you have disturbing, recurring, or obsessive thoughts about one particular area of your life?

16. Are you aware of any health habits that could endanger you later in life?

17. Do you make a conscious effort to spend time just laughing and having fun?

18. Do you consider yourself someone who has achieved a great degree of inner peace?

19. Do you feel comfortable with your financial debt structure?

20. Regardless of your present age, are you actively making plans for a secure retirement?

21. Do you have adequate life, health, disability, property, casualty, and liability insurance?

22. Do you have a contingency plan for unexpected emergencies?

23. Do you make a conscious effort to help others in your community through volunteer activities?

24. Are you in good physical health?

25. Looking at yourself through someone else's eyes, would you say: "This is a person who leads a balanced life"?

Scoring Give yourself four points if you scored "yes" on the following questions: 1, 2, 3, 4, 5, 6, 7, 8, 9, 11, 12, 13, 14, 17, 18,

19, 20, 21, 22, 23, 24, and 25 and "no" on questions 10, 15, and 16.

The following scale will give you a general picture of your overall state of balance.

92–100 Very well balanced

76–91 Moderately well balanced

37–75 One or more areas of your life is out of balance

0–36 Several areas of your life are out of balance—you need to do a great deal of work

Reaping the Benefits of Achieving Balance in Life's Four Critical Areas

Career

We talked a good deal about this issue in the first three chapters, and it may be useful to review those materials. Aside from evaluating the way you are tracking (see Chapter Three), it is important to assess whether the organization for which you work is providing the kind of environment you require to reach your potential (see Chapter Two).

To assess whether your career is in balance, ask yourself the following questions:

✦ Am I utilizing my best talents and highest skill levels?

✦ Do I keep up with trends and technological advances in my industry?

✦ Is my present job or career enhancing or impeding my future employability?

✦ Do I genuinely enjoy what I do?

✦ Am I comfortable in my present work environment?

✦ Am I being appropriately paid for my efforts?

Considering how much time and effort we spend on our careers, it makes little sense to develop a clock-puncher mentality. Whether you are self-employed or work for a large organization, it's important to keep in mind that the most important investment you can make is in yourself—and in your ability to create a career that reflects who you are. Remember, your true career lies within you—irrespective of whose name appears on the paycheck!

Finances

I meet many people who do not have peace of mind because their finances and debt structure are out of balance. Consequently, they are forced to scale back or simplify their lifestyle. Unfortunately, selling a home or turning other assets into cash is easier said than done when people find themselves caught in an unstable economy. To prevent getting caught up in such circumstances, it is best to presume that the economy is going to remain unpredictable and take measures that shore up your financial stability and security.

To determine how well balanced you are in this area, write the word "true" or "false" after each of the following statements:

SELF-EVALUATION EXERCISE: ASSESSING YOUR FINANCIAL FITNESS

✦ ✦ ✦

Instructions   Indicate if the following statements describe you by answering either *true* or *false*.

1. If I or a member of my family became disabled for 6 months or more, or if other unforeseen emergencies arose, I could continue to maintain a life-style comparable to that I am leading now.

2. I keep track of my income and expenses so that I usually know where I stand on a month-to-month basis.

3. I fill out a balance sheet—either on my own or with the help of a financial professional—and analyze it at least once a year.

4. I make investments on a regular basis with a predetermined amount or percentage of my income.

5. I have started preparing for my retirement and given serious thought to my financial needs during that phase of life.

6. I have an adequate amount of insurance to take care of myself, my family, and my possessions, should the need arise.

7. I have made an effort to understand how I can legally minimize my annual tax bite and have guided myself accordingly.

8. I have specific financial goals that I have set for 1 year, 5 years, 10 years, and 20 years from now.

9. I have thought about and executed any of the following documents my advisors and I deem necessary: an up-to-date will, a trust agreement, power-of-attorney document, health care power-of-attorney agreement, a living will.

10. My business and personal papers are sufficiently ordered and documented to be retrievable and understandable by someone else in my absence.

The more of the foregoing statements you are able to honestly answer as being true, the more in balance your finances. False answers indicate vulnerabilities in your financial planning that should be attended to.

Self

To attain balance in this area, you must consider the four factors discussed next.

---

1. The intellectual self
2. The spiritual self
3. The emotional self
4. The physical self

The intellectual self involves cultivating and stimulating your mind. We have had much to say about this dimension in our discussions on creativity and thinking (see Chapter Five).

When we engage in the various forms of thinking, we keep our minds sharp. This cognitive acuity helps us to make productive judgments in the face of adversity and emotional upheaval. As is the case with all aspects of self, it is important to exercise this area of your being as if it were a muscle.

Scientists have proven that we use only a very small percentage of our potential brain power. If you don't start taking better advantage of what's available to you, your intellectual self will begin to atrophy. If, in fact, you fail to invest the necessary time and resources to balance all four areas of your self, you risk throwing your entire system out of whack.

The spiritual self is the force that connects an individual to a higher power—or to a guiding or organizing force. This is the aspect of self that shapes a person's character and values—and gets to the heart of who he or she is. I'm aware that this is a very personal issue. But for me there is no higher priority than the care and feeding of the spiritual self. I find that, the richer I am able to make this aspect of my life, the more in balance everything else tends to be. By putting my spiritual self before all other considerations, I have a frame of reference for all my goals and a benchmark for measuring all my actions.

The emotional self is that part of our nature that deals with such positive feelings as humor, joy, love, elation, and confidence. On the darker side of the emotional spectrum we have anger, depression, jealousy, worries, and fears. It can be argued that some of the feelings listed are actually by-products of emotions, but such distinctions are unimportant in the context of balancing.

Unlike the spiritual self, which tends to be a supportive and stabilizing force, the emotional self is a temporary, ever-changing state that is subject to our circumstantial responses. For this reason, emotions are not especially useful for making long-term decisions. When the spiritual self takes priority over the emotional self, we tend to be more proactive and balanced—and not as reactive to prevailing conditions.

The physical self pertains, of course, to our degree of wellness and the extent to which we promote wellness through taking care of our bodies. We owe it to ourselves and our families to invest in our own health—and I'm not talking about spending big bucks on athletic equipment or pricey health clubs.

A brisk half-hour walk three to four times a week is all most adults need to maintain adequate cardiovascular fitness. In terms of diet, there is now sufficient data to give any interested person a number of alternatives for structuring a healthy eating plan. As for such physically abusive practices as excessive drinking and smoking, one needs to search for blind spots in the spiritual and emotional realms.

Although researchers are still trying to work out the specifics, there is an unquestionably strong relationship between a person's psychological health (which includes the spiritual and emotional) and his or her physical health. Corporations have learned, for example, that a relatively small investment in physical fitness and stress management can pay for itself a thousand times over in reduced sick leave and health care costs. But reducing stress through exercise and relaxation techniques is just the tip of the iceberg. In fact, the linkage between mind and body is one of infinite subtlety. Let me give you a case in point.

Have you ever held a grudge against someone whom you felt perpetrated an injustice against you? If so, you might be subjecting yourself to an unnecessary health risk. Psychologist Donald Hope is among those therapists who believe that forgiveness can have physical as well as emotional benefits:

"It looks contradictory to our self interest to let go of wrongs," says Hope. "But . . . trying to get even only leads to a vicious cycle of retaliation. In the long run, forgiveness is best for the forgiver—and the forgiven."[6]

Apparently, the health benefits of forgiveness work best for those who take the time to engage in a spiritual and psychological examination of the problem. Some therapists find that forgiveness can presage "a gigantic turnaround, a cleansing that can be called rebirth." The physical improvements reported by patients include sleeping more soundly, better digestion, and lower blood pressure levels.

Relationships

Relationships take into account a broad network of systems—all of which cry out for balance. As we noted in our exploration of response styles in Chapter Six, only the optimizer can develop truly balanced, win-win relationships. Individuals who are dominated by the other three styles are by definition in a state of imbalance. Such men and women have a variety of difficulties with relationships because they are concerned with fulfilling old needs and rectifying past hurts. The good news is that most people are capable of switching to more productive ways of relating to others.

To achieve harmony in the area of relationships, you must seek a balance between taking and giving. People dominated by nonproductive response patterns tend to keep score of who's doing what for whom, but optimizers understand how much you get by giving, which brings us back to our discussion of the relation between physical and emotional health.

In his book *The Healing Power of Doing Good*, Alan Luks presents convincing evidence that helping others—whether in one's community or in the workplace—produces a multitude of benefits for the giver. His research indicates that over 90 percent of people who participated in volunteer work on a weekly basis rated their health as being better than others of the same age. Survey respondents report reversals of chronic headache and lower-back pain and dramatic improvements in heart conditions.

In one Harvard study, psychologist David McClelland showed students film clips of Mother Teresa—perhaps the world's most renowned altruist—helping poor and sick people in Calcutta. Analyses of saliva samples taken from these students turned up increased levels of an antibody that has been shown to inhibit respiratory infections.

The exact benefit of simply observing altruistic acts may be debatable, but the overall rewards of helping are well documented. Can this kind of balanced, optimized behavior actually prevent certain types of cancers and other serious diseases? Some researchers think so. Alan Luks has plenty of evidence to support his observations that "helpers" can expect to reap the following rewards:

✧ A fortified immune system—better able to fend off disease

✧ Activation of positive emotions that underlie good health

✧ Reduction of negative, stress-related emotions

Luks's survey also shows that helping behavior can produce similar results in the workplace. He suggests several practical steps one can take in this context, including:

✧ Make an extra effort to help a coworker—even if it goes beyond the strict requirements of the job.

✧ Reach out to someone who appears to be in need.[7]

The idea of giving of ourselves to enhance the systems of which we are a part—be it our family, our community, our workplace, our nation, or the human race—seems to come naturally to optimizers. However, since the majority of us have been burdened by rescuing, manipulating, and/or controlling tendencies, we may first need to be taught the extent to which such seemingly pure altruistic acts also serve our own self-interest.

Now that you've been apprised of the many benefits you can reap from helping others, there's no reason to wait for anything momentous to happen. You need only do one thing to begin optimizing and achieving balance in the area of relationships:

Start taking positive action toward others today!

THE THREE ESSENTIAL
BALANCING TECHNIQUES

Defining What Is Enough

Many Americans seem to be obsessed with getting all they can—the most high-powered job, the biggest house, the flashiest car. There is a pervasive and, I think, destructive drive for acquisition that can even influence a person's choice of a spouse. Instead of looking for a loving relationship, for example, too many people are obsessed with credentials. This came up recently when I ran into Barbara, an old acquaintance from college:

"Carolyn, I'm getting married next month!" Barbara beamed.

"That's great," I answered. "All the best to both of you."

"Oh, you should meet him," Barbara said, pulling out a picture. "Isn't he the most handsome guy you've ever seen? And he's a top real estate attorney—a Harvard graduate, no less. After the wedding, we're going to live in his beachfront estate in Malibu."

Frankly, I hardly knew what to say. Part of me wanted to extend my condolences that she couldn't find someone she genuinely loved. But I'd run into this kind of thing many times before. Instead of telling me how she felt about the interpersonal relationship, Barbara was trying to establish a kind of point value. Good looking? That rates a "9." A rich attorney? At least a "10 plus." Who, I wondered, was this person trying to impress–me or herself?

This kind of "look how much I've got" mentality is perpetuated by advertisers trying to sell us products. Still, buying the products is one thing and buying into the message that your value as a person is determined by possessions is quite another.

Once this insatiable, *can't get enough* mind-set kicks in, any notion of being centered or balanced goes right down the drain. And, as we have seen, individuals and organizations who are in this kind of drastic imbalance are courting trouble. It's fine to set goals of success and profitability. On the other hand, individuals who decide they are going to succeed at all costs risk losing their friends, their families, their spiritual center, their health—and ultimately their material success.

Several years ago, my husband Ray and I came to the conclusion that we were sacrificing too much of ourselves and our family life for the sake of money and professional advancement. We were both doing well in our respective careers. Like many people, we figured we'd just keep working hard and acquiring more and better material possessions. After all, this kind of ego-driven behavior is what we grew up believing was the right way to get ahead.

Ray and I recognized that it was time to take stock—both separately and jointly—of where we were in each of life's major areas. This self-examination helped us determine how much money we needed for our life-style needs and long-term financial security. We proceeded to balance these factors with our needs and goals in other areas and readjusted our priorities accordingly. We will continue to monitor all the systems of which we are a part. Should one or more of them get out of balance, Ray and I will make the appropriate adjustments.

Just as each of us comprises a distinct system, we and our spouses make up complete or partial family systems. As we have observed elsewhere, corporations can also be viewed as family systems. And, like all systems, corporate leaders must develop a sense of how much is enough. The same kind of imbalances that afflict individuals can also adversely affect corporations that are ready to sacrifice all other considerations in the name of greater short-term profits. This one-sided, selfish approach makes them vulnerable to imbalances that severely erode the bottom line.

Several months ago, I was working with a corporation's senior management in deciding what the company's role in its industry would be over the next several years. The leaders of this company, which was very successful in its particular niche, were thinking about launching a massive expansion. Although I had not yet reached any firm conclusions, I suspected that such an expansion would not be in their best long-term interests.

"Has it occurred to you that you may be hurting yourself by going into debt trying to compete with much larger companies?" I asked the CEO. "Have you ever considered that you may be better off staying right where you are and concentrating on the areas in which you're already strong?"

"But, Carolyn," he responded, "that's not the American way!"

Notwithstanding the unbridled need to acquire more and grow ever larger, there is another important aspect of knowing how much is enough. As you interact with and determine your role in various systems, you must be able to *draw boundaries*. Failing to do so can cause you to become so enmeshed in a particular system that the lines between your identity and that of the system disappear.

This kind of thing is often apparent when you explore the dynamics in dysfunctional families. In such situations, there are no boundaries between the family system and its members. Everybody's business is everybody else's business—just as each member's problems tend to have a paralyzing effect on everyone else in the family.

As we have seen, the same kind of codependency can occur in the workplace. It can happen when we don't separate our own interests from those of the corporation, or when we allow work-related problems to bleed into other key areas of our lives.

Because the five lifeskills have a synergistic relationship to each other, those of you who have invested time in mastering the materials in previous chapters will already have a head start in using this technique. The tracking skills we explored in Chapter Three—such as creating a mission and setting priorities—will help you define what is enough in each area of your life. Likewise, the negotiating techniques discussed in Chapter Six will be valuable for setting limits and drawing personal boundaries.

Achieving Balance Through Diversification

Dr. Merl Bonney, a noted clinical psychologist who was my professor at the University of North Texas, made a statement I will always remember: *A mentally healthy mind has alternatives.* I suppose this was really a more elegant way of saying an old expression my mother used: "Never put all your eggs in one basket." Either way, the thought has relevance to all aspects of our lives.

Whether you're talking about finances, friendships, or career goals, it is essential to have alternatives and diversification. When you structure an investment portfolio, for example, it's wise to never put your money in one place or in one kind of instrument. Instead, it's better to spread the time frame out between short- and long-term investments. It's also wise, within the parameters of your comfort level, to spread the risk between instruments that have higher yields and greater margins of safety.

In Chapter Three, we talked about the importance of developing flexible skills that enable you to remain employable as you strive to reach your career potential. As new technologies and turbulent economic conditions cause shifts in the kind of know-how corporations consider most necessary, it is essential not to become too dependent on any one skill or talent.

In the 1980s, one often heard it said that we were living in an age of specialization. While it is still important to have specific talents that establish our value, we would do well not to become too attached to them. In the graphic arts field, for example, many experienced illustrators and designers in their forties and fifties are suddenly finding that they can no longer earn a living. Why? Because they never learned computer graphics—technologies that their younger counterparts are adept at using to get the same kind of work done faster and more cost-efficiently.

In one way or another, the same phenomenon is occurring throughout corporate America. Consider the following story that appeared in *Fortune*:

"A factory worker at a food company in Mississippi runs a cooker. Has for years. One day his company brings in computerized controls to regulate the temperature—a job he used to do by hand. There are dozens of commands to choose from on the computer screen. The worker knows how to read, but he can't master the machine. Today, the man is no longer a line worker. Instead, he pushes a broom."[8]

There are two ways to look at scenarios like these. From the point of view of the individual, it is essential to continue to upgrade and diversify our skills—whether through formal courses, on-the-job training, or life experiences. At the same time, it is clear that companies that intend to attract and retain the best people must provide a variety of attractive training opportunities. As I noted more than once on these pages:

Those companies that want to motivate the best people to stay have to help them develop the skills and allow them the freedoms that will enable them to leave.

Corporations and individuals that don't invest in the kind of training that fosters alternatives and skill diversity are, in effect, clinging to a sense of false security. Their refusal to look ahead is sure to cause painful imbalances in the future.

One of the most effective ways to avoid codependence in our interaction with any system is to maintain diversity in our relationships. We have seen that codependence—including the corporate variety—occurs when people become too reliant on another person or institution. At this point in our journey, I would hope that you recognize how unrealistic it is to expect any person or organization to fulfill your needs. Those who persist in carrying around such unfeasible expectations will be vulnerable to stress, depression, and a wide variety of addictive behaviors.

Maintaining diversity in relationships doesn't mean going out with a different person every night or having 200 friends. What the effective use of this balancing technique does entail is participating in appropriate resourcing groups so that you have a variety of people to call on for support, feedback, and professional advice. In terms of your individual relationships, whether in a business or personal context, the most important question to ask yourself is:

Am I optimizing—that is, engaging in win-win situations where the other person and I can both ask for and receive what we need from one another?

Altering the Balance as You Change and Grow

As we continue to evolve and improve our lifeskills, there are bound to be subtle and not-so-subtle shifts in the way we allocate time, reorder priorities, and pursue our goals. Whatever the proportion at a particular time, it's important that we engage in a conscious process of internal management. This is what enables us to achieve the kind of systemic homeostasis that makes us feel centered and in control of our lives.

As you evaluate where you are at a given moment in your life, you may not perceive a straight-line growth in a particular area. Indeed, there are bound to be times when it seems that you have regressed. If, for example, you were recently fired or suffered a financial reversal, you might look at that as something destructive to your sense of balance. As you've probably gathered by now, I don't look at setbacks that way—although they certainly can throw any of us off course momentarily.

When an apparent setback occurs, there are a number of ways to capitalize on the resulting imbalance. You can work on shoring up that area of your life. Or you can take the opposite approach and use these changes in circumstances to invest in an area you may have been neglecting. Either way, the most important thing is that you are in tune with your innermost feelings and the spiritual forces that enable you to view short-term changes in a broader perspective.

Of course, no matter how balanced and centered you feel today, you must recognize that your needs—as well as your relationship to various systems—are bound to change over time. As you grow older, for instance, you may find yourself spending less time on work and more time pursuing personal interests or volunteer activities. People who have children at a young age often invest a great deal of time and energy in their families. Later on, they find that they suddenly have the time and desire to pursue a career. This is what seems to be happening to many baby-boom women who are building successful careers in their forties and fifties.

It's important to keep in mind that, as we approach the new century, there are very few specific rules for how and when things are supposed to get done. Just as we see people launching careers later in life, there are also people who are starting their families at a later age and deemphasizing the importance of work. Remember, the order in which you pursue goals and the specific amount of time you invest in the various dimensions of life are far less important than staying true to your innermost core.

By continuing to work at mastering the five lifeskills we have explored, your life will continue to be enriched in a multitude of tangible and intangible ways. As your values deepen and the depth of your experience grows, you will attain a sense of balance and inner peace that pervades everything you do.

PRACTICAL EXERCISES FOR STRENGTHENING THE BALANCING LIFESKILL

✦ ✦ ✦

1. List in order the things that consume most of your time.

2. For the next week, write down the first thoughts you have upon waking up. Consider the extent to which you are acting on these thoughts.

3. While driving down the highway alone, do your recurring thoughts form patterns? Write these down.

4. Write down the dimension of your life that makes you feel (a) most peaceful, (b) least peaceful.

5. Write down your most profound fears and/or doubts with respect to each of these areas:

   a. Workplace and career

   b. Financial

   c. Social

   d. Family

   e. Personal

6. Look at your score on the life-quality index in Chapter Three. Investigate areas where you have three or more points of difference in your importance score versus your reality score. Rethink these issues in terms of your need for balance.

ENDNOTES

1. Patricia Aburdene and John Naisbitt, *Megatrends for Women* (New York: Villard, 1992).

2. Carolyn Corbin, *Strategies 2000*, rev. ed. (Austin, TX: Eakin Press, 1991).

3. Stephen R. Covey, *The 7 Habits of Highly Effective People* (New York: Fireside/Simon & Schuster, 1989).

4. Ona Robinson's observations regarding whispers and screams are from her "Successful but Alone," an unpublished paper.

5. Ibid.

6. Donald Hope is quoted in Thomas Fleming, "The Healing Power of Forgiveness," *Reader's Digest*, June 1988

7. Alan Luks with Peggy Payne, *The Healing Power of Doing Good: The Health and Spiritual Benefits of Helping Others* (New York: Fawcett, 1992).

8. The anecdote of the Mississippi factory was cited in Nancy J. Perry, "The Workers of the Future," *Fortune*, special issue, *The New American Century*, Spring/Summer 1991.

PART III

BRIDGING THE GAP BETWEEN KNOWING AND DOING

Chapter 8

Managing
Change

Any person or business seeking to optimize the future must learn to manage change effectively. This entails dealing with unexpected reversals and sudden shifts in circumstance. It is also necessary for individuals and organizations to initiate change if they intend to move ahead and grow. These self-generated changes can create their own adversity, which must be understood and managed.

Mastering the five lifeskills will give you a strong foundation for effectively managing change. My focus in this chapter is to show you how to build on these principles, and to help you develop new techniques for negotiating the kinds of changes we foresee taking place.

Becoming an Effective Change Manager

First, it is essential to recognize that we are all in a state of change. Although the differences might be subtle, no living organism is an exact replica of what it was yesterday. The same is true of organizations. There are so many external and internal variables that can affect and alter a corporation's strength and competitive position. A short list of external factors might include the state of the national, local, and global economies; technological innovations; and political upheaval. Internal factors include turnover in personnel; greater cultural and ethnic diversity; fluctuations in employee motivation; and the impact of business decisions.

As we move into the twenty-first century, we see organizational change manifested by increased corporate turnover, an overall slump in productivity, and a preponderance of indecision that has resulted in a depletion of constructive energy. On a more personal level, we find people contending with such deenergizers as family instability, reduced creativity, career obsolescence, financial turbulence, emotional stress, a sense of spiritual emptiness, and a crisis in self-esteem.

These manifestations are the result of shifts and transitions that are taking place all around us. To negotiate these changes, we must recognize their potential impact—even as we attempt to cope with the adversity they create. The following techniques, derived from the five lifeskills are especially useful in the area of change management.

Mastering the Four Critical Change-Management Skills

1. *Visioning.* Always keep looking ahead. Recognize that change is a fact of life and develop the futuring skills to

anticipate and envision probable events and their consequences.

2. *Assimilating.* Employ your resourcing skills to gather relevant data. Then use that information as a basis for optimizing situations and making indipreneurial decisions.

3. *Educating.* It is essential to foster learning in terms of both yourself and those with whom you come in contact. No matter how much you know, circumstances are changing too quickly for you to become complacent and self-satisfied. Information that is state of the art today may be obsolete tomorrow. That's one important reason we must actively seek knowledge that will enable us to implement change in our lives and in the systems with which we interact.

4. *Innovating.* With change comes new problems—and these require new and better solutions. Remember, the definition of an optimizer is someone who is able to turn potential problems into the seeds of innovation and creativity that enrich every aspect of life.

I was recently talking with Sara Recer, a friend who works in Hollywood with Carol Burnett's Kalola Productions. Sara also owns Recer Management Company, an organization that provides personal management services to people in the entertainment industry. In the course of our conversation, Sara and I both realized that people with careers in TV and film have always lived with the same kind of uncertainty that is now affecting almost all industries. Here's how Sara describes the situation in Hollywood:

"A few people control the TV and film industries—while the vast majority are constantly trying to find work. Even people who are well-known to the public invariably find themselves out of work at some point.

"Let's take TV. 'The Tonight Show' with Johnny Carson ran for over 30 years, 'The Carol Burnett Show' and 'Cheers' ran for more than 10 years. These are extraordinarily long runs for shows—and long times for people to have jobs. More often than not, a show will run anywhere from one year to five years. At that point, everyone connected with the show is out of a job.

"Talk about a performance-based industry. There are so many high-quality shows that are taken off the air because of low ratings. Many times, those numbers have more to do with when the show airs rather than how good it is. The network makes that decision. If that happens, all the actors and creative people are out of a job. It may not be fair, but that's the nature of this business. Anyone who sticks around for a period of time has learned to live with uncertainty."

I believe that the change-management skills that have long been needed to survive in Hollywood provide a good object lesson for people in all businesses—particularly those industries that were once considered to be relatively secure. Consider the following:

✦ Today, virtually every business must be performance-oriented to remain competitive.

✦ The ultimate success of any business is largely determined by the *customer ratings* it receives.

✦ The destiny of individuals employed by a particular organization is largely dependent on that company's ratings—and on the policies and actions of the organization's leaders.

✦ Ultimately, each individual must develop strengths in the area of change management so as not to become overly dependent on any one organization or position. Or, to put it another way: No matter what anybody else does, it's your show—so you'd better be prepared to get on with it!

OVERCOMING RESISTANCE TO CHANGE

Before we can institute change in our lives and businesses, it's essential that we recognize our capacity for resistance. Have you ever thought about why people and organizations expend so much of their energies trying to maintain the status quo? I believe the answer has to do with a pervasive tendency to remain in *comfort zones*—familiar places where we feel relaxed and in control.

Behavioral scientist Bob Bolton—founder of the consulting group Ridge Associates—defines comfort zones as "habitual behaviors developed over a period of years that have become easy and familiar to use." Because these recurring patterns or paradigms make us feel safe, "moving outside them entails varying degrees of discomfort and risk."

Comfort zones can be seen in our relationships with others, in our mind-sets, and in the way we do things. The desire for comfort and safety is not inherently destructive. It's only when such feelings are manifested in unadaptive behaviors and attitudes that they become counterproductive—and even dangerous. Taken to its extreme, a refusal to leave a comfort zone can result in codependence and in financial or personal bankruptcy. Let's take three brief cases in point:

✧ Jim finds himself enmeshed in a distressing relationship with his girlfriend. Things were going well for a while. But in recent months, the couple has been arguing constantly—saying a great many hurtful things to one another. Jim is so stressed out that his performance at work has been slipping. Jim recognizes that the relationship is, for all intents and purposes, over. Unfortunately, he cannot bring himself to end it.

Aside from not wanting to hurt his girlfriend's feelings and provoke a major scene, Jim thinks about how difficult it will be to find someone new. "Who knows," he asks himself, "if that relationship will be any better?" In effect, Jim has decided to remain in a comfort zone. But, ironically, as so often happens, one could hardly characterize his emotional state as *comfortable.*

✧ Fifty-five-year-old Angela has been making a good living as a writer since graduating from college. In recent years, she has had a problem working at a pace that generates sufficient income to meet her needs. Editors and colleagues have suggested that Angela could greatly increase her productivity by working on a computer instead of the electric typewriter she has been using for the last 20 years. Whenever that suggestion is made, Angela responds with a joke about the world being taken over by robots and machines.

Underneath the laughter, Angela really believes that computers are somehow sinister and dehumanizing. She can't imagine high-quality work coming out of "these monstrosities," although many writers she respects have been using computers since the 1980s. Philosophical qualms aside, Angela is fearful of the new technology. She doubts her ability to learn computers, even though people tell her that the process would only take a few weeks at most. Nevertheless, Angela decides to keep pecking away on her trusty typewriter. For the present, she isn't in enough pain to leave her comfort zone.

✧ As I've noted, people sometimes remain in comfort zones by taking actions based on established patterns that are not responsive to the demands of a particular situation. In the previous examples, Angela and Jim were not willing to take action to get out of their respective comfort zones. But the story of Braniff Airlines is one that demonstrates what can happen to companies and people who take inappropriate action simply because it fits their customary patterns.

A number of years ago, just after the airline industry had been deregulated, Braniff's CEO decided that this was a temporary situation that would soon be reversed. A man known for a somewhat impulsive management style with little regard for the feedback of those around him, this CEO proceeded to institute an almost unprecedented program of expansion. While most other airlines added 1 or 2 new routes, Braniff opened service to 16 new cities in a 30-day period. As Howard Putnam—the man who eventually took over for that CEO—recalls, the results were disastrous:

"Braniff's rapid and short-notice expansion required astronomical expenditures. Airport leases were negotiated at an accelerated pace with an exorbitant premium tacked on. Union contracts had to be amended so that service could be started quickly. This sense of urgency served to increase costs while reducing the airline's efficiency. In addition, many of the new routes had very low traffic volumes. They were unprofitable from the first day and their continued operations had to be justified from headquarters.

"To fly the new routes, Braniff had to order new aircraft immediately. Over four hundred million dollars was borrowed from 37 banks and insurance companies to place the necessary orders for airplanes from Boeing and engines from

Pratt and Whitney. As a result of the expansion, several thousand new employees were hired to fly the planes, board the passengers and maintain the aircraft. . . . Within a few short months of its expansion, the economy stumbled, air travel slackened, jet fuel prices soared, and interest rates ballooned to an historic 20%. . . . Before long . . . Braniff's once-sizable profits began to plummet into the red."[1]

As we approach the new century, it is more important than ever to develop the courage to act when circumstances so demand, and to exercise restraint when appropriate. Here again, we can see why mastering the lifeskills is at the heart of effective change management. It is clear that better resourcing and futuring skills could have helped Braniff's CEO anticipate changes others were predicting. Perhaps even more fundamentally, if this man could have recognized his automatic response tendencies and made even a small shift toward the optimizing mode, he might well have pursued a wiser course of action.

People who are governed by controlling, manipulative, and rescuing response styles tend to use these familiar patterns as comfort zones. This impedes their ability to handle change and to make decisions that are in their best interests. If there is a single key to effective change management, it rests in learning to become an indipreneur—one who is able to optimize all relationships and circumstances.

As we move from an entitlement-based society to one that is performance-based, people and businesses are being forced to confront change. Right now, the systemic changes in the way we live and work are causing a good deal of turmoil and pain. Ultimately, I believe that the net effect of this turbulence can be beneficial. To help you reap those benefits, I'd like to show you how to embrace and thrive on change.

Whatever your motivation for wanting to become a more effective change manager, the process is essentially the same. Change always involves the loss of comfort zones along with the rest of the status quo. This is true even when the change is positive and self-initiated. Either way, the change process entails the same steps which we will explore shortly.

DEVELOPING A SYSTEMIC APPROACH TO CHANGE

When I examine the ways an entity deals with change, I find it helpful to think in terms of systems. All systems in the universe are interdependent and interactive. Furthermore, each system exists within multiple environments. Every time there is a shift in any of these environments, some degree of change will occur in that system. This formulation applies to people, organizations, and nations. Let's take a closer look at this idea of a systemic approach to change.[2]

Every human being comprises a system that consists of numerous subsystems. For example, our bodies can be seen as a single system encompassing such subsystems as respiration, circulation, and digestion. Then, of course, there are intellectual, emotional, and spiritual systems—each containing their own subsystems. From this vantage point, every person can be viewed as a system existing within a complex systemic network—all of which are composed of elements or variables that work together to produce a specific purpose.

Let's now consider corporations and other organizations from a systemic vantage point. Ideally, an organization can be viewed as *the enthusiastic movement of two or more cooperating individuals toward a common mission.* In reality, however, we often observe the following:

✦ Stagnation—or movement that is anything but enthusiastic

✧ Control-based competition negating any chance for true cooperation

✧ Vague or ill-defined missions and goals

In evaluating an organization's capacity for change, we look at variables like clarity of mission, level of cooperation, and enthusiasm as components within an integrated system. When there is a shift in one or more of these variables, it can trigger change throughout the system. This, in turn, can cause changes to occur in a complex network of systems.

When Sears decides to close 150 stores and lay off 50,000 people, for example, that clearly affects the corporation as a whole, the displaced individuals and their families, and the workers who remain on the payroll. But, as I am going to demonstrate, this single instance of corporate downsizing is just the first link in a systemic and environmental chain reaction.

The Sears cutbacks will certainly affect the retail store industry. If, say, there is a K-Mart close to one of the Sears stores that are being shut down, this will cause an immediate change in its competitive position. Potentially, the Sears closings can effect K-Mart's overall position in the industry— which would, in turn, create further changes in the industry as a whole. Arguably, shutting down 50 Sears stores could have an impact on how much you and I pay for certain products. In any case, there is no question that we will be affected in some way.

When large numbers of people are laid off, local economies are bound to suffer. Consequently, people in other industries may be laid off. Many of these jobless individuals will receive unemployment insurance and other government entitlements, and this will show up in state and federal balance sheets. Inevitably, funds will be needed to cover these increased entitlements—which *will* come out of everyone's pocket. In addition, there is likely to be less money available to address such critical needs as education and highway repair.

In observing how systems interact, we can discern four distinct components: *input, processing, output,* and *feedback.* As the Sears example indicates, actions and events have a complex relationship—rather than a linear or straight-line relationship. Consequently, whatever I put into a system (i.e., the *input*) may not affect what comes out (i.e., the *output*) in a direct or predictable way. Consider this simple example.

Carl and Phil are coworkers. In the context of the present discussion, let's think of them as two interactive systems. Carl, believing that Phil made a careless error, issues an angry statement. That statement (Carl's *output*) becomes *input* to Phil's system. The question is: How will Phil respond—or what will his *output* be once he can *process* this *input*?

A stereotypical reaction for Phil would be to come back at Carl with another angry statement. There are, however, many other ways that Phil could respond. This would depend on a number of variables, including Phil's past experience, his values, and his automatic response style.

However he reacts, Phil's *output* will be received as *feedback* by Carl. Carl will then *process* this information, and use it as *input* to determine the way he deals with Phil—both now and in the future. If Phil comes back with a response that demonstrates even more intense anger, it may serve to escalate the war of words. On the other hand, if Phil agrees that he made a mistake and indicates a willingness to discuss it, Carl may be inclined to mirror that more productive approach.

As we examine the way systems interact, it's essential to remember that the consequences of *input, processing, output,* and *feedback* go beyond the systems that appear to be directly involved.

If, for example, Phil leaves the workplace bristling with anger toward Carl, he may allow those feelings to become *output* directed toward his family. Should that occur, Phil's family system would be affected—and another systemic chain reaction would begin. As is the case with an instance of corporate downsizing, a single interaction between two people can cause an imbalance that sets a complex change program into motion.

It is clear that all systems operate best in a state of balance or homeostasis. Change is a reaction to disequilibrium—a system trying to self-correct and get back into balance. Indipreneurial people and organizations tend to be adept at predicting and planning for change. Those mired in nonproductive paradigms, on the other hand, find change to be disruptive and painful. Optimizing those uncomfortable and potentially threatening circumstances is what becoming an effective change manager is all about.

THE SEVEN-STEP CHANGE PROCESS

The process of change can itself be viewed as a system composed of the variables illustrated in Figure 8.1: the *stimulus* that sets the process into motion is the input; *denial, recognition, acknowledgment, chaos,* and *enlightened leadership* become the process; *renewal* is the output; and the *environmental impact* is the feedback. This interactive system will use the *environmental impact* as the basis for adjusting toward a new state of balance or homeostasis. There are, of course, those dysfunctional individuals and organizations who get stuck in one of the early or intermediate phases of the process. Unfortunately, they are likely to experience the pain and turmoil change brings about without reaping its potential benefits.

FIGURE 8.1
✧
The Change Process

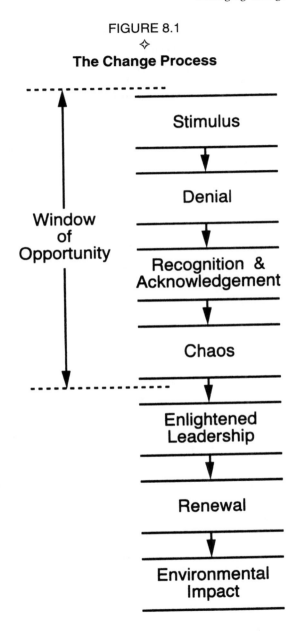

As we begin our exploration of the seven-step change process, it is important to keep in mind that there is often a window of opportunity during which time change can be intercepted or redirected. This opportunity—which may be available through the latter stages of *chaos*—has the best chance of yielding meaningful results early on in the process. The earlier the better!

Intervention—a term frequently used with respect to addictive behaviors—is also applicable to averting other systemic difficulties. If we are able to recognize conditions that are likely to create disequilibrium and dysfunction before they kick in, there are often things we can do to stave them off. If, however, we don't take advantage of that window of opportunity to *intervene*, the change process will take on a life of its own and proceed through the following seven steps.

Stimulation

Change is always triggered by an apparent stimulus—which is the marker for an underlying causal chain. For example, the sharp price rise in oil from the OPEC nations during the 1970s caused a threefold increase in what American consumers had to pay for a gallon of gasoline. Among the multitude of changes arising from this one stimulus was a demand for small, fuel-efficient automobiles. Unfortunately, the Big Three American automakers had committed so much of their resources to building large, gas-guzzling cars, they were unable to respond to this sudden need for change. At the same time, the Japanese had become adept at building cars that addressed the need for fuel efficiency.

Millions of Americans—including many who found it distasteful to support foreign economies at the expense of their own—began buying Hondas and Toyotas. The typical explanation for this decision went something like this:

"When I'm spending so many thousands of dollars for a single item, I feel that I owe it to myself and my family to buy the best product I can. When American carmakers can offer cars of comparable quality, I'll go back to buying their products."

Two decades later, Detroit is turning out some very good fuel-efficient cars. Nevertheless, American automakers are still struggling to overcome a pervasive perception that the Japanese offer a better and more reliable product. Did Detroit have a window of opportunity before the gas crisis of 1974 to start investing in fuel-efficient cars? Was an OPEC-driven oil shortage a predictable occurrence? As they say, hindsight is 20/20. Nevertheless, even as far back as the 1970s, there were people who were able to see the handwriting on the wall.

It is interesting to note that, in the wake of that first gas crisis, there was much talk of investing in alternate forms of energy to make America independent and less vulnerable to the whims of OPEC. But, within a few short years, American consumers grew accustomed to paying more for gas—and everything else. Before long, we stopped hearing about alternative energy sources, and Detroit began reporting that a growing number of consumers were once again buying big, gas-guzzling cars. Which brings up an interesting question: Did we learn from our pain or are we still mired in the second step of the change process?

Denial

Permit me to throw out a few more questions regarding this car business: Why did it take so long for American automakers to respond to the stimuli they were receiving? Why, for that matter, do so many people and businesses continue to act as if they have access to an undepletable energy supply? As we've discussed, there seems to be a pervasive reluctance to recognize and respond to change. Furthermore, I often find that, the greater the magnitude of the stimulation, the more formidable and entrenched the denial tends to be.

In helping individuals and organizations get through this phase of the change process, we break denial down into seven elements: *shock, numbness, robotic activity, rationalization, helpfulness, hope,* and *magical thinking.* In practice, denial can involve one or more of these variables functioning alone or in combination at a given time.

Shock is a kind of dazed feeling that often kicks in after a sudden or unexpected stimulation takes place. Imagine how you might feel if you had just been fired, or received a phone call that a loved one has died in an automobile accident. For the moment, you're not quite sure how to process this unexpected input. From a physical point of view, you're still the same person you were before you received the new information. At the same time, you feel removed from events that are taking place around you. Someone says hello, and you don't hear him. You drive through a red light and almost cause your own car to crash. These are all manifestations of shock.

Numbness is essentially an extended form of shock. Even months after traumas like the ones just described, you may be in a kind of trance—unable to feel or function very well. During this stage, there is a great deal of confusion concealed by a kind of insipid paralysis. Numbness is also sometimes experienced on an organizational level. When massive layoffs and closings are announced, for example, entire departments may manifest this form of denial. Work proceeds, but with less accuracy and at a slower pace than before. Lateness and absenteeism increase, as do instances of depression.

Robotic activity is another common symptom of denial. You continue to perform your everyday functions at work and go through your customary activities, but you're not truly present. In a sense, you are acting much like a robot who is adept at repetitive, automatic behaviors. If decision making or some form of creative thinking is required, however, these will not be forthcoming.

Rationalization, which gives the appearance of thinking, is really a verbal form of denial. When someone who has just been fired, says, "This is probably for the best," he may actually be right. But, even so, such words are being used as a shield against feelings of pain. Like other forms of denial, *rationalization* cannot be deemed as being negative or positive in and of itself. In any case, trying to use rational-sounding words to make sense of what has just happened is a common manifestation of *denial.*

Hopefulness is often seen during the later stages of denial. The initial shock has been absorbed, but *chaos* has not yet taken place. At times, *hopefulness* can be a sign that the person is trying to optimize the situation. In other instances, it can be a defense against recognizing the extent to which things have been shaken up.

During this stage, people are sometimes helpful and empathetic to others. They are in touch with their own vulnerability but, at the same time, have not fully absorbed the impact of what has happened. Hopeful people are, therefore, sensitive to the pain of others and find comfort in giving aid.

Magical thinking can take place in the wake of both negative and positive change. When adversity strikes, it is tempting to revert to a fantasy that someone or something will suddenly make things better. The person who has just been fired buys a lottery ticket, closes his eyes—and can almost envision himself winning that life-changing dollar prize. This same kind of *magical thinking* was the basis of a show called "The Millionaire" that aired during the early years of television.

The premise of that show was, that, each week, an anonymous billionaire-philanthropist selected a person who was undergoing some sort of difficulty. That individual was then given a million tax-free dollars. The only stipulation was that nobody, other than the recipient's spouse, could be told about this bonanza. The cost of telling was forfeiture of the money.

It's amazing how many of those lucky folks couldn't keep their mouths shut and wound up having to return the money. Meanwhile, the rest of us watching the program all had the same thought: *Just give me the million bucks, and see if I won't be able to keep it a secret!*

During times of adversity, it is much easier to hope and dream that someone will get us out of the mess. But, as every indipreneur recognizes, these are things each of us must do for ourselves. The other side of that coin entails recognizing the role *magical thinking* can play during times of positive change.

When a person falls in love, for example, there is often talk of *magic*. This is fine, as long as you recognize that no person or relationship can completely change your life and guarantee a happy and secure future. Nevertheless, the propensity of human beings to entertain such thoughts is yet one more indication of our capacity for *magical thinking*. This and all other forms of denial can affect organizations as profoundly as individuals—especially large corporations that have a long history of success.

When things are going great and profit margins have been growing annually, the climate is right for *magical thinking* to unveil its seductive charm. Look at IBM—a legendary corporate giant whose annual total revenues hadn't dropped since World War II. Suddenly, in 1992, the company found itself bathing in some $5 billion of red ink. Just before year's end, a massive downsizing program was announced.[3]

Again, it's easy to be a Monday-morning quarterback in passing judgment on the mistakes of others. Still, when literally hundreds of competitors are cloning your product and selling it for a significantly lower price, you would think that astute leadership would impose drastic measures—and fast!

Did Big Blue believe that its past successes ensured it a magical immunity to the certainty of change? Apparently so. When Harvard's Rosabeth Moss Kantor states that "feeling comfortable can create false security," and urges corporate leaders to "*promote* discomfort," she is effectively warning of the dangers of lingering too long in denial.[4]

Recognition and Acknowledgment

At some point, a few days—or even years—after denial takes hold, we will generally reach a point where we can recognize and acknowledge what has occurred. The man who has been told that his job is being phased out says: "It's time to take stock of where I am and figure out the most productive directions in which to move." Similarly, the corporate leader comes out of denial with words that show a real understanding of what has taken place.

"We don't pretend to have all the answers," now-deposed Big Blue chairman John Akers told an interviewer in the wake of the company's 1992 setbacks. "We're on a journey."[5] If IBM was arrogant in asserting its preeminence and denying its problems, that tune had surely changed.

Skeptics may wonder if such words are mere rhetoric, or if they really convey a new understanding of what has taken place. One can only hope that, when the stimulation is strong enough and the denial sufficiently protracted, those affected will recognize and start addressing critical changes that are taking place in their midst. Still, the magnitude of our resistance to change should never be underestimated. Even when our present way of doing things isn't the best way, at least it's familiar. As Jack Welch, long-time CEO of General Electric puts it:

"Change has no constituency. People like the status quo. They like the way it was. When you start changing things, the good old days look better and better. [That's why] you've got to be prepared for massive resistance."[6]

Chaos

Chaos signals the beginning of an attempt to regroup and negotiate the systemic changes that have been recognized and acknowledged. At this point, people want to do something about what has taken place, but are not quite sure of what needs to be done. There are any number of things that can happen during chaos. Depending on the scenario, a system may experience some or all of them.

There is tremendous stress during this phase in the change process. Feelings of depression, frustration, and anger are not uncommon. On the other hand, chaos can create an excitement that verges on mania. At times, the entire organization seems to be experiencing a kind of adrenaline rush that may be unwarranted. In some cases, this elation can result in ill-advised decision making. Irrespective of whether the pervasive feeling is one of excitement or depression, a good deal of conflict can be expected—from both individual as well as interpersonal perspectives.

People and organizations that exist in a chaotic state for too long will experience burnout and bankruptcy—even if that chaos is the result of positive developments. Whatever its causes, chaos is a predictable consequence of change. That means we have an opportunity to harness its turbulence and shape its influence. The expansion of T.G.I. Friday's provides a good case in point.

I've been working with this forward-looking organization in helping them manage the anticipated chaos brought about by an expansion plan that would more than triple the size of the organization. Friday's—which had 230 restaurants and 22,000 employees worldwide at the start of 1993—expects to have 700 restaurants and 70,500 employees by the year 2000.

"Successful companies must force change," says Dick Rivera, president of T.G.I. Friday's. "Making change can be chaotic and painful, but an organization that's looking to the future cannot afford to be fearful."

In citing an employee and manager retention rate that is 60 percent better than the industry norm, Executive Vice President Nick Galanos stresses that one of Friday's goals is to continue being the employer of choice.

"By anticipating the chaos that results from growth, we hope to make our expansion easier," says Galanos. "One of the things we think will help is listening to our employees and being responsive to their feedback and suggestions. In fact, we've installed an 800 number especially for this purpose. We welcome ideas and criticisms from all our team members. Even though some of the changes we are making may cause a certain amount of stress, we want *all* of Friday's people to feel that they will benefit from our rapid growth."

In my work with T.G.I. Friday's and other corporations, I have observed 15 behaviors, feelings and perceptions that are likely to occur during chaos. By anticipating these occurrences in advance, we can start working to control their impact before they happen.

Fifteen Markers of Workplace Chaos

1. A feeling that there is never time to do all that is expected.

2. A tendency to jump from one task to another without completing any one task at hand—and the resulting frustration.

3. Widespread instances of stress and burnout as indicated by such overt symptoms as absenteeism, lateness,

depression, and an overall lack of enthusiasm about work.

4. A perception of ambiguity concerning the expectations of senior leadership—a feeling that management is making too many decisions too rapidly and not communicating with people.

5. A sense of floundering and impending failure. Since people don't know what to expect, they suspect that the organization is attempting to conceal its problems—or that they themselves are responsible for some of those difficulties.

6. A general state of confusion and interpersonal conflict among employees and departments. This is often manifested by a kind of analysis paralysis. People on all levels seem unable or unwilling to make decisions.

7. Feelings of personal and organizational incompetence. People feel that they are not properly trained for their jobs and, therefore, are not competent to handle the tasks to which they are assigned.

8. Feelings of isolation from both management and peers. A sense that management is so concerned with its own problems that it has no desire or interest to communicate with the people.

9. A marked lack of indipreneurial spirit. Employees feel that they are not given enough latitude in making relevant decisions. Furthermore, the chain of command is too bogged down to make its desires known. Some companies try to deal with this gridlock by speaking the language of empowerment. Too often, however, those words are not supported by meaningful action.

10. A perception that adequate resources are lacking to do the job as expected. We often see this in companies that

have turnaround or convergent management. Operating with transitional or turnaround techniques while attempting to grow is a frustrating business. Recognizing the difficulties involved, therefore, is a critical first step. Still, many hard decisions need to be made to bring these polarizing forces into line.

Whenever there is polarization of any kind, we observe a tendency for all parties to retreat to the safety of their respective corners. Instead of dealing with the unfamiliar changes that are taking place, people tend to cling to safe solutions that have worked in the past. This may explain why there is so much nostalgia for the good old days of, say, the 1950s. A clear-eyed look indicates that there was plenty of chaos in that era. But, since that adversity has already been surmounted, drawing on solutions that worked way back when is yet another example of retreating into comfort zones.

11. A lack of focus or clearly defined goals. This makes people feel as if they are going around in a dysfunctional loop. As a result, a tremendous amount of tension and interpersonal conflict is generated.

Because people don't understand their mission within the organization, there is often a great deal of frustration and fear. These feelings tend to make people more entrenched in nonproductive paradigms. Rather than adapting a more optimized approach, individuals with controlling, manipulating, and rescuing tendencies are likely to become even more extreme in the ways they exhibit these patterns.

12. A request on the part of management that people sacrifice tangible incentives. At the same time, the rewards for this forbearance are vague and unspecified. In some cases, this is a cynical strategy on the part of manage-

ment to get something for nothing. Far more often, however, management itself has not yet defined those projected rewards well enough to communicate them effectively.

This scenario can be likened to one in which the people of a nation are asked by its leaders to tighten their collective belts. Implicitly, there will be some substantial rewards in the future—if not for the present generation, then for the ones to follow. But, more often than not, the positive changes that will result from those sacrifices aren't communicated to people as part of a vision that says: "This is where we need to go—and here is the roadmap for how we are going to get there."

13. A fear that mistakes will be punished to a far greater degree than productivity will be rewarded. This stifles the kind of environment that nurtures creativity and risk taking. Oftentimes, this kind of fear is not abated even after management institutes empowerment measures. Once people are punished for taking a risk, they generally require a lot of convincing before they're ready to believe that the same thing won't happen again.

14. A withholding of information while, at the same time, advocating a culture of collaboration and trust. As we noted in Chapter Two, people are bound to display a lack of motivation when a company's leaders are not forthcoming with vital information about the organization. When such a lack of disclosure is accompanied by a lot of rhetoric about trust and empowerment, a dysfunctional message is being introduced into the environment.

This situation is comparable to a family where parents tell the children, "we trust you," and then proceed to talk in hushed tones and keep their valuables under lock and key. Just as the children in such a family are likely to become dysfunctional, people who have to operate in an organizational system where conflicting messages are the order of the day are highly vulnerable to corporate codependence.

15. A work force that spends most of its time reacting rather than creating. During chaos, there are often many small crises throughout the workday. Consequently, people spend so much of their time putting out fires that they never seem to get to the important tasks that move them and the organization forward. I call this majoring in minors—a phenomenon I first observed as a young girl.

When I was growing up on my parents' farm, one of my duties was to feed the chickens. It didn't take me long to notice that, if there is feed on the ground, a chicken will go from one seed to the next—almost never looking up to see what's ahead. Because it is so busy following the seed, a chicken is only able to react to what is directly in front of it.

Another bird I observed as a youngster was the eagle—many of which were visible from our property. Now, eagles behave in a way that is totally different from chickens. This magnificent bird soars high above all the little things that are going on below. An eagle might find nourishment in all those seeds scattered on the ground, but he doesn't even bother noticing them. Instead, he adjusts to the various air currents as he rises high above the ground—setting his sights on things far more global than a bunch of seeds.

The thought struck me that a chicken never really gets anywhere because it lives one seed at a time. I call this peck-peck-peck style *majoring in minors*. The eagle, on the other hand, is able to travel long distances because it *majors in majors*. For an organization to soar, it must create an environment where people have the energy and freedom to concentrate on the big issues—rather than on the minutiae that take on an elevated importance during *chaos*.

Enlightened Leadership

Enlightened leadership signals the end of *chaos*. From an individual perspective, this phase occurs when *optimizing* begins to gain preeminence over less productive response styles. People who exist in a chaotic state for a period of time may experience a critical event that triggers this phase in the change process. An alcoholic, for example, who sees his life falling apart may choose to begin treatment before everything comes crashing down. Likewise, a person who has recently been fired may recognize that he has, in fact, been in a state of chaos for years, and that the time has come to become more indipreneurial.

Enlightened leadership can also come about as the result of some internal triggering mechanism. A person takes stock and recognizes that things are out of whack. Some gut-level, intuitive feeling says: "Look, I have to take control of events before they start taking control of me."

A parallel process can take place in an organization. When chaos gets out of hand, corporations sometimes bring in a new CEO or other senior person to move the organization forward. A new leader may come forth and say: "Let's get everything under control. Here's what's wrong. Let's start setting up a plan that gets us out from under this confusion and chaos." *Enlightened leadership* can also come from one or more persons within an organization who are able to come forth with a visionary plan of action.

Once a person or organization has come under *enlightened leadership*, a new window of opportunity for optimizing change is introduced into the system—which brings us to the next-to-last phase in the process.

Renewal

Renewal consists of two components—*focused mobilization* and *homeostasis* or balance. For the sake of clarity, we will explore these two closely related factors as separate entities.

FOCUSED MOBILIZATION *Focused mobilization* is the stage in which an entity comes up with new ways to operate within a renewed system. The first step is to evaluate all available options. What alternatives are available? Which ones are feasible?

To help answer these questions, we employ a variety of *resourcing, futuring,* and *optimizing* techniques. Organizations may form internal committees or retain outside consultants to help them make decisions. As individuals, we can call forth a wide range of resourcing groups to assist us in addressing the renewed system. Before decisions can be made, there is likely to be a good deal of negotiation required, so those skills will be important at this juncture.

Focused mobilization is a time when a good deal of discovery and innovation can take place. Oftentimes, these creative functions are accomplished by taking a variety of ingredients from several different sources and *blending* them to form a new product or service—even a whole new organization. Once we have gone through the foregoing steps, we are likely to find that we have a synergized system that is greater than the sum of its parts.

HOMEOSTASIS *Homeostasis* is achieved when the system has once again returned to a balanced state. At this stage in the change process, there is a sense of freedom and real exhilaration. The frustration, depression and burnout that were so pervasive in *chaos* have been greatly reduced. The renewed organization has a motivated work force—one that knows what is expected and feels up to meeting the challenge. People feel focused and secure about their jobs. In general, everyone throughout the organization has a sense that things are predictable and under control. A new comfort zone has been established.

Environmental Impact

For the moment, this regained sense of comfort and well-being are as welcome as a peaceful sunrise after a hurricane. We can once again observe the renewed system in terms of its impact on the complex systemic environment in which it interacts. The current state of homeostasis will tend to foster comfort and balance throughout that environment. This, it is hoped, will lead to a positive chain reaction.

So it is that the recovering alcoholic, having curtailed his dysfunctional behavior, now has an opportunity to have a positive impact on his family, on his community and on his work environment. In the same way, the renewed corporation can potentially be a source of strength to its employees, its community and to the public at large.

Renewal is a wonderful place to linger. Before we get too complacent, however, it's critical to keep in mind that another stimulus can be introduced into the system at any time. Once that happens, we may find ourselves right back in the throes of the seven-stage change process. This is not necessarily undesirable—it's just an inherent part of living and doing business.

For better or worse, we cannot stay in any comfort zone for too long. Why? Because the complex systemic network to which we are connected is always shifting. This is, perhaps, more true today than at any time in the past.

Two or three hundred years ago, the paradigm of people's lives did not shift all that much. For the most part, the systems within which people were born remained fundamentally the same until the time of their death. An individual's physical and emotional systems may have changed, but the systemic network within which they existed remained in a fairly balanced state.

Today, our systems are changing so rapidly that there is hardly any time to embrace comfort zones. Like it or not, we have to face the fact that any homeostasis we are able to achieve is only temporary. To maintain a semblance of balance in our lives and businesses, enlightened leadership is needed on a consistent basis.

Where, you may ask, will we find this leadership? How can we foster it in ourselves and others? My answer is this: master the five indipreneurial lifeskills, and you will own a most effective compass for negotiating the systemic changes that can strengthen or derail us at any time.

Optimizing the Future Through Positive Change

I mentioned earlier that a window of opportunity exists, during which time the change process can be altered or forestalled. There are four approaches that can be taken within this window:

Initiate Change

By using futuring techniques to determine that change is about to take place, individuals and organizations are able to move directly into *enlightened leadership* and take positive action. What you are essentially doing in this instance is creating a model for a renewed system through the visioning process. At that point, you are able to provide the stimulation needed to initiate self-generated change.

Whirlpool Financial Corporation (WFC) is the financial services subsidiary of Whirlpool Corporation, a leading manufacturer and marketer of major home appliances. Even though WFC was not experiencing pain or chaos, the company recently initiated a series of changes to refocus its strategic and financial direction. Here's how Harry A. Gossett, vice president of corporate services, explained the move:

"We recognized that maintaining our leadership position in the twenty-first century would require the courage to embrace change and create our own future. By initiating, rather than reacting to change, we were able to align our operation more closely with Whirlpool Corporation's global plans.

"Among other things, we decided to phase out of aerospace and drop most of our commercial business. These steps might have seemed drastic at first. But, in the long run, they will allow us to concentrate our resources and take a new and more focused approach."

Counter a Trend

There are times when we can recognize that a trend has been set into motion. The stimulus may have just kicked in, or the system may already be mired in chaos. Since the window of opportunity for intervention is often accessible into the latter stages of chaos, it may be possible to short-circuit the process. This approach is gaining acceptance in treating certain emotional dysfunctions.

A number of recent studies have indicated that some forms of alcoholism and depression have a strong genetic component. To the extent that such predispositions can be identified, it may be possible to stave off some of the environmental factors that may exacerbate these conditions.

This opportunity to forestall potentially destructive trends is also available to corporate leadership. To change direction, however, leaders must be able to future and optimize—and not use denial as a way of perpetuating maladaptive comfort zones.

Go With the Flow

There are times when seemingly negative change can provide important lessons and opportunities for growth and innovation. We have discussed the possibilities that are often embedded in adverse situations. Indeed, there are times when riding out the waves of change is the fastest way to get to higher ground. Still, there are many factors to consider in how you choose to negotiate change.

The first step is to evaluate honestly your own feelings. Then you need to determine how these personal factors fit into the larger system.

I've seen people ride out corporate chaos and reap rich rewards when the organization returned to homeostasis. I've also seen other instances where individuals forced themselves to tolerate more stress than they were able to handle. By using the balancing techniques in Chapter Seven, you will be able to assess the most productive and appropriate change-management option.

Vacate the System

If you are in an organization that is mired in chaos and dysfunction, it might not be possible for you to effect change unilaterally. Under the circumstances, it may be advisable to vacate that particular system. However, I must offer a word of caution in this regard.

Before you pick up and go, it is important to recognize the source of a particular problem. For example, I've seen many unhappy people go from job to job—even though they worked for outstanding indipreneurial companies. Similarly, I've known other individuals who continually move from city to city because they can't find what they're looking for internally.

I believe that such actions are manifestations of denial or flight rather than genuine attempts to optimize the future through positive change. Nevertheless, there are times when you can spot trouble ahead and honestly do not wish to be part of the trends you see coming. In such instances, removing yourself from the situation just might be the wisest course of action.

---

*S*ELF-AWARENESS EXERCISE: *IS IT TIME TO INITIATE CHANGE?*

✦ ✦ ✦

Instructions This exercise has no right or wrong answers. Allow your responses to be governed by your intuitions and gut-level observations. Use these in combination with the lifeskills and change-management techniques we have explored to decide whether it is time to initiate change.

1. Name all the systems or organizations of which you are a part. For example: family, work, school, community, and so forth.

2. Identify the system that appears to be most out of balance at the present time.

3. List all the variables or components of that system. Then write down your answers to the following questions:

  a. What is the desired output?

  b. What particular input or combination of variables initiates the system?

4. Is the output satisfactory to you? If not, review the input(s) to see which one(s) could be altered to yield a different result.

5. Which other variables in that system might need alteration?

6. Using the four change-management skills—that is, *visioning, assimilating, educating,* and *innovating*—how might you change the system to create more balance?

7. Can you identify one or more ways that this out-of-balance system might be affecting other systems of which you are a part? If so, how can they be altered?

ENDNOTES

1. The Braniff story appears in Howard Putnam with Gene Busnar, *The Winds of Turbulence: A CEO's Reflections on Surviving and Thriving on the Cutting Edge of Corporate Crisis* (New York: Harper Business, 1991).

2. My ideas about taking a systemic approach to change came together at a seminar, "The Power of Choice," sponsored by the San Diego chapter of the World Future Society. The seminar was held at a World Future Society convention in Anaheim, California in August 1992.

3. IBM's problems are detailed in Cynthia L. Kemper, "Embracing Organizational Change: Can we turn new management rhetoric into reality?" *Colorado Business Magazine*, March 1992; cited statistics credited to *U.S. News & World Report*.

4. Rosabeth Moss Kantor is quoted in "Six Certainties for CEOs," *Harvard Business Review*, March/April 1992.

5. John Akers' quote is cited in Cynthia L. Kemper, "Embracing Organizational Change: Can We Turn New Management Rhetoric into Reality?" *Colorado Business Magazine*, March 1992.

6. Jack Welch is quoted in Noel M. Tichy and Sherman Stradford, *Control Your Destiny or Someone Else Will* (New York: Doubleday, 1993).

CHAPTER 9

DEVELOPING THE CONFIDENCE AND SELF-ESTEEM TO BECOME AN INDIPRENEUR

We've covered a good deal of ground in our journey together, and I know there's much to think about as you continue to pursue your personal and business goals. We, as individuals, will continue to change—as will the systems of which we are part. Every year—indeed, every day—we are being asked to confront new and more formidable challenges. The question is, will you be prepared to surmount them?

Unfortunately, many individuals and organizations are not well prepared; that's why I envision a good deal of pain and trouble ahead. My concern in this regard has motivated me to develop The Center for the 21st Century—and to write this book. Teaching the indipreneurial lifeskills has become an important part of my professional and personal mission. I believe that, the more I can do to strengthen the systems of which I am a part, the richer my life will be. It is my hope that these chapters have convinced you that it is advantageous to adopt that perspective.

The indipreneurial lifeskills we have explored provide a framework for optimizing the future. These principles and techniques have little resemblance to traditional academic courses that address separate disciplines. Instead of providing you with specific memorizable information, they give you a synergistic paradigm for thinking, learning, and living.

Let's assume that you've thoroughly absorbed each of the chapters in this book. You've done all the self-evaluation exercises, devoted sufficient time to mastering all the techniques. If so, you may be wondering if this effort guarantees that you will be successful—a winner in all that you attempt. While specific results can never be assured, I am comfortable asserting that mastering the lifeskills is the best way to maximize your chances. The investment you make in tracking, resourcing, futuring, optimizing, and balancing is fully comparable to investing in your health.

Most of us know one or more persons who eat only healthful foods, exercise regularly and avoid tobacco and alcohol. Do these good health habits guarantee that a person won't contract a serious illness and live longer? Not necessarily. We occasionally hear of people who are 100 pounds overweight, never exercise, chain smoke, never see a doctor—and die in their sleep at the age of 90.

If you wish, you can assume that you will be one of those lucky folks who can get away with any kind of indulgence—and maybe you will. After all, even scientists can't seem to agree on exactly which foods inhibit or promote which diseases. Nevertheless, the thrust of the evidence has led most informed people to conclude that good health habits increase the chances of leading a longer, healthier life. Based on my work with individuals and organizations, it's clear that mastering the lifeskills has a comparable effect. Learn to use them wisely and your chances of optimizing the future will be immeasurably improved.

Again, it's important to keep in mind that, in the short run, the fruits of your labors may not always be apparent. In spite of your best efforts, all sorts of adversities can pop up in your business and personal life. When that happens, confidence and self-esteem are the underlying forces that enable you to maintain perspective and keep moving ahead. My purpose in this concluding chapter is to strengthen those forces.

HOW TO INCREASE YOUR SELF-CONFIDENCE

Developing the assurance to do anything well takes training, education and practice. If, for example, you were to decide to become an airline pilot, you would be required to spend many hours in flight simulation. This part of the training process is designed to build confidence—*before* a pilot ever flies a real plane. In any area of life, simulating future activity gives you the experience and practice to negotiate the unexpected with confidence.

As you observe people who've attained mastery in any area of life, you will notice their ability to improvise their way through problems and unanticipated situations. Somehow, the experienced jazz pianist hardly misses a beat when the singer he is accompanying spontaneously decides to change keys in midsong. Likewise, the skilled pilot navigates his plane through turbulent air currents—and the passengers never realize that anything is amiss. Such facility in any endeavor is learned—the result of practice and repetition.

While the lifeskills may not be as technically specific as playing the piano or piloting a plane, confidence in applying them is achieved in much the same way—through practice and repetition that fosters the assurance that whatever problems may arise can be addressed. As you take stock of yourself, try to discern your level of confidence in the various areas of your life.

Are you especially good at a certain aspect of your job? Do others look to you for help and guidance? Are you adept at a particular hobby or other activity? Try to trace your history with respect to that area of mastery, and contrast it with an area in which you lack confidence. More often than not, you will find that the degree of practice and the quality of your previous experience are the key determinants of your self-confidence in a particular area. As an illustrative example, I'd like to contrast the attitudes of two neighbors—Jeff and Frank—with respect to their confidence levels in the area of fixing things.

Jeff is extraordinarily mechanical. If he has an electrical problem in his house or if something is wrong with his car, Jeff can almost always get to the bottom of it. His next-door neighbor, Frank, freely admits that he is "totally inept" when it comes to using his hands. Consequently, he is always asking Jeff for help. In observing how Frank approaches, say, a minor problem around the house, Jeff has noticed that he has absolutely no patience. Because he lacks confidence in his ability, Frank presumes that he is incapable of resolving the problem, and typically gives up trying in two minutes or less—at which point he asks Jeff for help.

Even before Jeff starts evaluating the problem, the most casual observer can see that his attitude is exactly the opposite of Frank's. Jeff is completely relaxed—and in no particular hurry. He *knows* the problem will be solved, even if it takes several hours. Jeff has had a knack for things mechanical since he was young. These skills were valued and encouraged by Jeff's father and other family members. As a result, Jeff is confident in his abilities and has the inner belief that enables him to tackle obstacles and problems as they arise.

As you might expect, Frank has a completely different history when it comes to fixing things. His father, an immigrant from Eastern Europe, was very mechanical. However, the family very much wanted Frank to be a lawyer or teacher. The first time Frank showed a disinclination for using a hammer and screwdriver, his parents told him: "Don't worry about not being mechanical. You're not going to make your living with your hands anyway."

When the need arose, Dad was always there to fix things for Frank. Consequently, the boy grew up describing himself as "a complete klutz" in this area. His parents' prophecy was self-fulfilling. Frank did become a successful attorney. Nevertheless, whenever a screw needs to be replaced, Jeff is sure to receive an urgent phone call.

Is there an area in which your confidence is so low that you feel totally dependent on others? Frank's feelings about his mechanical ability may not hinder him in his chosen field. Nevertheless, his feelings of incompetence in this one area can potentially have a strong impact on his life.

Frank has never changed a flat tire on his car and feels incapable of learning how. Should he ever be driving at night in a deserted area, his refusal to become more mechanically competent could pose a serious threat to him and his family.

In such a complex world, there are many areas where we must rely on the expertise of others. Nevertheless, I submit that it is important never to allow yourself to become completely dependent on anyone, whether you're dealing with a car mechanic, an attorney, a physician—or the corporation for which you work.

To cut the cord that renders us helpless and dependent, we must take responsibility for every aspect of our lives—even if we are *interdependent* on a complex network of people and systems. It is essential to recognize, however, the vast difference between dependence and interdependence.

When two people become interdependent, they share power and resources with each other. But in a dependent relationship, one person abdicates to someone else. Relationships that thrive on positive interdependence are those in which people are able to bring out the best in one another. When such situations are allowed to thrive, each individual complements the other as both move closer to fully realizing their respective potentials. As your self-confidence continues to increase, you tend to become less dependent—and more interdependent—on others.

As far as I'm concerned, building self-confidence in such areas as futuring and optimizing is much the same as in seemingly mundane areas like using a screwdriver or changing a tire. The key lies in developing self-assurance in your problem-solving abilities in specific areas—and generalizing those skills to other relevant areas.

In a sense, the lifeskills we have explored on these pages can be viewed as screwdrivers and hammers—tools with which we can build the future we envision. But, as with any other skill, you must take the time to go through the necessary steps. The time you devote to learning the specific lifeskills techniques will enable you to access a process for fulfilling any mission and realizing any goal. Let me now show you how to use these principles to improve your self-confidence.

EIGHT CONFIDENCE-BUILDING TECHNIQUES

1. In evaluating your relative confidence in various aspects of your life, examine your childhood memories. As you pinpoint the areas in which you have high and low confidence levels, try to recall your earliest experiences, and how certain incidents were positively or negatively reinforced.

Make a list of every aspect you can think of. Rank your confidence level from 1 to 10. Write down your two or three earliest memories in that area, and your overall feelings about them. As you analyze how your feelings of competence developed, ask yourself which of those low-confidence areas are having the greatest impact on your life. Then begin using the following techniques to strengthen them.

2. Take a risk by branching out in an area in which you feel underdeveloped and dependent on others. Set a specific, accomplishable goal and give yourself a deadline. Then go for it! Take a class that will afford you training. Set up a resourcing group where you can exchange your skills for those you want to strengthen. This is a wonderful exercise for developing interdependence. Use the researching techniques in Chapter Four to gather more information about this area. After you've met your deadline, take some time to enjoy your accomplishment.

3. Approach someone you perceive as being an expert or authority figure and ask for his or her advice or support on a project that interests you. People who lack self-confidence erroneously believe that asking for help is a sign of weakness or incompetence. Here again, it is important to remember the difference between dependence and interdependence. When you ask someone for advice or support, you may feel that you are bugging or distracting that individual. I submit that there's no need to feel that way.

Most successful people have gotten where they are by using variations of the resourcing techniques in this book. More often than not, they enjoy being approached. Many have had mentors, and like providing guidance and direction to others who share their interests. In fact, a number of eminent individuals have expressed dismay that they are rarely asked to share their knowledge and wisdom. By approaching people who have distinguished themselves, you indicate confidence—not only in yourself, but in the resourcing process as well.

Whenever you approach somebody, you must respect their right to say no. In some cases, they are simply too busy. On other occasions, they might be overwhelmed with requests. This is especially true in so-called glamour or high-visibility fields.

If, for example, you try to approach a Hollywood star or any kind of media celebrity, he or she may well decline to speak to you. Instead of taking this as a personal rejection, put yourself in that person's place. Imagine how you might feel if dozens or even hundreds of people approached you each day. The more empathy you can convey to the person you are approaching, the better your chances of receiving a favorable response.

While you should always take a positive approach, it's essential to accept a *no* answer graciously, and not take it as a personal rejection. People who lack confidence tend to personalize everything. The self-confident person, on the other hand, understands that a negative response is not a reflection on him, or a sign that his approach was ill advised. It's important to recognize that other people have considerations and parameters that are not always obvious.

Instead of being shattered by an apparent rejection, try to use it as the basis for discovery and further information. Oftentimes, a little more patience and homework is all it takes to turn that *no* into a *yes* on a subsequent request.

4. Volunteer for activities that utilize skills in which you feel confident. As we saw in Chapter Seven, giving to people in need can have an overall psychic and physical benefit to you. By sharing your strengths with others without

asking for specific compensation, you enhance your self-image while improving the systemic environment in which you live.

Another good confidence builder is to volunteer your services in an area of low confidence. How, you may wonder, can people with problems help those with similar difficulties? In fact, this is the basis for such groups as Alcoholics Anonymous and Overeaters Anonymous. Furthermore, this same phenomenon is taking place in the helping professions.

I am aware of a number of psychotherapists, for example, who specialize in helping others deal with the very problems they themselves are trying to resolve. One of the most successful psychologists working with substance abusers is herself a recovering drug addict. An eminent psychiatrist—now deceased—who specialized in helping men with sexual dysfunctions was known to have chronic problems with impotence.

There are two ways to view this phenomenon. On the face of it, one can argue that those who are seeking to resolve specific problems are hardly in a position to help others with similar dysfunctions. On the other hand, it's possible that the only way a person can walk in your shoes is by walking in those same shoes herself. By that reasoning, a person who has dealt with a problem is uniquely qualified to understand the plight of another who is undergoing that same difficulty.

5. Write an article about yourself as if you were a journalist interviewing *you* about an award you've received for your accomplishments. Write down as many positive things as you can say about yourself. Try to see your weaknesses as good points. If, for example, you have difficulty accepting praise, interpret that as modesty and humility. Write down every adverse situation you have overcome in attempting to achieve your goals.

Keep this article in an accessible place. Make it a point to read it and update it periodically. Whenever you doubt yourself or feel a lack of confidence, read it aloud.

6. Never fall into the trap of comparing or contrasting yourself with others. The people who make TV commercials get big bucks for making us believe that we are in competition with some kind of abstract ideal that tells us how we are supposed to look, act, and live. On this basis, it is hoped that we will buy a certain car or suit of clothes, or drink a certain brand of soft drink. Whether we do or don't, all outside comparisons are hollow and meaningless. Ultimately, we are in competition only with ourselves. Let's take a closer look at this issue.

A celebrity appears on the TV screen. That person is beautiful, wealthy, successful. While it's true that many of us covet those attributes, would we really want to be that person? In almost every case, the answer is no. In our consumerist society, it's easy to confuse pieces of another person with his or her totality. The late Elvis Presley provides a good case in point.

For years, millions of people idolized Elvis. Many still do. He was, perhaps, the most important icon of his generation—handsome, sexy, talented, successful, and fabulously wealthy. It's almost impossible not to admire the man's specific attributes, but would you really want to be that person—someone who was so lonely and miserable that he essentially gave up on his own life?

Before you envy someone their assets, take the time to look at the whole picture. In most instances, you'll find that you wouldn't be willing to change places with that person—even if such a thing were possible. Ultimately, your only choice is to accept and build on what you have. This is the only card you can play, so you might as well play it confidently.

7. Identify and optimize your unique skills clusters. Just as we tend to envy others their desirable attributes, there is a pervasive tendency to evaluate our own strengths in ways that are too specific. Skills clustering is a far more innovative and useful way to think about your talents. You may, for example, be aware that you are good at analysis, assimilating data and organizing data. To optimize these skills, it is important to combine them in an integral way that is of use in the world.

One of the most powerful attorneys in the entertainment business is purported to have been a relatively mediocre student in both high school and college. In fact, this person was told by a teacher in a high school law course that he would "never be able to become an attorney."

Even as a very young man, this individual was supremely confident. He sensed that his academic grades were a minor issue. The whole idea was to get through law school and pass the bar so that he could put his unique skills cluster to productive and profitable use. Said skills cluster consisted of the following:

✦ An uncanny gift of gab

✦ An innate sense of salesmanship and negotiation

✦ A gut-level feel for people

✦ A love of show business

✦ An unrelenting drive to succeed

In terms of the procedures traditionally associated with successful lawyering, this man has never been in the top half of his profession. He is weak at drawing up contracts and hasn't been to court in over 20 years. Nevertheless, he is the best at what he does, in great part because he was able to identify and optimize his unique skills cluster.

The tracking principles we explored in Chapter Three are especially relevant for identifying your unique talents. Resourcing groups provide an excellent outlet for brainstorming and developing innovative ways to strengthen and combine those skills. This clustering process builds self-confidence by giving you an opportunity to synergize existing skills and apply them in new and potentially more rewarding ways.

8. Recognize any tendencies to exaggerate your shortcomings. Each of us has a variety of strengths and weaknesses. The question is, to what extent do you allow them to affect your life? Open your local newspaper on any given day, and you're bound to find examples of people who allow themselves to be derailed by a relatively minor flaw or problem. At the same time, there are men and women who overcome serious handicaps and achieve greatness.

As we will see in the next section, self-esteem is a key factor in how we view our strengths and shortcomings. A person with high self-esteem is generally able to isolate his weaknesses or turn them into strengths. On the other hand, the individual with low self-esteem often tends to diminish strengths and maximize limitations. Before we explore the underlying reasons for this, I'd like to share some suggestions for dealing with both real and perceived shortcomings.

HOW TO TURN WEAKNESSES INTO STRENGTHS

✧ Acknowledge your weakness. Rather than denying or attempting to camouflage a particular shortcoming, try to face it head on. Then ask yourself if this particular characteristic is making any real difference in your life. To the extent that you can control a characteristic or attribute that is holding you back, take positive action to rectify it. If, on the other hand, there's nothing you can do, acknowledge your feelings and go on from there.

✧ Some weaknesses cannot be ignored, because they present a real block to a goal we may want to achieve. In that case, it may be necessary to reevaluate and change goals. The college football player who suffers a debilitating injury, for example, will have to abandon his goal of becoming a professional. Nevertheless, there are many productive things he can do with his life—once he reassesses his skills clusters.

✧ When you identify a rectifiable weakness that is holding you back, do everything in your power to change it. Resourcing and optimizing are two especially relevant lifeskills in this regard. If, for example, your lack of education or training is preventing you from advancing in your career, make it a point to shore up in that area. If you identify a weakness in some aspect of your work, you may want to retain an expert or create a braintrust where skills can be exchanged.

Confident people who understand their weaknesses are not afraid to take appropriate action. A self-confident executive who is weak at computers, for example, surrounds himself with people who are strong in that area. On the other hand, I've seen executives who are afraid to acknowledge their weaknesses ignore festering problems or hire "yes people" who further weaken the system.

✧ Turn an apparent liability into an asset. The country singer Mel Tillis has a stutter that might have prevented a less confident person from pursuing a show business career. Not Mel Tillis. He took that stutter and integrated it into his singing to the point that it has become a trademark. Tillis can now sing beautifully without a stutter, and has worked hard to overcome the problem when he speaks. The stuttering still surfaces on occasion, but Mel Tillis has essentially turned this apparent weakness into a strength. In the process, he has become an inspirational role model to others with similar problems.

✧ Use the weakness as a way to build character. We've talked about the importance of embracing the path of most resistance. Every time we overcome a weakness or a setback in our lives, we strengthen our entire system. In a sense, the process is very much like the one that takes place in muscle building. To strengthen and build your muscles, you have to reach a certain resistance point. The same principle applies to building character.

Many of us grew up valuing the path of least resistance. What we are now learning is that we are much more likely to get what we want by traveling the road of *most* resistance. Look closely, and you will find that there are few, if any, overnight success stories. Show me a winner in any aspect of life, and I'll show you someone who has overcome both external and self-generated adversity.

Embracing the hard road and seeking the path of most resistance provides a number of benefits. In addition to helping us build character, it is an invaluable asset for leading and role modeling. Furthermore, as we delve into the complex question of self-esteem, you will discover even more subtle and unexpected rewards. But before we do that, I'd like you to complete the following short questionnaire.

---

*S*ELF-AWARENESS QUESTIONNAIRE: *ASSESSING YOUR SELF-ESTEEM*

✦ ✦ ✦

Instructions Score each statement with a "0" if the statement does not agree with your perception, "1" if you partially agree with the statement, and "2" if the statement offers an accurate description of how you usually feel. Remember to give yourself a score of 0, 1, or 2 to each of the following 20 statements.

1. On the whole, I feel good about my body and physical appearance.

2. When I am with a group of friends, I usually feel comfortable and able to participate fully in the goings-on.

3. I feel good about the kind of work I do and about my overall level of performance.

4. I fit right in with my colleagues and/or workplace peers.

5. As I look back at my childhood, I recall that my parents made me feel loved and valued.

6. When I was growing up, I felt proud of my family, the way we lived, and our position in the community.

7. As an adult, I feel that my family accepts me and provides emotional support.

8. When I make a request of an authority figure—whether in or out of the workplace—I can accept his or her refusal without taking it as a personal affront.

9. My spouse or significant other has an investment in making me feel important and special.

10. Most people who know me respect me.

11. When I make a decision, I stand behind it and don't spend a lot of time agonizing about what might have been.

12. When I am with my peers, I feel at least equal to them in most respects.

13. I feel as if I am making a significant contribution to the systems of which I am a part.

14. When attending a social function, it is relatively easy for me to approach a group of people and introduce myself.

15. When I am around people who outrank me in terms of such credentials as job position, I feel comfortable that there is no need to prove myself.

16. When something I attempt doesn't work out, I generally don't blame myself.

17. When I am with my family of origin, I feel connected.

18. In general, I am able to accept criticism without becoming defensive or depressed.

19. I feel that I deserve all the good things that have happened to me in life.

20. I feel that I've learned and grown from the setbacks I have faced in my life.

Total ___

Scoring Now, add up your total scores and place your score beside the word *total*.

34–40 = Very high self-esteem; congratulations!

22–33 = Relatively good self-esteem; look for specific patterns and opportunities for improvement

15–21 = Self-esteem needs a good deal of bolstering

7–14 = Significant improvement is needed in this area

0–6 = Low self-esteem in a number of areas

HOW TO RAISE YOUR SELF-ESTEEM

Self-esteem is closely akin to the question of confidence, but it has taken on a much more profound meaning. Many mental health professionals now believe that a person's level of success cannot rise above his or her level of self-esteem. The bottom line is, if you feel that you are not worthy of something, you will prevent yourself from attaining it—even if it is handed to you. Let's take a moment to consider the magnitude of this statement.

As you look at the people you perceive to be winners, ask yourself if they exhibit the slightest doubt that they deserve every ounce of success they have obtained. Now consider people whom you consider to be underachievers or unable to fulfill their potential. How do they conceive of their place in the world?

I know a number of people who fit the latter description. Many of these individuals are quite talented; some are even brilliant. Still, as I look at them, there seems to be a key element missing—a kind of glue that provides cohesion and a forward thrust. More often than not, the element these people are missing is self-esteem.

Fear of failure is one theory that is forwarded in explaining why some people don't achieve all of which they are capable. But, for me, *fear of success* is the concept that gets closer to the heart of how low self-esteem can undermine one's professional and personal life. How, you may wonder, is it possible for anyone to be afraid of succeeding? After all, that's what all of us want—or is it?

Dr. Martha Friedman, author of *Overcoming the Fear of Success*, believes that this dynamic affects people across the socioeconomic spectrum. And, in some cases, the effects can be disastrous.

"In its more intense form, fear of success can wreck careers and ruin marriages, even lead to an early death," says Friedman. "Even its more benign manifestations can significantly impair an individual's ability to achieve his or her potential, or simply to enjoy life."[1]

Dr. Friedman believes that the people burdened by fear of success equate achievement with gaining something they don't deserve. To cope with this guilt or fear of inevitable punishment, the person takes measures that assure failure—or at least reduce the possibility of achievement. Unless one is able to recognize the source of the problem, he or she may never understand why things never seem to materialize.

"People who are afraid of success will back away from advancements, protesting that they don't have the ability when they clearly do," Dr. Friedman observes. "In wrecking any hope of success, employees may also subtly sabotage their work by procrastinating, failing to meet deadlines, and even showing up late for the job. They may unconsciously alienate coworkers, sabotage themselves by spending all day taking personal calls on the telephone, or . . . drink . . . more than they should at lunch."

In addition to the personal toll extracted by the fear of success, Friedman believes that American business is paying a high price for such problems. "Workers afraid to excel in their jobs tend to hurt productivity—even the development of a company's future leaders may suffer."[2]

In taking the measure of your own self-esteem, it may be helpful to consider the extent to which fear of success may be causing you to "arrange for your own unequal opportunities."[3]

The self-awareness questionnaire on pages 302–304 can help you pinpoint specific areas where you may be undermining yourself. But there are some overriding questions I'd like you to consider:

✧ Are you leading the life you really want?

✧ Are you fulfilled in your career and your personal life?

✧ Do you feel good about where you are and where you are heading?

If your answer to one or more of these is "no," you might want to look into the possibility that you are allowing fear of success to derail you. While the causes of this fear are generally rooted in childhood, the condition can often be dealt with through increased self-awareness and mastery of the indipreneurial lifeskills we have explored.

Interestingly enough, one particularly effective technique for countering fear of success relates to our discussion about improving self-esteem by embracing the path of most resistance. Dr. Friedman supports this idea when she cautions of the dangers of getting too much too soon. "Success is easier to integrate if you have worked hard for it and maybe even suffered a little for it. Then you can say, without fraudulence, that you deserve it. You've paid your dues."[4]

ENHANCING SELF-ESTEEM THROUGH BALANCING AND RESOURCING

Our sense of self-worth or self-esteem is linked to socioeconomic as well as psychological factors. Traditionally, men found their self-esteem through work, women through relationships and family. As we approach the twenty-first century, many of these distinctions have broken down. Women continue to establish their value in the workplace, just as men have assumed a far more active role in rearing children and caring for the home. The key factor for both genders with respect to self-esteem is balance.

As all aspects of our systemic environment continue to change, maintaining a balance in life's major areas will provide an ever-more-daunting challenge. To sustain high levels of self-esteem, it is essential to keep improving the lifeskills and adapting them to these constantly shifting circumstances. One technique I find particularly helpful in this process is participating in a self-esteem resourcing group.

Unlike some other resource-connector groups, self-esteem groups don't necessarily have to meet regularly or on a formal basis. In many cases, there are only three or four participants who can be contacted individually or collectively. There are certain people who energize us by providing affirmation and support. Whenever you feel your self-esteem subsiding, you might speak with one or more of these individuals on the phone, or get together for lunch.

In the course of your resourcing, you may discover that one group member gives you self-affirmation in your personal life, while another lends support in times of work-related difficulties. Although the people in your group are not likely to be mental health professionals, the support and affirmation they offer can be every bit as therapeutic. I believe that, if more men and women actively resourced in this way, there would be a lot fewer people in need of professional help.

FOSTERING SELF-ESTEEM
THROUGH STRONG VALUES

To maintain the kind of balance that promotes high self-esteem, individuals and organizations must have a stable system of values. These can come from spiritual or religious beliefs, from ethical standards of what is right and wrong, or from present or preexisting cultural models.

One of my clients, the Clovis Unified School District (CUSD) in California, uses *Sparthenian* principles to instill values in its students. Each year, this ethnically and socioeconomically diverse district presents its Sparthenian award to students who best exemplify the physical and mental disciplines associated with the ancient cultures of Sparta and Athens.

"The Sparthenian award is at the heart of our program," says now-retired superintendent Dr. Floyd B. Buchanan, who originated the idea. "It rewards effort and achievement in academics, sports, student leadership, the arts and community service."

Can the self-esteem of young people be improved by reinforcing a strong and stable system of values? The folks at Clovis have proven that it can.

Some might argue that schools should not be in the business of teaching values. If that's the case, where can young people turn for direction in learning to differentiate right from wrong?

Traditionally, such values were conveyed by the family. But today, a significant number of children are growing up in broken or single-parent homes. One study found that parents spend "an average of 15 minutes per week of 'meaningful dialogue' with their children who glean values from peers or television." In another survey, two-thirds of high school students said they would lie to achieve a business objective.[5]

Can young people who demonstrate such a total lack of ethics and values be expected to have high levels of self-esteem? I think not. I expect that the Clovis Unified School District will serve as a model for American education. Indeed, *The Wall Street Journal* ran a feature on the outstanding results CUSD has achieved. I take this to be a tacit recognition of the impact values-based education can have on the future of American business.

If today's young people think it's okay to lie and cheat to get ahead, how well does this bode for the future of corporate America? We must never lose sight of the fact that corporations are made up of individuals. When the people in an organization are lacking in ethics and self-esteem, dysfunction and corruption will be the order of the day. Progressive school systems like CUSD understand the pervasive effect this unhealthy situation can have on every aspect of our future. That's why they have decided to work on altering the system right now.

"Our present superintendent, Dr. David Sawyer, is broadening the vision of a system where everybody wins," says CUSD's public information officer Ellen T. Matsumoto. "We believe that encouraging students to develop values and try their best reduces fear of failure and enhances self-esteem. This system works. Our dropout rate is well below the national average. By 1995, our goal is for 90% of our students to be academically prepared to enter college if they so desire."

Clovis promotes seven values in its classrooms: honesty, respect, responsibility, dedication, self-respect, perseverance and concern for others. To reinforce their efforts, parents are asked to participate in a six-week Family Wellness Survival course. In addition, teachers are expected to role-model the values they teach. Apparently, this approach is working. A study tracking the effects of the Clovis approach over a four-year period found that students showed "significant improvement in helpfulness and cooperation, and ranked higher in these areas than control groups."[6]

I believe that all people and organizations are capable of fostering the kind of enlightened leadership demonstrated by the Clovis Unified School District. Whether or not they will do so is, of course, another matter. In the final analysis, though, the most important issue is what *you* will do to enhance your own self-esteem and strengthen the systems of which you are part. As we have seen, optimizing the lifeskills we have explored hinges in great part on a person's feelings of self-worth. That's why I'd like you to take a few moments to reflect on the following:

---

*S*ELF-AWARENESS EXERCISE: DO YOU LIKE AND TRUST YOURSELF?

✦ ✦ ✦

1. Do you have a feeling of quiet peace and satisfaction about life? If not, identify the sources of your inner turbulence. Review Chapters Five, Six, and Seven for some measures that can be used to correct this unrest.

2. Do you feel that, no matter what happens, you can somehow make it? If not, write down those circumstances you fear can derail you. Utilize the futuring, optimizing, and balancing techniques we have developed to create scenarios of these situations.

3. Do you have faith in your ability to solve problems when they occur? To the extent that you are in doubt, work on mastering the tracking and futuring lifeskills, and in building your self-confidence.

4. Do you have a strong sense of who you are? Or do you need constant approval or affirmation? If you are having problems in this area, review the section in Chapter Six that focuses on moving into the more optimizing response mode.

5. Would you characterize yourself as someone who has strong values that cannot be compromised? If not, you may want to look at how this may be undermining your self-esteem.

We've come to the end of our journey, and, frankly, I find myself searching for the right words with which to close. The principles and techniques I've shared with you do not provide a quick fix or a panacea—but, as you know, that never was my mission. Taking the giant steps that enable you to remain strong and independent is an ongoing process. And, while the necessary lifeskills are the same for everyone, each of us must make it happen in our own way—and at our own pace. That's why I want you to trust your process while recognizing that the future is in your hands.

I've told you that I am a spiritual person who believes in a higher power. Nevertheless, I assume full responsibility for my life choices—and I urge you to do the same, whatever your religious and philosophical beliefs.

When I was in college, my friends and I often had philosophical arguments about free will and fatalism. Obviously, these were never resolved. Given the realities of the world in which we live, however, I would suggest that you consider how the late author Isaac Bashevis Singer responded when the question of free will versus fatalism was put to him:

"This is an issue which has been argued about throughout the ages. Nevertheless, if a fatalist and a person who believes in free will should both happen to be crossing a busy street when the light suddenly turns from green to red, you'll notice them both running just as fast to avoid being hit by the oncoming cars."

To me, this says that, whatever one believes, human beings must conduct their lives as if there is free will. In the end, there is no choice but to proceed as though our actions really do make a difference. That's why I hope you will always strive to make choices that are based on courage and positive values—not mistrust and self-doubt.

If you'll use the lifeskills I've shown you, and trust your process each step of the way, there's no question in my mind that you'll be able to take the giant steps across the breach that separates fear and uncertainty from courage and opportunity.

I look forward to seeing you on the other side!

ENDNOTES

1. Dr. Martha Friedman is quoted in "Surviving Success," *Manager Magazine,* Fourth Quarter 1982.

2. Ibid.

3. Dr. Friedman's comment regarding arranging for one's own unequal opportunities is quoted from a coauthor interview.

4. Dr. Friedman's comments regarding slowing down the process of success is quoted from her book, Martha Friedman, *Overcoming the Fear of Success* (New York: Warner Books, 1980).

5. The studies regarding the time parents spend with children and high school students who said they would lie to achieve a business objective were cited in Sonia L. Nazario, "Right and Wrong: Teaching Values Makes a Comeback, as Schools See a Need to Fill a Moral Vacuum," *The Wall Street Journal*, September 11, 1992.

6. The study tracking the effects of the Clovis approach over a four-year period was cited in ibid.

TO CONTACT CAROLYN CORBIN:

Carolyn Corbin can be reached for keynote speeches, seminars, training sessions, and consulting assignments through the

Center for the 21st Century
3001 LBJ Freeway, Suite 105
Dallas, Texas 75234
(214) 484-2985 Dallas area
1-800-788-3199 Outside Dallas

The Center for the 21st Century identifies emerging trends and targets training programs that position its clients in the right place **before** the right time.

New programs and delivery systems are constantly being introduced in order to respond to changing global and workplace conditions.

The Center specializes in such critical workplace issues as change, chaos, diversity, competitiveness through cooperation, creativity and humor, learning how to learn, lifeskills for personal and professional success, globalization, international marketing, economic development, developing new products/services, and creating the "indipreneurial" organization—to name a few.

INDEX

T